# SMALL PULP AND PAPER MILLS IN DEVELOPING COUNTRIES

# Small Pulp and Paper Mills in Developing Countries

*Edited by*
**Jörg Becker**

*Foreword by*
**Sam Pitroda**

*Published for*
**KomTech GmbH,
Frankfurt and Solingen**
*by*
**CONCEPT PUBLISHING COMPANY, NEW DELHI 110059**

ISBN 81-7022-392-X

*First Published 1991*



*Published and Printed by*
Concept Publishing Company
A-15-16, Commercial Block, Mohan Garden
NEW DELHI 110059 (India)

*Lasertypeset by*
Microtech Advance Printing Systems (Pvt.) Ltd.
H-13, Bali Nagar,
NEW DELHI 110015

# FOREWORD

PROFESSOR JÖRG BECKER and his associates deserve great praise for organizing a workshop on Small Pulp and Paper Mills using non-wood fibres in developing countries, in New Delhi during April, 1988.

Paper products have been part of the process of human development for centuries. Paper is used not only for the printed matters, such as newspapers, magazines, books, computer print outs, but also for packaging and processing many products and services. Paper relates to not only education, information and knowledge but also economy, expansion, growth, production, distribution and delivery systems. It is one product that creates an impact on the political, social and economic fabric of any modern nation.

Paper technology is very complex. It involves ecology, environment, chemistry, machine tools, controls, electronics, communication, information, computers and many other complex disciplines. The need for paper products has increased significantly in the last several decades. World over, there is a shortage of paper including news print, because of limited traditional raw material and its impact on the environment. Paper products have increased significantly in the past and the pressure has been felt especially in countries where the need is even greater.

Paper as a product is essential to provide literacy, education and information which in turn are fundamental elements in the process of development. Literacy and information are required not only to modernize and transform societies, but also to improve self-esteem and self-confidence in an individual. Even today, literacy is one of the most fundamental forms of communication. Literacy is also connected to poverty elimination and new jobs.

I remember from my personal experience, that while I was growing up in a small village in Orissa, in India, good quality paper was indeed a precious commodity. In primary school, we learned to write on cardboard slates. Every piece of good paper was worth saving for the occasion. About twenty years later, when I went to the US, I saw children there growing up with an abundance of paper supply. Kids were constantly busy with paper cutting, pasting, sketching, painting, writing etc., as if there was no end to the paper supply. Now, 20 years later, back in India, I find that an ever increasing paper requirement, world over, has had a significant impact on our ecology and environment, especially in developing countries. The pressure to find alternate raw materials, new technology, new processes, re-cycling methods etc., is building up all over the world.

In my own telecom business, which involves predominantly silicon technology for communication, I find a tremendous use of paper for printing telephone directories. Every time I see large bulky telephone directories for metropolitan areas, it reminds me of the fact that thousands of trees must have been cut to provide these telephone directories and "let your fingers do the walking", to find products and services. Occasionally, I ask myself : "Is it possible to put these telephone directories on silicon chips for easy access by everyone?" Could this be an alternative at this stage? Will it help improve the environment a bit? As a result of these questions, I see a need to ease pressure on the environment by putting many of the paper products on silicon micro chips and modern memory devices. Paper-less offices and factories are now being implemented in the western world. However, the impact of this on the environment is hardly visible or appreciated.

I am not saying that the world needs less paper. I am one of those who firmly believe that environment issues are already getting complex and global, and demand new technologies to produce paper without disturbing our trees, forests and the ecology. And it is in this context that the work presented in this volume by various experts from all over the world and edited by Professor Jörg Becker becomes important and essential.

World over, there is a trend to decentralise, deregulate and de-governmentalise decision-making, distribution systems and developments. The small pulp and paper mills concept will enhance this process of decentralisation. This indeed would bring about competitiveness, lower costs and new jobs in the remote areas closer to the raw materials and manpower.

Only through these kinds of innovations and new initiatives, will paper technology and products continue to grow to meet ever increasing demands and applications. No matter how much effort we put into, developing modern electronics technologies to incorporate large silicon chips to move information faster and cheaper, paper technology and paper requirement are here to stay. The use of paper cannot be replaced. However, the use of electronic information systems and the way in which we produce paper today, with improvements in the innovation and new technologies, can lead us to preserve more trees and improve our environment in the future.

We should not forget the fact that the process of deforestation has been so rapid, with no effort to re-plant the areas, that the overall effect has been devastating. Wooded areas have been shaved off drastically in the drive to meet demands for paper and other wood products for the growing consumer markets. Now sensitivity to this has increased significantly. This has created awareness and pressure for global restrictions and technical alternatives.

I am sure the work by Professor Jörg Becker and his colleagues presented in this volume will enhance the understanding and application of new alternatives and their environmental impact in all developing countries.

New Delhi, August 1990 SAM PITRODA

# CONTENTS

## III. DIFFERENT COUNTRY REPORTS



## IV. POLLUTION CONTROL AND PROCESS TECHNOLOGY



## V. OUTLOOK

# INTRODUCTION

THIS READER presents the results of two research projects which were undertaken separately, but which were related in content with each other. I supervised these projects together with the English paper engineer Arthur W. Western, and under contract to the German Agency for Technical Cooperation (GTZ). The first project was an attempt to develop a model for the relationship between cultural paper and the Third World. I worked on the economic, political, social and cultural framework problems, while Arthur W. Western drew up a concept for technical solutions.[1] The second stage of our GTZ-study had a more concrete, practical orientation; together with colleagues from Third World countries, we aimed at the evaluation of paper mills which complied at least with the following two criteria: 1. annual production of approximately 10,000 tonnes, 2. using non-wood pulp as raw material.

This reader contains the different evaluations which emerged within the framework of our second GTZ-project.[2] These were presented during the workshop "Small Pulp and Paper Mills in Developing Countries", which was held in April 1988 in New Delhi. The reader also contains the other papers presented at this workshop, and has been further supplemented by articles by Roger Grant, Manfred F. Judt, S.L. Keswani, Günther Schildhauer and Hans Rahm. Here I would like to emphasise three important points.

1. Over the past few years, the long discussions taking place in the Third World have thrown up considerable criticism of European concepts of *appropriate technology*. The most common criticism can be summed up as follows: "It is easy for someone who drives a Mercedes to recommend that others should ride a bicycle." Such criticism demands our serious consideration. It is indeed unacceptable that politicians, business people and engineers in the Third World should be expected to be satisfied with whatever philosophy of technology happens to be fashionable in Europe. All that the GTZ-colleagues, Arthur W. Western, and myself can do is to

present readers in the Third World with our arguments and offer options. Of course, the selection or evaluation of these is not in our hands. Taking as examples two large industrial projects within the paper producing industry in Third World countries, I would like to present in summary the difficulties and the conflicts of interests which can arise with such projects. The examples are the Bai-Bang paper mill in Vietnam and the Southern Paper Mill in Mufindi in Tanzania.[3]

Both these mills projected 60,000 t/annum paper production. Both of them have met with the following problems:

- The Vietnamese project cost US $ 266 million, i.e. more than double what was originally forecast. The same applies to the mill in Tanzania.
- Both mills are technically so complicated that they can only be run with the aid of expatriates, the result being that the largest percentage of salary costs goes to expensive experts from the US or Europe.
- Both mills are so large in volume that the transport infrastructure, for delivery of trees and despatch of paper, is much too inadequate to deal with these procedures.
- The mill in Tanzania has become the largest energy consumer in the whole country, and it is the high energy costs for both mills which have pushed the price of paper up so terribly high in these two countries.
- Because import control policy for paper in Tanzania has not been coupled with a policy for local paper production, paper coming from abroad can be sold at US $ 370/t, thus undercutting the local paper price of US $ 700/t.
- In planning the mill in Tanzania, the African extended family was totally "overlooked", with the result that 10,000 people now live in the factory village and not the forecast 1,800. Thus problems arise due to the lack of food-supplies, play-schools and schools, not to mention doctors etc.
- The paper mill in Tanzania has made factory workers of many farmers. The result is that the wives of these former farmers have much more work to do on the farms without them.

These are just some of the important reasons why large industrial projects for paper production in Third World countries are so questionable.

2. My criticism of the paper mills in Vietnam and Tanzania touches on a second, for me, important point, namely the *role of the social sciences* in these discussions. It is not so much a particular technology which alters a society, or which permits a paper mill to function profitably. What is more significant is the social network into which this technology is embedded. In other words: any discussion about small-scale paper mills in developing countries must necessarily begin with a discussion of the political goals being aimed at. As for paper production, the following questions must be asked: Which labour market is at my disposal and how do I wish to influence this market from the industrial-political point of view? How does my industrial policy effect the problem of foreign debt? How large is my potential market and what is the actual purchasing power of my clients? What are the social consequences of building a factory in an agricultural area? Who will pay for the possible ecological damage? The social sciences can be of help in answering these and other related questions. But the social scientist can only reach concrete decisions in cooperation with an engineer who can tell him whether there are any possible technical solutions. Furthermore, the questions which emerge from a social science point of view must also be put at the level of mill operations and organisation. Sam Pitroda and his Centre for Development of Telematics in India showed just how important these points are. When asked about his success he said:

> "I have believed for a very long time that we have a tremendous amount of scientific talent in this country. These guys are as smart and capable as you can find anywhere in the world. The only problem is to motivate them – give them a goal, provide the right environment for them to work in, and let them get on with what has to be done. The problem has never been a technological one – it was always a managerial challenge."[4]

This also applies, without reservations, to the paper industry.

3. Finally, and above all, the main point of this reader is to draw up a catalogue of concepts and arguments which need to be considered regarding *practical and concrete matters*, particularly in the technical area, with the aim of improving the position of small-scale paper mills in developing countries. This means, first and foremost, the

achievement of better operational profitability. With this task in mind, I would like to say something about the role of my consulting company KomTech Ltd. KomTech Ltd. is an independent centre specialising in research on communications and technology problems, be these in the Third World or in my own country. Our aim is to carry out critical research, i.e., we are not bound to the GTZ, or to any manufacturer of paper machines, or to any large European paper mill. Thus my first request during the New Delhi workshop was that we discuss the problems openly, which might mean touching on sensitive topics or even unpleasant points of criticism. If conflicts are simply ignored, critical research and political advice are almost impossible.

My second request was that we apply ourselves to practice-orientated recommendations. Both Arthur W. Western and myself felt that we should concentrate in particular on the following technical problems:

- Chemical recovery
- Continuous digestion
- Fibre and water recovery
- Instrumentation
- Ecological consequences.

With this special emphasis on ecological matters, the New Delhi workshop was committed to the same concerns as those which occupied the paper engineer Professor Dr. Walter Brecht, who from 1931 to 1971 built up the Institute for Paper Manufacturing at my university, the Technical University of Darmstadt, modernised it, and helped to train many generations of paper engineers in Germany and from abroad. As the son of a paper manufacturer and brother of the famous German writer Bertolt Brecht (1898-1956), Walter Brecht (1900-1986) had a perspective which was both comprehensive and interdisciplinary. His writings on water pollution arising from the paper industry are still standard works in this scientific field[5]. Shortly before his death, he referred once more and with emphasis to the fact that the paper industry ought finally to learn from, and accept the consequences of the 1971 Club of Rome study "Limits to Growth".

Neither the New Delhi workshop nor this reader would have been possible without the moral and financial support of many different institutions. Thus my thanks go to the Germany Agency for Technical Cooperation (GTZ) in Eschborn/Germany, in particular to Wolfgang von Fumetti, Walter Jahn and Henriette Mende. Also to the Central Pollution Control Board of India and the Indian National Productivity Council, both in New Delhi/India, and to the UNESCO International Programme for the Development of Communication (IPDC), Paris/France, which latter took on the travel expenses related to our workshop. A special word of thanks goes to Sam Pitroda for writing the foreword to this book. And last, but by no means least, my thanks to the authors for their contributions and their cooperation.

In his foreword to my first paper study, the late Nobel Peace Prize holder, Seán MacBride wrote:

> "Everybody in a position to influence governments or international organisations, should take up as a matter of urgency the question of afforestation and of producing wood pulp or adequate substitutes. This is an important and an urgent task."[7]

This exhortation still applies!

Frankfurt, December 1990 JÖRG BECKER

## REFERENCES

1. Jörg Becker: *Paper Technology and the Third World.* Economic Conditions and Technical Alternatives. With a foreword by Seán MacBride, Brunswick and Wiesbaden: Vieweg Publishing House 1988; summary in this reader on pp. 61
2. Cf. the articles in chapter II, pp. 61
3. Cf. the following critical assessments: "Schwedens grösstes Dritt-Welt-Projekt", in: *SÜDOSTASIEN aktuell*, Nov. 1986, pp. 563-564; Anthony Ngaiza: "Paper at a Price: Southern Paper Mill Tanzania", in: *Ambio*, 5/1987, pp. 280-286.
4. Quoted after "The hi-tech gift of Sam Pitroda", in: *Business World*, Sept. 14-27, 1987, p. 40.
5. Cf. Walter Brecht and Fridolin Zippel: *Wege zur Verbesserung des Wasserhaushaltes von Papierfabriken*, Darmstadt; Eduard Roether Publishing House, 1963.
6. Cf. Walter Brecht and Hanns-Lutz Dalpke: *Wasser, Abwasser, Abwasserreinigung in allgemeiner Sicht und in der Sicht der Papier-und Zellstoffindustrie*, Biberach an der Riss: Güntter-Staib Publishing House 1980.
7. Seán MacBride: "Preface", in: Jörg Becker: *Paper Technology and the Third World*, op. cit., p. 5.

[illegible]

[illegible]

[illegible]

[illegible]

[illegible]

# ONE

# GENERAL SITUATION

# 1

JÖRG BECKER

# PAPER TECHNOLOGY AND THE THIRD WORLD

## Global Restrictions and Technical Alternatives

### 1. Introduction

THE TRITENESS of the statement that a fish cannot swim without water stands in crass contradiction to the public and scholarly interests of communications and media researchers and book specialists in the use of, and research on, paper as the raw material for the technological basis of all printed matter (books, newspapers, comics, magazines, computer printouts on paper etc.). The general disinterest regarding this question demonstrates a general bias on the part of the Western media and book researchers, who with their idealistic and non-materialistic tradition,[1] would sooner involve themselves in disputes over the content transmitted by the print media than reflect upon the economic, political and technological conditions that make possible the production, distribution and delivery of the contents communicated by the medium of paper.

If one differentiates the mass media by the basic production techniques employed by the print media on the one side, and the electronic media on the other, then the raw material, paper, is for the print media the equivalent of the raw material radio frequencies, for the electronic media. Paper is a product of fossil energy resources which has common qualitative characteristic with radio frequencies in that neither fossil energy resources nor the number of utilizable frequencies of electromagnetic waves can be increased. The worldwide energy crisis recognised since the beginning of the seventies, had as one result that the problem of paper supply as the basis for the provisioning of a print medium in many aspects came to resemble very closely the battle for access to, and distribution of, other raw materials of finite resource availability.

In the following, the assumption is made that it would be more practical if in a discussion of the democratic aspect of the international press and book system (bias, literacy campaigns, free flow of information etc.) the international battle for distribution of cultural paper be examined and considered.

All discussions of the international struggle involving the distribution of raw materials must nowadays be carried out within a multi-factor framework. Also the question of the supply of cultural paper of various nations and groups would soon become defined, since partial diagnosis and therapy would lead the whole problem into a cul-de-sac, as economic, political, technological, ecological and social causes and effects must by weighed together.

In conflict with, and complementary to, other debates on raw materials — e.g. minerals — the debate over the provisioning of cultural paper has an additional dimension. As far as cultural paper is concerned, it is not only a question of seeing the materials from an economic but also from an ideological point of view. It is on this double characteristic of economy and ideology that the whole debate depends. Man's right to inform and to receive information that is socially relevant, is directly linked with the type and quality of cultural paper supply to a nation or group (as far as the print media sector is concerned).

The Third World, and in particular Black Africa, is especially disadvantaged as regards cultural paper supply. In discussions of the most varied dimensions concerning the supply of cultural paper, the figures show greater disadvantages for the Third World when compared with the disadvantages which are also experienced by regions within the industrial countries. The situation in the Third World is only comprehensible within the framework of a wider international analytic concept insofar as in principle it is only to be altered within the framework of a discussion over a *New International Economic Order* (NIEO) and a *New International Information Order* (NIIO).

Indeed, a fish can swim if there is water; but the very presence of water does not specify which, and how many, fish may swim in it — in which direction they can swim — nor for how long they can survive. In order to ensure a just and equal distribution of cultural paper to all nations and groups, certain fringe conditions must be fulfilled in order to give the water a "democratic" dimension.

## 2. Global Aspects: The Triangle of Economics, Politics and Ecology

In his 1979 contribution: *Education about the Third World and its Development Problems*, Upper Volta's renowned social scientist Joseph Ki-Zerbo made the following points:

> "What can be in the interest of the masses? Surely the gratifying of basic needs. This is fundamental to all development concepts. One should take care, however, not to reduce basic needs to the absolute minimum necessary to stay alive. The basic human rights, like freedom of opinion, are a part of them, which does not mean, however, defining the basic human rights necessarily in accordance with Western concepts of law and morality (. . .). This leads me to a further principal characteristic of development Cultural identity."[2]

If one concurs with such conclusions, it becomes clear, that the successful search for identity and the establishment of communication must be regarded as essential parts of a basic needs strategy. To avoid misunderstanding it needs to be stressed that there can be no abstract basic need for paper, books, TV broadcasting or microchips, but only for such that can adequately guarantee the historically grown need for communication. In this historically qualified sense there is a basic need for cultural paper in many Third World countries and in many regions within these countries. The current shortage of paper in the Third World increases foreign book penetration, leads to conflicts of identity, weakens the education system, undermines the plurality of press opinion, makes political censorship easier and puts a strain on the foreign trade balance.

The reasons for the Third World paper shortage are manifold. In essence they are a function of the globally, externally originated conditions of the paper market. The five most important conditions will now be dealt with.

### *2.1. Development of Energy Costs*

From 1973 till 1980 the world pulp and paper industries were burdened by ever-increasing energy costs, especially for oil and related products. Pulp, but especially paper production requires an enormous quantity of energy. According to a World Bank study pulp and paper production are counted among the energy-intensive branches of industry;[3] it is one of the branches in which the energy costs account for between 15 and 50 per cent of the total costs per production unit. Even if the paper branch is less energy intensive than, for example, the metallurgic industries, still, on average, to produce one tonne of paper 1–2 tonnes of black coal or 0.7 to 1.4 tonnes of natural gas are required.

Drastic reduction of energy should be the first necessary consequence for the Third World. Another World Bank study assumes that smaller paper mills can save up to 11 per cent and bigger ones 12–15 per cent in energy costs in Third World countries.[4] Smaller mills can save energy through better insulation and heat exploitation. Bigger mills should use their waste heat better, introduce simpler changes in the production process and use more energy-efficient equipment.

### *2.2. Development of Paper Prices*

In the 1960s and 70s the prices of cellulose, pulp and paper increased at the same rate as other industrial goods in the developed world. The prices for pulp and paper increased to a lesser degree in the US, whereas cellulose was an exception since its price went up by 60 per cent in real terms as compared to the producers' price index for industrial products. This high level has been more or less maintained. This differentiated development of paper and pulp prices on the one hand, and cellulose on the other, can also be applied to other industrial countries which possess a national manufacturing capability for cellulose paper and pulp.[5]

The Third World's "Commodity Terms of Trade", e.g. the relationship between the cost of raw materials and that of the cellulose produced in the US, developed in a rather different manner in the years between 1969 and 1980. In an analysis the prices of 10 raw materials supplied to the industrial countries by the Third World were compared to the price for the US "special alpha and dissolving grades" cellulose; these were based on *fas* prices (= free alongside ship). Iron ore, tea, rubber, jute, copper, coffee, tin, cacao and cashew nuts were able to maintain their "terms of trade" in relation to cellulose from 1969 to the mid-70s. From 1975 on the prices for coffee, tin, cacao and cashew nuts increased to significantly that the resulting "terms of trade" net profits could not be ignored. Over the same period of time the conditions for tea, iron ore and rubber worsened. Already from 1973 onwards the barter relationship concerning the export commodities copper and jute deteriorated drastically.

FIG. 1.1: 'Terms of Trade' (commodity terms of trade) for selected raw materials from the Third World in comparison with US cellulose (1960 = 100)

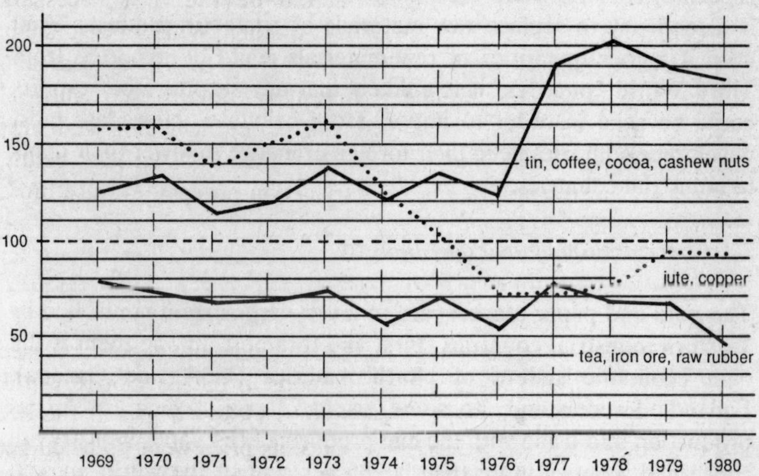


*Source:* United State Department of Commerce; Statistical Absrtract of the United State, Washington, DC: United State Department of Commerce 1975- Estimates by the author.

The world economic crisis of 1980, which still continues in most developing countries, has on the whole changed the "terms of trade" relationship between the above mentioned Third World export products and US-cellulose to the disadvantage of the former. The statistics for 1981 and 1982, which are the most recent available, show that almost all Third World export goods suffered "terms of trade" losses. Only iron ore and jute could be seen to have achieved a slight improvement. As opposed to this the barter value of such Third World export products as copper, tin, cacao, cashew nuts, coffee and rubber, suffered a considerable and at times even catastrophic decline.

If the Third World intends buying the same quantities of US-cellulose as before, it will therefore have to export higher quantities of raw materials. Even if the Third World countries are able to do so, they will most probably not have markets for larger quantities of these products. The demand for raw materials remains weak.

Hence we may proceed on the assumption that the industrial countries' capacity of absorbing raw materials has now been reached, especially so since there their markets are saturated and since there is a tendency to replace raw materials by synthetic products. And even if higher quantities of raw materials could be exported from Third World countries, it is unlikely that any surplus from exports could be used in order to import more cellulose. Nowadays most developing countries need their foreign exchange to lower their debts to industrial countries.

### *2.3. Concentration in the Paper Industry*

The pulp and paper markets are to a very large extent controlled by Western industrial countries. First and foremost among them is the twin economic system of North America (USA and Canada), Finland, Sweden and, to some extent, Japan, which, as far as production and trade with the end products of the paper industry are concerned, control more than 80–85 per cent of the world market. Diverse anti-trust suits against the paper industry are among the many indications of the extraordinarily high degree of concentration in this branch of industry.

With a regional concentration to Scandinavia and the USA the 100 largest pulp and paper companies controlled about 46 per cent of the world production of paper and cardboard in 1975. In 1980 their share had increased to approximately 51 per cent. Their share of market pulp was around 70 per cent in 1980. Whereas pulp production seems more concentrated than total production of paper and cardboard, it can generally be said that if one were to split up market domination and world-wide control according to the enormous diversity of various end-products from paper and pulp, the degree of concentration would increase many times over. For some qualities total world production is in the hands of a few concerns only.

Even if the Third World has at no time produced more than 6 per cent of all chemical pulp, some countries, especially Brazil, India, the People's Republic of China, the Philippines and South Korea, were able to increase their production considerably in the last few years. Whether this form of economic growth benefited the Third World generally, or even the population of the actual country, is doubtful. The beneficiaries were on the whole the North American — Scandinavian producers, who are building up the pulp and paper industry in some Third World countries by means of their capital and know-how, their technology and their advisory capacity. The recently constructed pulp mill CELLUCAM in Edea, Cameroon, for example, in important points shows a model of technology transfer which one can designate "pseudotransfer" in the words of Ignacy Sachs.[6] Although more than 50 per cent of CELLUCAM shares are in the hands of the Cameroon government, a Swedish pulp and paper company, which is only minimally involved financially in CELLUCAM, gained the marketing rights for the paper meant for export. In this way transnational paper concerns have a considerable influence on the marketing and worldwide distribution of pulp produced in the Third World. Even if in some cases growth can be ascertained, it is doubtful whether one can speak of *A Third World* paper or pulp production.

### *2.4. Wood Resources in the Industrial Nations*

Expenditure for wood forms the biggest single cost item in the production of paper and pulp. Proportionally and globally wood accounts for about a third of total variable costs of pulp production — they vary from 50 per cent of costs in Sweden to 25 per cent in Brazil. So it is clear that changes in world-wide afforestation very soon have an effect on the price calculations of paper products. As approximately 80 per cent of the world's pulp production presently takes place in the Western industrial nations, the destruction of forests in the Third World will only peripherally influence world paper prices.

More interesting is therefore a glance at the ecological economic stability of northern forest areas. Conspicuous in this context is the fact that nearly all global models of recent years — from the "Club to Rome" to "Global 2000" — take a stability of these forests for granted. In view of the damage to forests in North America and Europe caused by the complex disease — acid rain —, one cannot share this optimism any more. Despite the difficulties listing all the damages of acid rain in concrete form, the following approximations are nevertheless of interest.

The OECD has made calculations on the basis that approximately 3 to 5 per cent of a GNP must be included in any estimate for "repairs" to dying forests. In the USA an amount ranging from 6 to 35 billion USD would thus be necessary to avert the economic damages of acid rain, and an additional amount of between 2 and 12 billion USD would have to be spent by power stations to convert their present plants.

The efforts of acid rain and of diminishing forests on global paper prices is difficult to estimate, as a complex series of factors have to be considered. The West German trade paper *Das Papier Magazin*, however, warns about the effects of acid rain:

> "For technological reasons only green wood is used in the production of wood pulp. We get it in the form of the so-called inferior wood when forests are thinned out (a forestry necessity to encourage the healthy development of hard and valuable timber). If young trees succumb, our supply of green wood is in danger. Diseased trees that have reached a certain level of disease can no longer be utilised by us."[7]

This development will have the following consequences for the Third World: The damages caused in the forests by acid rain as well as increased expenditure for anti-pollution measures will push up paper prices world-wide with serious consequences for the Third World. Only recently one further effect was drawn — public awareness by West Germany's largest forest proprietor, Johannes, Prince Thurn and Taxis: Price pressure on northern forests will lead to an increased destruction of tropical rain forests in the Third World.[8]

### *2.5. Future Market Developments in Industrial Nations*

The global consumption of cultural paper clearly demonstrates the gap between the Third World and the industrial nations, well-known also from other problem areas. As far as the consumption of cultural paper is concerned the Western industrial nations show themselves as glaring surplus societies, whereas the consumption of cultural paper in the Third World (and many socialist countries of Eastern Europe) shows the typical characteristics of a deficiency economy.

One can drastically illustrate this relation between deficiency economy and surplus society in the following way: Whereas in 1980 Black Africa aimed at a book production of 120 pages per person per year (and did not achieve this aim), a Scandinavian household gets more than 200 pages of advertising material in four colour printing delivered to the door free and unasked for in two weeks. Although the theoretic and empirical mutual relations between deficiency economics and surplus societies are multicausal, and a solution to the conflict potential between the two economies cannot be found simply by the surplus societies passing a "little" of their "more" on to the deficiency economies, the question should be looked into here whether a reduction in paper consumption in industrial countries could lead to more favourable wholesale prices for the Third World.

According to all available prognostic studies the demand for cultural paper for books, press and magazines in the industrial nations will continue to grow, though not as fast any more as in the sixties and seventies. The following prognosis by the consulting company of Arthur D. Little for the late eighties can serve as an example of such studies:

> "Printing and writing papers in general will continue to be the fastest growing products in the pulp and paper side of the forest products industry. We expect the demand for coated groundwood papers to continue to increase at about 5 per cent per year through the 1980s. Demand for this product is rising because of shifts in advertising decreased, but also the spread in the cost of advertising expenditures from television toward the printed media. Not only has the amount of prime-time television available for advertising decreased, but also the spread in the cost of advertising between broadcast media and print media is steadily widening. We expect some continued cyclicality in the demand for coated groundwood papers as a function of advertising linage demand swings during business cycles, but we expect the magazine expenditure revival of the past four years to continue into the 1980s."[9]

If considerations on the future development of the cultural paper market in Western industrial countries also include changes in the technological field, we find the following picture: Although magnetic data carriers are cheaper and can absorb many more data than paper, they can hardly begin to make up for the functional advantages of the conventional print media. Other technological innovations will increase paper consumption even more: Photocopying and computer technology increase demand for paper. Whereas in 1970, 1.5 billion normal photocopies and 1.2 billion photocopies on coated paper were made in the FRG, in 1977 the numbers have increased to 10 billion normal photocopies and 1.5 billion on coated paper. These changes amount to an annual increase of approximately 23 per cent. A further component, which will ensure an increase in paper consumption is connected with the increase in the number of computers, electronic printers and world processors. Interestingly enough, an increase in paper consumption corresponds to an increase in electronic printers.

Expressions such as the "paperless office" or even the "paperless society" thus turn out to be superficial slogans which are being propagated in the interest of suppliers of electronic services, which have very little in common with empirically verifiable reality, especially since as a result of the world-wide economic crisis, the automation of offices is taking place at a much slower rate than feared by some and hoped for by others. Most prognoses predict a rate of increase of 2 to 3 per cent a year for cultural paper in Western industrial nations up to the year 2000. The result is that one cannot assume that the Third World may profit from a saturation of northern markets.

The five most important influences of the world paper market on the Third World may then, from a development policy point of view, be summarised into the following five propositions:

1. Only paper industries with the lowest possible demand for imported technology, energy and raw materials can bring about real aid for the Third World, since no further burdening of the foreign trade balance of these countries can be allowed.
2. Of the three cost factors–technology, energy and raw materials — the one offering the least chance of saving is the primary energy needed in the production of pulp and paper.
3. For many Third World countries the terms of trade for paper imports have rapidly deteriorated in recent years. This is especially true of countries exporting tea, raw rubber and iron ore. Yet, even in the case of a more favourable development of terms of trade, one cannot assume that board masses of

consumers within a Third World country will be able to buy imported paper more cheaply than at present.

4. The continuing tendency world-wide towards concentration and oligopolization of the pulp and paper manufacturing industry in North America, Scandinavia and the Common Market brings no hope for positive trickle-down effects from a national paper industry boost in Third World countries.
5. The economic consequences of damages in forests in northern hemisphere countries, the increasing costs of anti-pollution measures, plus the still growing (thought somewhat more slowly) demand for cultural paper in industrial nations (photocopies and computer printouts) will further increase the world market prices for paper to the detriment of the Third World.

From these five propositions one can draw two distinct conclusions:

1. An improvement of the paper situation in the Third World is possible only if there are simultaneous structural changes in international technology and raw material policies, in other words changes in the direction of a New Order dealing with economic and information problems as demanded at the beginning of this paper.
2. Although theoretically and politically there are many reasons for the desirability of such changes only a very limited awareness of the importance of the demands for a New Order can be deduced. That is why a different conclusion should be drawn from the analysis of global conditions: Since the international energy and raw material policy structures cannot be changed in essence — at least there are no political forces for such processes visible in the near future — it seems sensible that the Third World, far more than is the case at present, have second thoughts about its own potential and own raw materials for the production of pulp and paper.

### 3. Technological Alternatives for the Third World

Large transnational paper companies do not invest in the production of pulp and paper in Third World countries since access to natural resources and other conditions inhibit large-scale development. It is more profitable and more secure to export to these regions. Some of the larger machinery manufacturers in conjunction with international consultants or general contractors are able and willing to supply new mills on credit terms to Third World countries who can provide financial guarantees and have sizable resources of fibre.

But almost by definition only a few oil-rich countries can satisfy these conditions and the record of such installations has not been wholly encouraging. The costs of building such plants are higher than normal as the need for import and the costs of freight are raising capital costs over variability level. The efficiency of such mills seldom reaches the level attained in the industrialised world as the limitations in human resources necessitate operations to be supported by expensive expatriates and imports of materials also making the direct production costs higher than normal. As a result it is usually necessary to increase prices by tariff protection and paper is not, as it should be, cheap.

Large scale production is inappropriate for Third World countries for other reasons than the sheer magnitude of cost. The most concentrated source of fibre, wood, upon which the whole philosophy of scale has been founded, is seldom available in sufficient quantity of suitable species, and requires enormous infrastructural development when it is available, much beyond the financing capability even of government sponsors. Wood is necessary to support maximum scale in pulp or paper manufacture, but it is no longer economic to cut down trees for paper alone; an economic mill today has to be integrated with timber production, calling for even greater capital investment.

Apart from wood, which can almost be disregarded for most Third World countries, non-wood fibre resources, predominantly agricultural wastes, offer the best prospects but they are seldom available in sufficient concentration to support scale as it is currently understood. Straw, bagasse and bamboo are the most readily available fibre sources; there are others, in particular areas, such as reeds.

It is possible to attain large to medium scale from these materials but there are restricting factors which can make scale impossible or inappropriate. Merely non-wood fibres such as bagasse, straw or reeds are not sufficient for paper production because of the inherent weakness of the fibre which is shorter than that from coniferous wood. Long-fibre support, from 15 to 40 per cent of total fibre, is needed according to paper substance and quality and is unlikely to be available in the quantity required to support scale within economic range. It may, even for a small mill, have to be collected from scattered sources over quite a wide area, or imported. Among non-wood fibres, bamboo alone is of sufficient strength to be used as the only fibre raw material in paper-making but for this reason readily available resources have almost everywhere been used up.

The size of the market is also a limiting factor to scale. Even where the total market is sufficient to support large scale, the distances involved for distribution and the inadequacy of road or rail services can make sales prices too high — a number of small mills, strategically sited, may be more viable.

Natural resources other than that of fibre also have a bearing on scale. The manufacture of paper can require up to 80 tonnes of water per tonne of paper produced and have a correspondingly large effluent treatment and disposal problem. Sites where water in sufficient quantity to satisfy scale is available are very difficult to find in most Third World countries.

Fuel to produce process steam is required for cooking the fibre and drying the finished paper. The quantity is significant, around 1.5 tonnes of oil or the equivalent as coal per tonne of paper produced from a fully integrated mill. It is unlikely to be available in the quantity required to satisfy a large mill, except in oil-rich Third World countries, and it is even more unlikely that the sources of fibre, water and fuel jointly will be so situated as to make collection and transportation remunerative.

A reliable source of electric power is also required, as much as 1 MWh/tonne of paper produced, depending on fibre and paper quality. It is almost by definition unlikely to be available in a Third World country, in quantities sufficient to support large-scale production. With higher costs of capital and fuel consumption a mill can be self-sufficient in electric power and the large mill is usually equipped for total or partial independence in this respect. By current general standards the wood-based mill has natural advantages in terms of fuel consumption, and as a consequence also in the use of electric power. There is usually wood waste and bark available as supplementary fuel, particularly when a lumber operation is associated. Efficient chemical recovery producing high-pressure steam is also practical and can thermally satisfy pulp production requirements with a margin for paper. It can also provide stream with a power generating potential above its own strict requirements.

These advantages are termed natural, because they are, and have been exploited for wood. It was not always so; the pulp and paper industry of today was built on sulphite pulping without chemical, recovery and this continued up to the last war. The effects of this on lakes and rivers are still being experienced in Canada and Scandinavia. Mountains of bark in Canada and Scandinavia also still exist as a memorial to the wastefulness of an industry which developed on the principle that fossil fuels would always be cheaply available. Changing standards and values inspired by popular pressures forced the developments in chemical recovery and fuel conservation which now apply to the wood-based pulp and paper industry. The costs in research and development were high, but could be afforded by an expanding and profitable industry; they were essential for its survival. The non-wood pulp and paper industry has similar natural advantages, but these have not yet been exploited to the same degree for lack of funds and application.

Broadly speaking, wood is not likely to contribute significantly to the need of Third World countries, except in such favourable areas as exist in the climatically suitable regions. Africa and South America are perhaps the most probable locations. Even in these areas, although long-term prospects can be seen to exist in re-forestation with suitable species, short-term prospects are not good unless they can be realised economically on a small scale. The costs for large scale development are intrinsically too high to be afforded, and the market is too small to absorb the output. Exports is no solution, as has already been recognised. The world is already saturated with high quality pulp sold at prices below production costs.

The immediate future for the Third World therefore lies mainly in the exploitation of existing non-wood materials. In general terms these are straw from wheat, rice or maize, bagasse, from the sugar industry, and bamboo.

Taking the last first, where *bamboo* exists within economic range it is already fully exploited. It is a self-sufficient source of fibre, very versatile and not requiring long fibre support. It can even carry a proportion of short fibre material. The paper industry in India has largely been based on the utilisation of bamboo. However, it is not planted by man but grows naturally in tropical forests and its utilisation depends on low cost labour for collection. Its use is only likely to be extended when presently inaccessible forest areas are opened up, enormous infrastructure costs are involved here. Consideration has been given to plantations of bamboo but the cold truth today is that no raw material, even wood, can primarily be grown solely for paper; the costs are too high. The fibre must be available as a by-product from other industries and this narrows the choice.

*Straw* is the most commonly available fibre and it is an agricultural by-product. The total quantity available would contribute to very considerably the paper-making requirements in Third World countries, but it is estimated that scarcely more than one tenth of the overall quantity produced is normally surplus to other uses, varying from cattle bedding to fuel for cooking. It is ironic that in some industrialised countries with little paper-making fibre resources, vast quantities of straw are wastefully burnt annually because other uses are limited and current technical limitations make its use for paper uneconomic. Where collection is organised rationally, straw-based mills can achieve scale up to 100 kt/year of paper but mills of much smaller capacity can be economic in suitable circumstances, to the mutual benefit of paper mill and farmer.

*Bagasse* is also an agricultural by-product wherever sugar is produced from sugarcane, and it is an excellent and versatile source of fibre. If the paper mill can be located adjacent to the sugar mill the cost of delivered fibre compares favourably with that of almost any other material. However, bagasse is also the traditional fuel for the cane sugar industry. Efficiently burnt, (even unprocessed bagasse with about 50 per cent moisture), there could be a bagasse surplus at all sugar mills varying from about 20 per cent at fully refined sugar mills to more than 50 per cent from sugar mills producing unrefined sugar. The efficient burning of bagasse, however, implies efficient boilers which are not always present; in addition, storage and handling arrangements must be made for the surplus, with further costs involved. In consequence many sugar mills use their boilers to provide such stream as is necessary, and as incinerators for the bagasse which remains. Properly organised, the duties of collection and storage can be undertaken by the paper mill. If the bagasse could be wholly or partially dried before burning and the sugar mill or paper mill is equipped to burn the pith which must be removed, the thermal effectiveness would be greatly improved. Under these circumstances it is not an impossible concept to imagine a combined industry requiring no supplementary fuel for the sugar mill and a viable paper mill alongside with reduced fuel requirements. But although this is a very real possibility, much development and research will be necessary to achieve it.

Where replacement fuel (which may also mean new boilers) is available, bagasse mills can achieve considerable scale and there are a number with paper production exceeding 100 kt/year. Mills of this scale are becoming more frequent as a result of the development of newsprint production from bagasse in recent years. Newsprint is vital for the press and therefore is imported at high cost even by the poorest of countries.

## 4. Technical Limitations to Paper Production from Non-wood Fibres

Non-wood fibres, as indicated above, are already supplying about 60 per cent of the paper consumption in Asia and China, and the proportion is estimated to increase. But since consumption rates in these countries are low, the amount produced is also low, much less than that needed. There are technical limitations to efficient production of quality paper from non-wood fibres which have discouraged investors and sponsors. It should be added here that very similar limitations once applied to the international wood-based paper industry in its formative years, but they have been overcome by applied effort and research.

The first problem is *inefficient chemical recovery*. Wood-based mills today use a highly effective and economic process, conserving about 95 per cent of the cooking chemicals and in consequence reducing not only production costs but also achieving acceptable effluent standards. In addition, the process provides steam at pressures which can generate electric power, considerably reducing energy costs.

Non-wood fibre pulping produces cooking liquors which contain silica. Its presence increases the viscosity of the liquor when it is evaporated so that it cannot be concentrated to the same degree as the liquor from wood, and hence it is less effective in combustion. In addition, silica can produce sealing which is almost impossible to remove and this limits operating temperatures. There is great need for an effective and economic process for removing silica from cooking liquors. One has been developed and is operating in the Rakhta Mill in Egypt. It is said to be very effective, but being the first, it is obviously, at this stage, a production prototype needing continuing improvement and refinement. A reliable and effective plant would not only raise evaporation and combustion efficiencies, but would also permit recausticising lime recovery, reducing production costs and the costs of effluent disposal.

The second limitation, which does not apply to bamboo, is the *need for long fibre reinforcement.* In this respect bagasse has advantages over straw but still requires long fibre support. If imported kraft can be afforded, the straw or bagasse based mill can produce an excellent range of papers, competitive in quality with the best, but this situation applies only to the oil-rich Third World countries. For the rest, which is by far the greatest portion, it is necessary to find cheap local materials which can be used as substitutes. Cotton waste is excellent but in very short supply, localised to specific areas where cotton is grown. Other textile fibre wastes can be used such as jute, sabai grass or sisal, but again supplies are limited.

The most promising source of long fibre for Third World countries is kenaf. Its value as long fibre is such that it is one of the few materials which can be grown in suitable areas solely for use in paper. A comprehensive study on the potential of kenaf carried out in recent years in USA suggest that it can actually be grown for newsprint production in that country and could achieve greater yield from a given area at lower cost than wood. For Third World countries its growth, for cattle fodder and long fibre pulp in combination, is under serious consideration and seems the most promising route to follow.

The combination of long fibre shortage and the limited availability, within economic range, of the main fibre source, plus the scarcity of fuel and power, limits the scale of operations in all but a few selected situations. It is also limited by transport distances for the finished product. To many authorities, accepting without question the belief that scale is essential for viability, this is enough to inhibit investment. In reality it is only in one respect that the small, non-wood based mill suffers and that is in chemical recovery.

The modern recovery boiler is a very efficient and sophisticated unit capable of handling the liquors from pulp mills with a capacity up to 1 kt per day as unbleached pulp. It is less efficient at levels below 400 t/day and almost impossible to build in its known form much below 150 t/day. Taking into account additives and moisture contents, this indicates that a paper mill should be producing as much as 60 kt/day to include an effective chemical recovery which contributes steam in excess of its own and pulp mill needs.

A more reasonable scale, taking into account size of the market and other limitations referred to above for Third World countries, would be around 10 kt/year and this was the level set by the Indian government in their plan to encourage paper mills to use indigenous fibres. Chemical recovery is available and economic in terms of chemical costs at levels down to 15 t/day as pulp, but these units are consumers and not generators of steam, and the efficiency of chemical recovery is also less, from 15 to 25 per cent. There is need for effective small scale recovery, but it is unlikely that attempts to scale down the traditional wood-based recovery units will be undertaken. There have, however, been encouraging develop- ments. The Babcock Krauss Maffei kiln approach and the Sulzer, France, separated combustion approach. But the latter has now been delayed for lack of funds, and financial limitations are undoubtedly restricting progress in what is probably the most significant field.

Non-wood paper-making does have some advantages which compensate to a degree for the disadvantages. Fibre preparation is more simple, less capital intensive, cooking is quicker and chemical consumption, ignoring recovery, is normally less. Adequate bleaching can be achieved by a simple 3-stage process whereas wood requires 5-stages, costing more in capital investment and chemical preparation and consumption. Refining power for non-wood fibres is also considerably less than that required for wood and this is a significant factor in overall energy requirements.

Apart from chemical recovery and contrary to general belief, *scale has virtually no advantages to offer Third World countries.* It is inappropriate for the reasons which have been given, and socio-economically less rewarding. Capital costs are higher, intrinsically, and the total financial burden one which is beyond reach for most private enterprises and unattractive to governments. Scale can offer a reduction in manpower which is its greatest attraction for industrialised countries with their high wages, but in Third World countries labour costs will be higher in large scale production because of the expatriate component required plus the need for greater levels of skill and experience in all departments.

For Third World countries the need is for efficient paper mills based on indigenous fibres which can offer viability to investors from first commissioning, something which the modern giants cannot achieve even in industrial countries. It is possible at an appropriate scale. Capital costs can be lower per unit of production at scale around 10 kt/year, because sophistication and expensive materials for construction are not necessary to anything like the extent required for the large units. Quality and production efficiency can be achieved without the need for highly trained personnel or expatriates. Energy costs per unit of production can be lower, naturally because of the fibre characteristics and also because of lower speed, an essential component of scale which is energy intensive in terms of electric power and energy used in the process of drying. Pressing efficiencies are improved as speed is reduced, because water removal is a function of time.

The enormous potential market for paper in Third World countries offers prospects for standardisation of mill design which can still further reduce capital costs and training needs. This opportunity is not open to large scale production.

The level of paper consumption achieved in the Western world around the year 1900 would be, for want of a better definition, a reasonable target for Third World countries and still many times greater than present standards. It is interesting to look back at the machines of that era. They were virtually standard, around 2 to 3 m in width, running at speeds around 100 m per minute. They were cheap and easy to operate, becoming the foundation on which the present industry has been based.

The Third World needs something similar as a basis for their industry and could have it in improved form, taking advantage of the genuine advances in technology which have been achieved. They must use indigenous fibres, and, in the short-term at least, this means non-wood fibre sources for the majority of installations. The two major problems restricting progress are effective chemical recovery at small-scale production, and a reliable source of long fibre support. There is evidence that the former problem is possible to solve. The need for long fibre can be reduced by suitable machine design and economic speed, but the overall situation will still need substantial improvement. Kenaf may be the answer. This and many other possibilities should be thoroughly investigated on an industrial basis.

The paper problem for developing countries will not simply disappear. The need will remain as long as communications and education persist; the ultimate decline in the use of plastics as oil supplies are exhausted is likely to increase the demand for paper, culturally, commercially and industrially. No Third World country can hope to improve its press and publishing system without an improvement in paper availability, but it can only come from the exploitation of its own potential.

There is good evidence that small-scale paper mills based on indigenous fibres can be viable in Third World countries without excessive protection, even if the standards of productive efficiency are lower than would be considered acceptable by Western standards. There is no fundamental reason why standards should be lower, but it will need effort beyond what can be provided by the industry in its present state, to bring about the achievable improvements.

## REFERENCES


1. Cf Heikki Hellmann, Kaarle Nordenstreng and Tapio Varis: *Idealism, Aggression, Apology, and Criticism: The Four Traditions of Research on International Communication.* Paper presented to the XII Congress of the LAMCR, Caracas, 1980-08-26/29.
2. Joseph Ki-Zerbo: "Unterricht über die Dritte Welt und die Probleme ihrer Entwicklung" in: *Die Dritte Welt in Schule und Jugendarbeit,* ed by Jörg Becker, Frankfurt: Haag & Herchen 1980, p. 20.
3. Cf Beak Consultants Ltd: *Environmental Considerations in the Pulp and Paper Industry,* Washington, DC: The World Bank 1980.
4. Cf *The Energy Transition in Developing Countries,* Washington, DC: The World Bank 1983.
5. Cf George H Boyd III: "Production Costs and Competitiveness in Industry, in: *European Pulp and Paper in the 80's,* ed by the Financial Times, London: Financial Times Conference Organisation 1982, pp. 59-65.
6. Calculated after: US Department of Commerce: *Statistical Abstract of the United States,* Washington, DC: United States Department of Commerce 1984, table 806.
7. Quoted in: Carlos Contreras: *The Transfer of Technology to Developing Countries,* Caracas: Instituto Latinoamericano de Investigaciones Sociales 1978, p. 28.
8. Hans Wolfgang Jäger: "Die saure Quittung", in: *Das Papier Magazin* 7/1983.
9. Quoted in: "Waldsterben: Dem Überfluss folgt Mangel", in: *Süddeutsche Zeitung* 1984-01-17, p. 11.

# 2

BORJE KYRKLUND

# WHEN AND WHY IS SMALL-SCALE PULP AND PAPER MANUFACTURE VIABLE

## 1. Introduction

OVER THE past fifteen years or so the minimum size of a financially feasible market pulp mill has doubled. At the same time the investment in that kind of mill has increased by about ten times. This development is due to what is commonly referred to as the "advantage of economies of scale". Rising manufacturing costs result in efforts to keep the fixed operating costs as small as possible in relation to the variable costs. For instance, the labour requirement for operating a pulp mill producing 100,000 t/annum is about the same as for one which produces 300,000 t/annum. In fact, with today's advanced technology and automation, the labour requirement in a modern mill is considerably smaller than in the smaller optimum-size mill 10 to 15 years ago.

In the field of paper manufacture, the economies of scale have had a similar effect on the optimum size of paper mills and normally this is considered to be a general trend today. On the other hand, financing of pulp and paper mill projects has become increasingly difficult because of their capital intensiveness, the fluctuating market and the high risks which seem to be involved in such an investment.

In the industrialised world, especially in Scandinavia and North America, there is therefore a tendency toward formation of increasingly larger enterprises through mergers. Accordingly there seems to be very little scope for the individual entrepreneur to enter into this industrial sector with a mill of his own. Nevertheless, there are still small mills in many countries which are viable enterprises although the reasons for their viability may vary considerably from one mill to another.

The Food and Agriculture Organisation of the United Nations (FAO) and the United Nations Industrial Development Organisation (UNIDO) are both involved with development of pulp and paper industries. Expressed in a somewhat simplified manner, FAO is concerned mainly with wood-based pulp and paper, whereas UNIDO deals with pulp and paper derived from agricultural residues. The two organisations have, over the years, cooperated on the development of small to medium-sized pulp and paper mills through identification of constraints and attempts to find means for eliminating them. In the case of UNIDO, work has, to a large extent, been carried out on a technological level, such as research into desilification of black liquor, whereas FAO has been more concerned with techno-economic evaluations of various technological developments in this field. Joint meetings have also been organised on this subject on several occasions, for instance in New Delhi (1978), Manila (1980), Bangkok (1985) and Alexandria (1986).

## 2. What is Small?

The question that immediately arises in the context of discussions of small-scale mills is the definition of "small". A market pulp mill of 150,000 t/annum, if built today, would be considered "small". On the other hand, a fine paper mill with the same output would be considered large. Similarly a fine paper mill based on straw as raw material and producing 50,000 t/annum would be considered to be large, if not *too* large, to be financially viable. If the same mill used wood as raw material, it would again be considered small. Therefore, seen from a purely technical point of view, what is "small" depends to a large extent on the product and the raw material.

Another technical parameter which influences the selection of optimum scale of operation is the process technology used. For instance, economies of scale have traditionally a very pronounced influence on the size of a market pulp mill, as shown in Fig. 2.1. Thus, the investment cost per unit output decreases sharply with increased size of operation until a levelling-off effect can be noticed at higher production rates. In mechanical type pulping processes, the economies of scale are much less pronounced as far as the pulping process is concerned. On the other hand, the technology of paper-making is about the same whether the raw material is mechanical pulp or chemical pulp, and this has its bearing on the economies of scale of integrated paper manufacture regardless of pulping process.

As a simple rule of thumb, the "small" mills referred to in this paper would have a capacity of 35,000 to 70,000 t/annum for integrated production of bulk grades, like newsprint, linerboard, sack kraft, etc., from wood. Small-scale production of printing and writing paper would be 10,000 to 35,000 t/annum, and certain waste-paper based operations could have a capacity of below 10,000 t/annum.

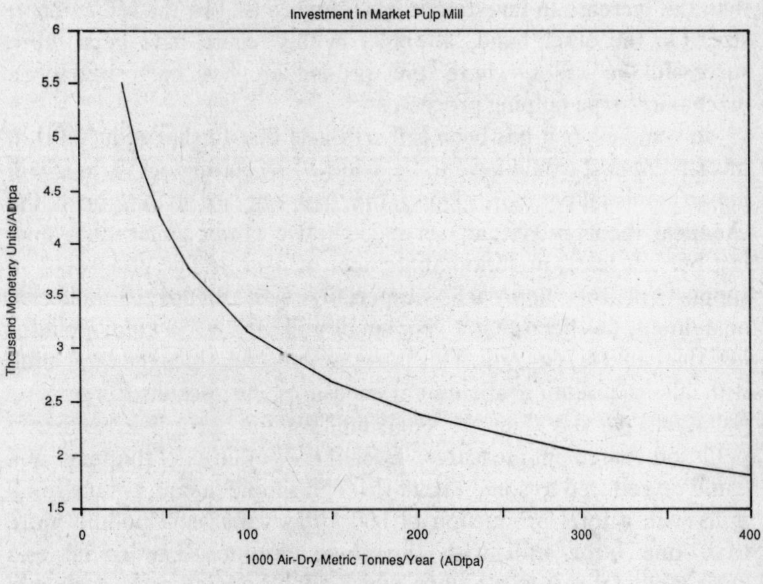


FIG. 2.1: Economies of Scale

## 3. Cost Reduction Through Technical Design

To achieve reductions in the effect of the economies of scale, many attempts have been made to simplify the design of the mill. The efforts in changes in design have in general been based on the assumption that, by reducing instrumentation and simplifying the processing of the fibrous raw material, considerable savings could be made. Most of such approaches have failed to produce the expected result. The reason for this is quite obvious. In a mill of today's technology, producing paper and integrated with chemical pulp manufacture from wood, the investment in instrumentation is about 5 per cent and the investment in the actual fibre line is only about 30 per cent of the total investment.[1] Thus, in the extreme case of achieving a 50 per cent reduction in the cost of instrumentation and in the fibre line in general, the overall investment requirement could be reduced by somewhat more than 15 per cent. It is evident that this would still be insufficient, especially since this saving is usually less than the increase in investment per tonne caused by the reduction in size. On the other hand, attempts in this regard have been more successful in cases where the production has been based on mechanical-type pulping processes.[2]

In some cases it has been fully realised that further reductions in investment cost would have to be achieved by cutting out various mill departments altogether. Thus, the first one to go has been the chemical recovery system; second, captive power generation; and, last but not least, pollution abatement measures. The philosophy in support of this approach, especially with regard to pollution abatement, has been that a very small mill of, say, 30 t/day pollutes less than a 800 t/day mill. This is not exactly true since the large mill, with all its pollution abatement measures, in fact discharges less pollutants per day than the small mill without recovery system and pollution abatement measures.[3] Even if the pollution of the small mill could be reduced to some extent through simple means, twenty small mills with a total production of 600 t/day would still pollute more than one large mill with the same output. The social and environmental cost to a country which adopts a blind small-scale mill policy under such circumstances can be considerable.

## 4. Selection of Project Parameters

There is an old saying that it is not the great income that makes a man wealthy but the small expenditures. The first step to improving the viability of a small-scale pulp and paper mill operation is, therefore, good housekeeping so that the cost of operation is kept as low as possible. This, of course, is valid for any size of operation, but is even more important for small mills which tend to have, relatively speaking, a higher fixed cost per tonnage produced and very often also higher variable costs. For instance, lack of chemical recovery, although saving investment and debt service expenses, also increases the variable cost of production. The only means for ensuring viability, that are available for direct control by the entrepreneur of the company, relate to:

(a) selection of raw material for pulping or paper-making;
(b) type of process (for instance, chemical or mechanical pulping, or entirely new solutions applicable to certain raw materials on a comparatively small scale);
(c) level of technology used;
(d) selection of product.

To the last item could be added the possibility of forward integration with converting industries; for instance, manufacture of folding boxboard integrated with box manufacture and printing. Horizontal integration can also be used to improve the viability of a small mill; for instance, by having a small pulp and paper mill integrated with a sawmill or, in the case of agricultural residues, integrated with a sugar mill, using bagasse as raw material.

The product mix needs, or course, to be selected with due consideration given to the market and its requirement on quality for that particular product. Lack of sophistication was already mentioned as one means of reducing cost and this is obviously possible to the highest extent if the product is unsophisticated as well. In that case, an "unsophisticated" raw material can be used through application of unsophisticated technology to produce such a product, provided there is a market for it. There is an obvious difference in requirements of raw materials, technology and quality between an operation producing cheap wrapping paper from mixed waste-paper, and another which produces high-grade printing and writing papers using wood or agricultural residues as raw material. These factors in general have a much higher impact on the viability of small-scale manufacture of a specific type of paper than modification of detailed design parameters for a mill producing a specific grade of paper. However, within one grade and one type of mill, attention given to design characteristics may contribute to lowering the cost of investment and production. In that context, use of second-hand equipment can be instrumental in reducing the investment cost and, in some cases, second-hand equipment is the only possible solution, since sufficiently small-scale equipment of the kind required may no longer be produced or may be too costly to produce today.

**5. Product Prices**

One set of measures for improving the viability of small-scale pulp and paper-making relates to government policies and geographical locations. Paper has to be sold at a price which is competitive in financial or economic terms with paper produced outside the country. The geographical location of some land-locked countries is such that imported paper may cost, in foreign exchange, more than twice the price charged on international markets. If paper is produced within the country, minimising the drain on foreign exchange, the economic benefit derived from this operation on a national level could well warrant maintaining the higher price of paper to ensure viability of the domestic paper manufacture. In such instances, however, the government needs to review the situation from time to time to ensure that unnecessary feather-bedding of the paper manufacture is avoided. Otherwise, adoption of this as a long-term measure might lead to inefficient operation.

The government may also wish to have domestic paper production to ensure a minimum self-sufficiency for its educational and communicational needs within the country. For such reasons it may, therefore, allow a higher price to be charged, and introduce measures for import restrictions or protective customs tariffs. Here again feather-bedding needs to be avoided, but the effect is the same as in the previous case, that an operation which, under other circumstances would be unviable, becomes financially and economically feasible.

**6. Know-How**

The three variables that ultimately determine the viability of any scale of operation of pulp and paper manufacture are investment, manufacturing cost and price of the product. These factors may, in turn, be affected by items such as choice of process, mill design, raw material, cost of power, and product quality. In order to achieve a viable operation, the factors which affect the three main variables need to be optimised. Some ways of doing this have already been mentioned but a very important aspect of this needs special attention.

Normally, in developing countries, the investor has to rely on outside know-how for implementation of his pulp and paper project. This means payment of high fees to expatriate consultant companies for preparation of feasibility studies and for engineering of the process. Secondly, foreign companies need to be involved in supply of equipment, civil works and installation of equipment. Finally, an administration contract needs to be signed with an expatriate company for operation of the mill once it is built. All this expatriate assistance is provided at a certain cost which, in some cases, may even double the investment compared with what it would be in an industrialised country where the necessary expertise would be available locally. Availability of know-how in the country itself, therefore, has a very strong bearing on the viability of a pulp and paper enterprise, especially if its capacity is in the small to medium size. Some developing countries are very fortunate in this respect and India is definitely one of them. A pulp and paper mill in India can be built almost 100 per cent with Indian expertise. In fact, there are examples where the expertise has been 100 per cent Indian, as well. Thus, in a country like India, where know-how is available for preparation of feasibility studies, planning and construction of the mill, equipment manufacture and mill operation, the costs of establishing a pulp and paper mill are no doubt minimised. Under those conditions and by provision of incentives, the pulp and paper industry can set its own patterns for development of this sector.

The patterns arrived at under those conditions may, at first sight, seem interesting examples to be followed in other developing countries. Here, however, one easily falls into the trap of trying to copy blueprints of one solution to an entirely different environment. This can lead to the same kind of disappointments as when developing countries try to build blueprints of pulp and paper mills from industrialised countries.

What, then, about transfer of technology from one developing country to another by using the know-how available in one country to develop an adapted form of technology for another country? This is, no doubt, the road which shows most promise although there are several pitfalls in this approach as well. Proposals to this effect have very often neglected the fact that, although trained labour and personnel at all levels are available at very low cost in the originating country, their cost, by the time they are in the recipient country, may have risen considerably. For instance, the salary of a senior engineer in India is insufficient to pay for housing for his family in many developing countries. Accordingly, his salary would need to be doubled, it not trebled, and this would go for the rest of the expatriate personnel as well. In addition, the staff may not have been exposed to international conditions and tend to try to transfer their own solution as such to the new country.

A mixed approach has been used in some instances for transfer of technology through cooperation of international consulting and contracting companies with corresponding companies in a developing country where know-how exists. India has, in this way, been involved in some projects in Africa and South-East Asia. This seems to offer some promise, although it is still too early to draw any definite conclusions. In any case, through this approach, the recipient country has the benefit of the international experience of consulting and contracting companies as well as the developing country experience of the cooperating country.

## 7. Conclusions

The points listed in this paper for consideration in the discussion of small-scale pulp and paper manufacture do not point to any revolution in the validity of the concept of economies of scale. However, they show that, under certain conditions and/or by selection of the right combination of product, process and raw material, viable small-scale paper manufacture still has a place in the supply of paper to the markets both in the industrialised world and in developing countries.

In some developing countries, with good facilities with regard to technical know-how in the design and manufacture of equipment, design and construction of pulp and paper mills, and know-how in their operation, further improvement in the viability of small-scale manufacture can be achieved. This depends on very specific conditions where normal rules of viable production do not apply. Countries with such specific conditions can, however, contribute significantly to the transfer of technology to other developing countries. Even without such specific conditions, manufacture of pulp and paper on a considerably smaller scale than that considered normal can be a fully viable alternative. No general rules can, however, be given for how this can be achieved. The success or failure of efforts to establish smaller scale pulp and paper mills depend entirely on local conditions and each case has to be studied specifically.

## REFERENCES

1. FAO: Establishing Pulp and Paper Mills — A Guide for Developing Countries, pp. 23-29. FAO Forestry Paper 45, Rome (1983).
2. FAO: FAO Advisory Committee on Pulp and Paper, 24th Session. FO:PAP/83/Inf.13, Rome (1983).
3. Kyrklund, B.: Are Pollution Abatement Measures Necessary in Small-Scale Pulp and Paper Mills? Paper presented by UNEP Consultative Committee on Pulp and Paper (1980).

# 3

ROGER L. GRANT

## OPTIMUM IS BEAUTIFUL
### Small Mills can Work

THE SENTIMENT "small is beautiful" has received little more than polite interest from our industry. Small wonder. Juggernaut mills make spectacular reading, and their creation and operation provide work for many suppliers and engineers. For the eventual mill owner, large scale appears to be a built-in means of counter-acting unfavourable economic influences. Reprint of an article from the magazine *Pulp & Paper International*, December 1987, pp. 51, with the kind permission of the author and the publishing house. As the article is a few years old, the author sent us the following statement: The main title of the article "Optimum is beautiful" remains forever true. However, the external factors relative to which a mill concept is optimum—be they economic, market or technological—are changing. One example of such a change since the article was written is the installation of large new units, the expansion of existing ones, and the closure of some small old ones. The outcome is a move to higher mill capacities in Figs. 3.1 and 3.2. An example of a change in market conditions is the fragmentation of traditional paper and board grades. Among technological changes, CTMP has gained acceptance as a near-softwood-kraft-quality pulp and processing is being extended into less common wood species. Superimposed one these trends is the ever-changing relationship between pulp and paper prices. These examples serve to underline the point that the word "optimum" refers not only to the scale of a mill, but to its total concept.*

Few things can be extrapolated indefinitely. since costs took off at the end of the 1960s, a small but growing school has been questioning the wisdom of increasing scale, in the context of both developed and developing countries. The recent saturation of certain markets has focused additional attention on the subject. Other industries have similarly been studying their own operations.

Little has been published of an economic nature on the question of scale, and this article attempts to help fill the gap. It is, of course, necessary to make numerous generalisations; this should not cloud the fact that every mills has its own individual economics.

By way of clarification, the article refers primarily to the optimum initial capacity of the new greenfield site mill. However, expansions are a recognised means of improving a mill's economics, and the principles discussed here generally apply. Further, we need to explain three terms that appear frequently in the text:

* "Capital burden" is used to denote the sum of interest and depreciation.
* "Unit," as used in "unit power cost," etc., refers to the cost of power per tonne of mill output. Mill output can be regarded as synonymous with mill capacity for the present purpose.
* "Optimum," The optimum scale of mill is the most acceptable mill size when all influencing factors have been taken into consideration. As we shall see, it is not necessarily the scale giving the maximum financial return.

Figure 3.1 permits us to take a broad initial view of the subject. In essence it summarizes the range of mill scale that is "viable": according to the relevant market, finished product and fibrous raw materials available. Each range of mill scale is represented by full lines for the most commonly encountered local circumstances and by broken lines for those less commonly encountered.

Wheat straw and esparto grass mills usually fall into the lower part of the "bagasse" range. Mills producing paper for export are usually integrated with pulp mills of capacity similar to the range shown for export pulp. Their slush pulp is generally either totally converted into a single family of grades (mechanicals or linerboards) or else fragmented between a limited number of products (writings and printings, coated and market pulp). This does not apply to paper specialities, which can of course be produced competitively in smaller scale mills.

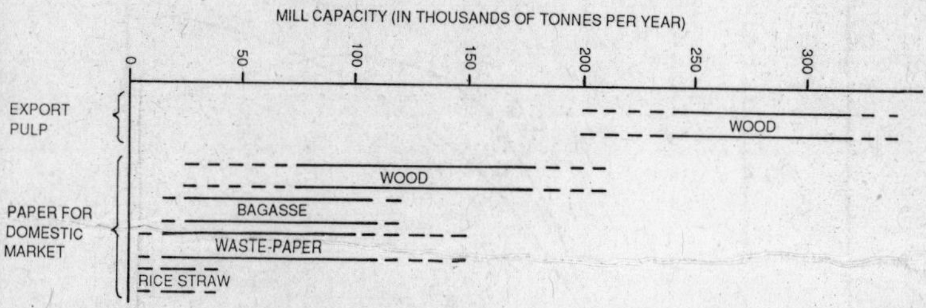


FIG. 3.1: **Viable levels of mill capacity according to market, finished product, and fibrous raw materials**

Two factors stand out as influencing the mill scale range. One is the protection that import duties can provide in the domestic market, but not in the international (export) market. The other is the total cost of pulping as related to the selling price of the finished paper product. To illustrate the latter, rice straw is generally cheaper than wood and requires less expensive processing to produce papers of similar acceptability to the market of a developing country.

Figure 3.1 in fact shows the mill scale ranges within which acceptable financial returns are produced. Let us now look more closely at the elements that influence this return. In round terms we can classify them as being of three types, according to how their unit cost varies with mill scale.

The unit costs of two elements, namely capital burden and salaries, decrease fairly markedly with increasing mill scale. We shall return to the relationship between capital burden and mill scale below. As for salaries, the decrease results from few additional staff being necessary as the mill scale increase.

The following elements are essentially independent or semi-independent of mill scale: pulping chemicals, purchased pulp, paper additives, steam and power, wages, consumable and maintenance materials, and water and effluent treatment chemicals. To the extent that their unit costs do change with scale, they usually decline.

This leaves three principal elements: wood, waste-paper and finished product delivery cost. Due to the delivery component they have in common, all three generally increase with increasing mill scale. Thus wood and waste-paper have to be brought in from

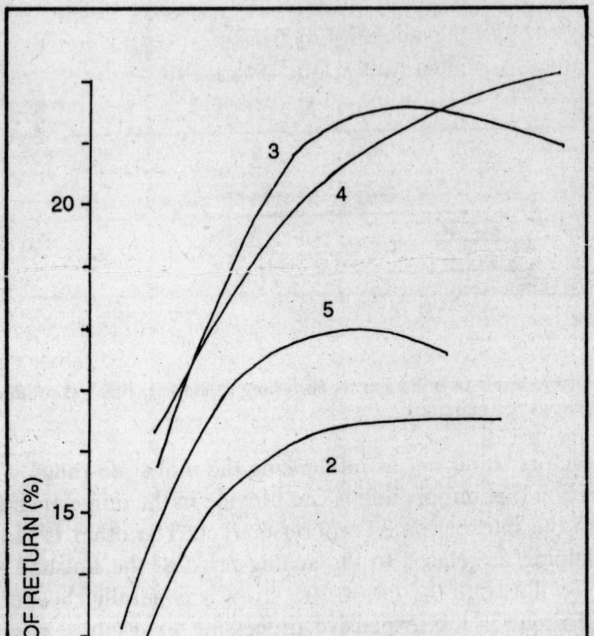


FIG. 3.2: Influence of mill scale on the rate of return for mills making: 1. unbleached kraft pulp from pine: 2. bleached kraft pulp from pine and birch: 3. unbleached Mg sulfite pulp from spruce; 4. newsprint from spruce pulpwood and purchased unbleached sulfite; 5. corrugating medium from birch pulpwood and purchased kraft pulp

progressively greater distances, and the finished product transported to customers increasingly far afield. The actual pattern of cost increase will of course depend on the respective distributions of fibrous raw material availability and finished product demand.

The picture of increasing mill scale is thus one of competing economic influences leading to the likelihood of an optimum mill scale for each set of circumstances.

### 1. Rate of Return (ROR) Curve and its Implications for Investors

To see how these influences interact, it is convenient to borrow from Eklund's work.[1] The purpose of his original article was to demonstrate the superior economics of forest industry integrates. His data have been used here to derive Fig. 3.2. Basically it illustrates the influence of mill scale on the rate of return on capital (ROR – cash flow per investment requirements) for five different types of mill. Three of the curves show fairly flat peaks, one levels off, and one keeps on climbing, albeit at a decreasing rate.

The maximum ROR, in all cases except the newsprint mill (Curve 4), occurs at around the 900 t/day level. From a technical viewpoint, this corresponds approximately to the then-current limit for a single pulping line. However, from a financial point of view, 900 t/day may not be the optimum scale. For example, for Curves 1, 2 and 5 it might be decided to adopt the 600 t/day level. The ROR would then be only 1 per cent lower, but the capital requirement would be reduced by 20 per cent. Market saturation considerations might also support this approach.

The absolute level of the curve is also relevant. Thus, for example, mills showing a high rate of return (Curves 3 and 4) could be accepted at a lower tonnage level than those showing a lower return (Curves 1 and 2).

Eklund's data refer to hypothetical mill models representing Finnish conditions in 1969. Since then, ROR has dropped, thus effectively lowering the curves in Fig. 3.1. The models have also been tested against actual Scandinavian conditions. Steeper curves resulted where larger one-line production units had become technically feasible or wood transportation costs proved more favourable. "Steeper curves" initially rise somewhat more steeply and flatten further to the right of the diagram.

The bulk of Finland's production is exported and it is worth pointing out the correspondence of scale between the wood pulp mills in Figs. 3.1 and 3.2. It is also worth drawing a rough parallel with the large export pulp mills being created in some developing countries and suggesting that they might be better off around the 600 t/day level than near the 900 t/day level. In their domain there are the additional considerations of raising the necessary capital and the influence of poor mill performance on the country's economy.

Bagasse, wheat straw and esparto grass, which are normally pulped in horizontal continuous digesters, usually show a maximum at the 200 t/day level. This corresponds to the largest such digester currently available. In addition, due to the slower drainage of these materials, the brown stock and bleach plant washers are approaching the largest sizes manufactured. At low tonnage levels acceptable returns can be obtained using batch digesters. In fact in practice there can be more than one maximum on the curve, albeit at different levels or ROR.

Rice straw is usually cooked in relatively small batch digesters and so does not benefit to such a degree from the scaling up of a single line. In addition, rice straw black liquor cannot be recovered because of its high silica content, so that a large volume may be difficult to dispose of.

From what has been said so far, it is evident that the absolute level and shape of the ROR-versus-mill-capacity curve are highly relevant to the selection of optimum scale. If the curve is pitched at a high absolute level due to such factors as favourable unit costs, selling prices or capital burden, an acceptable financial return may be achieved at relatively small scale. In the developing countries, incentives, such as high import duties (up to 75%) and tax holidays, are provided to make this possible. The actual shape of the ROR curve depends on the interplay of the various influencing cost elements as the scale of the mill increases.

Often developing countries wish to export a part or all or their production so as to turn their local raw materials into hard currency. Equally often, the additional delivery cost and unprotected selling price serve sharply to reduce the financial return.

## 2. Geographical, Technical and Economic Variations

Different processes in our industry are variously described as capital intensive, raw material intensive and energy intensive. From a financial viewpoint this means that the unit capital burden, raw material or energy cost accounts for a significant proportion of the total delivered cost of the finished product. It is also possible for a process to be intensive in more than one of these cost elements, although they may be mutually exclusive. As for labour intensity, large numbers of people are often employed in developing countries, particularly for raw material collection and finishing operations. Yet, due to low prevailing wage rates, they do not make a significant impact on the total economics.

A few examples serve to illustrate these three forms of intensity. For a large new market pulp mill on the US west coast operating on cheap wood (mainly residues) the cost of such wood might be around 20 per cent of the delivered pulp cost, while the unit capital burden could be double that. By contrast, a similar new Scandinavian mill, with its higher wood cost, could be paying around 40 per cent for its wood and about the same in capital burden.

TMP plants are said to be energy intensive. Operating on cheap wood residues, a small TMP plant (50 t/day) might have about equal unit costs for wood, power and capital burden, say 25 per cent each. At the 150 t/day level, capital burden would drop to 15 per cent and the other two components increase to about 30 per cent each. When operating on roundwood, the wood cost is proportionately greater.

Parenthetically, one can note that old mills, with little or no outstanding loan debt and essentially written-down assets, appear to have a small unit capital burden but correspondingly greater unit costs elsewhere. Inflation accounting philosophy, which bases depreciation on the replacement value, shows that this picture is rather misleading.

The fact that unit energy costs are semi-independent of mill scale permits us to narrow the field down to two prime influencing elements, namely capital burden and raw material. Since delivery is common to the delivered price of wood and waste-paper, as well as to the mill netback (sales price minus delivery), it is more useful for the present purpose to consider delivery alone. Capital burden and delivery are usually the main opposing factors that produce maxima in our ROR-versus-mill-capacity curve, and it is therefore worth examining the effect of scale upon them.

Let us consider capital burden first. In engineering generally there is the "power of 0.6" rule-of-thumb guide to costs, which effectively says that doubling the capacity of plant increases the capital cost by around 52 per cent. This is necessarily an approximate average figure. In our industry, extreme values of about 30 per cent and 90 per cent can be encountered. Kraft pulp mills with a single Kamyr cooking line lend themselves to low percentage figures, while mechanical pulp mills give high values.[1] In these two cases, increased scale is achieved by different physical means. In the first case, one set of units (digester, etc.) is enlarged to around the 1,000 t/day level, while in the other case the number of individual grinder or refiner units is increased. Paper mills costs increase at around the 60 per cent level. Obviously the inclusion of an additional unit (pulping line or paper machine) to achieve higher capacity pushes the percentage figure up somewhat.

From the point of view of financial return, it is the unit capital burden that counts. The 60 per cent figure for paper mills corresponds to a reduction of unit capital burden by 20 per cent when the mill size is doubled. Similarly, the above extreme figures of 30 per cent and 90 per cent translate into reductions of 35 per cent and 5 per cent, respectively. However, since the 30 per cent equipment configuration may well have a higher absolute unit capital burden at the lower scale, higher absolute unit capital burden at the lower scale, these scale reductions help bring them closer together.

For small-scale versions of usually large-scale equipment, the unit capital burden accounts for a particularly large proportion of the delivered cost of the finished product. This is the principal reason for the rapid initial rise in the Fig. 3.2 curves. It follows that small-scale installations should not be purely scaled-down versions of larger mills, but rather should use an appropriate level of less capital-intensive technology where possible.

It is unfortunately more difficult to make generalisations about delivery costs. This results partly from the fact that the distribution of fibrous raw material availability and finished product demand are different for every mill, and partly from the combinations of possible transport methods. One can say that the cost of transporting wood, with its high moisture content, is usually the most significant factor. For low yield processes (chemical pulp), the impact on unit wood costs is greater than for high yield processes (mechanical paper). However, since the unit capital burden of the former tends to be reduced by increases in scale to a greater extent than the latter, there is a certain offsetting influence here.

For transport by ship, handling at both ends is quite expensive and best value per unit of distance is usually obtained on the longer sea hauls. The cost of land transport is more closely proportional to distance. For transport of all forms of finished product the effect of higher energy prices has reduced somewhat the attraction of shipping to distant markets.

### 3. Present State of the Art of Building Small Mills

Having discussed the principles, let us now examine the present state-of-the-art with respect to small mills. We will start with the Krafft paper machine, for it elegantly illustrates our criteria for small scale (see Fig. 3.3 profile inset). It is noteworthy that all five machines are installed in developed countries (Netherlands and Fed. Rep. Germany). The machine is usually at its best located next to a large corrugating plant. There it can use the broke waste from the plant directly and buy in the balance of its waste-paper requirements. Thus delivery costs on both raw material and finished product are kept to a minimum.

For the reasons outlined in the inset box, capital and operating costs are also low. In fact the unit capital burden of such a mill equals that of one with a larger and faster paper machine of about three times its capacity. Contributory factors in the saving of capital and energy are the relatively narrow deckle and low speed. The latter also helps to reduce clothing and manning costs. Production of the machine as a fairly standardised item on suitably sized machine tools also adds to cost efficiency.

The machine as a concept is a breakthrough, although it contains no new technology. Rather it is the product of good economic analysis of the cost elements in combination with sensible engineering approaches to minimize them. In some respects it is a scaled-down version of large-paper-machine technology, while in other respects a different approach has been taken.

The Kraft machine falls into the lower end of the range for "Waste-paper" shown in Fig. 3.1. The figure similarly summarizes the current state of the art with respect to scale. Waste-paper and rice straw can already be made into certain paper grades on an adequately small scale. In this context small MG an reconditioned secondhand paper machines are used extensively to produce waste-based products in the lighter substances.

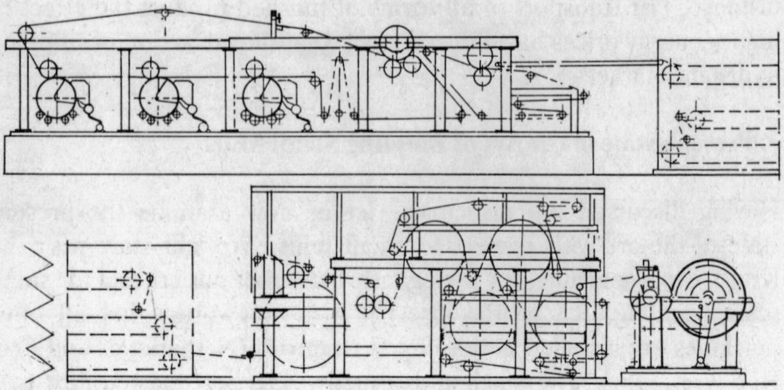

FIG. 3.3: Profile of the Krafft paper machine and its uses

**First of the mass production machines? Simple design and frequent orders — five so far installed — could make the Krafft paper and machine suitable for many small mills in industrial countries. Above dryer section, top wet-end.**

The machine drives its name from the manufacturer, Carl Krafft & Söhne of Düren, Fed. Rep. Germany. Typically it produces waste-based corrugating medium and testliner in the basis weight range 100-300 g/m$^2$. Since it has three to five formers, other multiply grades within this range can also be run. The maximum trim width is 2.45m, thus making it suitable for similarly wide corrugators. However, wider deckles, up to 5.0m, are possible to accommodate combinations of corrugator widths. Maximum machine speed is intentionally kept low at about 180 m/min. Typically the output of salable paper is around 70 t/day at and average basis weight of 120 g/m$^2$. At present five machines are in operation.

A simple waste plant is designed to treat the grades of waste-paper available plus any purchased pulp. The paper machine commences with three to five formers. Fans, rather than vacuum pumps, maintain the vacuum. In the event of a wet end break, automatic controls clear the broke and start production again. A double-nip press is followed by a high-pressure felted press.

The pre-dryer section is of particular interest. The expense of dryer cylinders is circumvented by adoption of a Dornier dryer. The paper web is carried on a light wire-mesh conveyor and fans circulate the drying medium under controlled evaporation conditions. Heating up to 260°C may be by indirect (steam or circulating oil) or direct means, but direct heating with gas, where available, usually gives optimum economics. Power consumption falls into the range 10-30 kWh/tonne of production. Relatively tension-free drying enhances paper quality. The dryer tiers can be stacked so as to fit available space.

Upon leaving the pre-dryer, the web wraps around a 2m-diameter drying cylinder. This serves to enhance the surface of linerboard. There follows a size press (optional) which can be used to improve the CMT properties of corrugating medium, and four or more 1.5m-diameter after-dryers. The machine is driven by a thyristor-controlled DC drive.

The machine house is also simple. No basement is required and the machine itself can be housed within a volume 10m wide by 75m long by 8m high. Steam requirements are generated in a small heater so that the boiler house is eliminated.

Manning is also low, for the machine can be tended by two men. Where two machines are installed in close proximity, one winder can serve both machines.

For the other main non-wood fibers (bagasse, wheat straw, bamboo, reed and esparto grass) the economic level is somewhat higher and the capital involved can represent a problem for developing countries. The situation becomes even more acute in the case of wood, although the viable level can be reduced somewhat by integrating with residue-producing sawmills. Thus this is the area where technological improvements are most needed.

One aspect of the problem is chemical recovery. The conventional recovery boiler is not economic until around the 2000 t/day (of pulp) level and at present there is no really inexpensive alternative available for smaller tonnages. In the existing approaches (Babcock Krauss-Maffei, Broby, Copeland and Zimpro) savings in capital are sometimes achieved at the expense of heat recovery, and they all require recausticising (and possibly a lime kiln) if the caustic soda is to be regenerated.

TMP plants have been installed at impressively low scales. Thus of those announced to date, about 30 per cent have been below the 100 t/day level and 65 per cent below the 200 t/day level. We have already shown that their economics are relatively insensitive to scale. Rather, their justification is based on TMP's ability to displace chemical pulps. Suitable cheap wood residues and inexpensive power naturally help the economics.

The other main area where there is a need for new thinking is that of non-integrated paper mills. Simply stated, the requirement is for a mill that can profitably produce paper on a small scale from purchased pulp. Dry forming was expected to make this possible at one time, but has not fulfilled its initial promise.

### 4. Pilot Plant Machines and their Unsuspected Potential

Extrapolating the argument for small machines, it can be seen that the pilot-plant-scale paper machines (Fig. 3.3) located at research establishments and academic institutions may indeed be viable commercially. Normally they are both used in-house and rented to out-side users. To the extent that their operating time is not fully taken up, they might usefully supplement R&D budget funds.

Capital outlay should be little or none, since most of the equipment probably already exists. Many of these machines are already highly automated. Supplementary automation might be justified to permit automatic running, including use of the "night shift." Automatic shut-down of the system could occur in the event of a break. The necessary raw materials could be obtained at bulk prices from associated companies. Imaginative products of a high added value, such as notepaper with a personalised watermark, would be marketed either locally or through associated company sales organisations. Given the paucity of these machines and their low individual output, world overcapacity is unlikely to be a problem. Small scale coaters and other pilot plant equipment might similarly play a part.

## REFERENCE

* Reprint of an article from the magazine *pulp & paper international*, December 1987, pp. 51, with the kind permission of the author and the publishing house. As the article is a few years old, the author sent us the following statement: The main title of the article "Optimum is beautiful" remains forever true. However, the external factors relative to which a mill concept is optimum — be they economic, market or technological — are changing. One example of such a change since the article was written is the installation of large new units, the expansion of existing ones, and the closure of some small old ones. The outcome is a move to higher mill capacities in Figures 1 and 2. An example of a change in market conditions is the fragmentation of traditional paper and board grades. Among technological changes, CTMP has gained acceptance as a near-softwood-kraft-quality pulp and processing is being extended into less common wood species. Superimposed on these trends is the ever-changing relationship between pulp and paper prices. These examples serve to underline the point that the word "optimum" refers not only to the scale of a mill, but to its total concept.

1. Eklund, R. and Kirjasniemi M. "An Approach to Economic Planning of Forest Industry Integrates," *Paper Trade Journal*, 153(45):54, 1969.

# 4

MANFRED F. JUDT

# CHEMISTRY PROBLEMS WITH NON-WOODY MATERIALS FOR PULP AND PAPER-MAKING IN DEVELOPING COUNTRIES AS SEEN BY UNIDO

THE USE of non-woody materials in pulp and paper-making is increasing in developing countries, where the expansion rate of pulp production will be twice as high as in developed countries by 1995. There is a need for more research and scientific understanding of such phenomena: Desilication of black liquors, lignin modifications, vessel picking, black liquor viscosity build-up, high-yield pulps with good strengths and flexible fibres from non-woody materials. Recommendations are given on how, by closer co-operation between R&D Centres in developed and developing countries and better selected research subjects for overseas' students, a better understanding of the chemistry problems of such materials could be gained in the future. UNIDO's role could be that of a catalyser.

## 1. UNIDO's Function within the UN-Family

UNIDO a, member of the United Nations Organisations, is 20 years old and started operations in Vienna on 1 January 1967. Its mandate, according to the United Nations General Assembly resolution 2152 (XXXI) of 17 November, 1966, is to promote and accelerate the industrialisation of the developing countries by:

- Encouraging and extending, as appropriate, assistance to the developing countries for the development, expansion and modernisation of their industries;
- Assisting developing countries in establishing and operating

industries to achieve full utilisation of locally available natural and human resources, and contributing to self-reliance;

- Providing a forum and acting as an instrument to serve the developing and industrialised countries in their contacts, consultations and negotiations;
- Developing special measures designed to promote co-operation among developing countries and between developed and developing countries.

To co-ordinate the work within the UN-family, also in the pulp and paper field, there is an "Agreement setting out guidelines for co-operation between the Food and Agriculture Organisation of the United Nations (FAO) and UNIDO in the field of industrial development".

According to the spirit of this agreement it is UNIDO's responsibility to care for the existing pulp and paper industries in the developing countries, and to help to promote the usage of non-woody fibrous materials world-wide. On the other hand, it is FAO's responsibility to care for the forestry sector and to promote the usage of softwoods and hardwoods in green-field pulp mills in the developing world.

The responsibility of the pulp and paper department within UNIDO is to work through the governments of the respective countries and provide the following services upon request: UNIDO shall:

- Supply governments, mills and institutions, with experts who, through their experience, will assist in increasing the production and usage of more pulp and paper;
- Carry out opportunity and pre-feasibility studies for new pulp and paper mills using non-woody fibrous materials;
- Advise, through experts, existing mills on how to produce more efficiently and also how to diversify their production using more indigenous fibrous raw materials and waste-paper;
- Provide general information on all phases of pulp and paper-making supported by a data bank;
- Help to finance and operate pilot plant units where specialised technologies will be developed;
- Help to train and educate nationals from developing countries in appropriate and new technologies and in scientific research

of interest to those countries;

- Invite experts from developing countries to attend international conferences or arrange such conferences in specialised fields for such experts, to make them better acquainted with developments in pulp and paper-making, and help them to apply this knowledge in their home countries, thereby also creating partnerships between mills and research and training institutions amongst developing countries.

## 2. The Future of the Pulp and Paper Industry

Only a few months ago FAO[1] in its paper "The Outlook for Pulp and Paper to 1995" confirmed that the pulp and paper industry will be a growth industry, and from Table 1 one can see that in the *developed* countries this growth rate will be 3 per cent per annum up to 1995, but it will be 5.1 per cent in the developing countries, and in the Far East it will even be 6 per cent per annum. This means that a lot of additional pulp/paper capacities will be built in which a wide variety of fibrous raw materials including non-woody fibres will be used.

TABLE 1: Past and Projected Annual Growth in Production of Paper

*(per cent per year)*

| | Actual | FAO | |
|---|---|---|---|
| | 1970-82* | 1982*-90 | 1990-95 |
| *World* | 2.7 | 2.7 | 3.4 |
| *Developed Market Economies* | 2.2 | 2.5 | *3.0* |
| North America | 1.9 | 2.0 | 2.2 |
| Western Europe | 2.3 | 2.5 | 3.3 |
| Oceania | 3.0 | 1.8 | 3.3 |
| Others | 3.1 | 4.1 | 4.6 |
| *Developing Market Economics* | 7.8 | 2.9 | 5.1 |
| Africa | 6.6 | 1.8 | 4.8 |
| Latin America | 6.7 | 3.0 | 4.5 |
| Near East Africa | 0.5 | 0.9 | 6.2 |
| Near East Asia | 10.0 | 2.8 | 5.1 |
| Far East | 10.2 | 2.7 | *6.0* |
| *Centrally Planned Economies* | 3.8 | 3.9 | 4.5 |
| Asia | 7.0 | 5.4 | 5.4 |
| Europe and USSR | 2.7 | 3.1 | 3.9 |

82* = 1980-1984 average

## 3. The Future of Non-Wood Plant Fibre Usage in Pulp and Paper-Making in Developing Countries

It should be remembered that up to 140 years ago the only fibres used for paper-making were from non-woody agricultural products such as wool, linen, flax, cotton, straw, etc., and to a large extent from recycled rags. Only recently have softwoods and hardwoods begun to be used for pulp and paper-making. Today these fibres have taken over 93 per cent of the market.

But there are large areas in the world, like the Middle East, North Africa and Central Asia, which do not possess indigenous supplies of wood, but have plenty of agricultural residues like straws, bagasse, reeds and graminees, like bamboo.

At the EUCEPA Symposium in Madrid in 1974 Atchison[2] showed that there was a world potential of 1000 million tonnes/annum of different non-wood materials but only 5.4 million tonnes of pulps were produced. In a more recent paper[3] he gives a breakdown of non-wood fibre pulp capacities by country and this production has increased in 1986 to over 11 million tonnes/annum. The world production of wood pulps was about 190 million tonnes in 1986.

So there is no shortage of non-wood materials in developing countries.

When one looks at the scientific literature on the chemistry and the physics of such plant fibres one is shocked by its "under-development". Of course, why should wood chemists work with annual fibres when 93 per cent of the world pulp and paper production is based on wood-fibres? But looking ahead, the growth rates of pulp and paper-making in developing countries will be two times higher than in developed countries.

Therefore allow me now to pinpoint problems which do need research work. Solutions will help the existing mills to make their production more scientific and cost-effective, and they will help the new 10 to 15 million tonnes of extra capacity needed until 1995 to do a better job in the developing countries.

In Table 2 Mc Govern[4] collected data from which it can be seen that most non-wood fibres have fibre dimensions which are longer and thinner than the fibres in northern hemisphere hardwoods. These characteristics are valued by paper-makers, because very smooth paper-surfaces, for example can be made with such fibres.

TABLE 2: Approximate Dimensions of Various Wood and Non-wood Fibres Used in Paper-Making[5]

| Fibrous Material | Length (mm) Range | Length (mm) Average | Diameter (mm) Range | Diameter (mm) Average | Reference in[(4)] |
|---|---|---|---|---|---|
| Bagasse | 0.8–2.8 | 1.7 | 10–64 | 20 | 18 |
| Bamboo | 1.5–4.4 | 2.7 | 7–27 | 14 | 18 |
| Cotton Lint* | 10.0–40.0 | 18.0 | 12–38 | 20 | 20 |
| Esparto | 0.5–1.6 | 1.1 | 7–14 | 9 | 18 |
| Kenaf, Bast | 2.0–6.0 | 5.0 | 14–33 | 21 | 20 |
| Woody | – | 0.5 | – | 38 | 17 |
| Jute | 1.5–5.0 | 2.0 | – | 20 | 8 |
| Manila Hemp | 2.0–12.0 | 6.0 | 16–32 | 24 | 20 |
| Reeds | 0.3–4.0 | 1.2 | 3–32 | 12 | 23 |
| Sisal | 0.8–8.0 | 3.0 | 8–41 | 20 | 20 |
| Straw, Cereal | 0.7–3.0 | 1.5 | 7–27 | 13 | 18 |
| Rice Straw | 0.6–3.5 | 1.5 | 5–14 | 8.5 | 20 |
| Temperate Woods | | | | | |
| Coniferous | | | | | |
| Tracheids | 2.7–4.6 | – | 32–43 | – | 9 |
| Deciduous | | | | | |
| Fibres | 0.7–1.6 | – | 20–40 | – | 9 |

* Linters are shorter (6 mm), more cylindrical, and have thicker walls than lint fibres.

## 4. Some Open Questions in Pulp and Paper-Making with Non-Woody Materials

### *4.1. Plant Science — Silica Content*[6,7,8]

The plants bamboo, bagasse, reeds, straws have increasing percentages of silica in their plant structure which in pulping and chemical recovery causes many problems like: (a) scale formation in evaporator tubes, (b) hard smelt deposits on furnace walls of recovery boiler, (c) slow settling rate of recausticised white liquor, and (d) make lime sludge unsuitable for lime mud reburning.

As a result the chemical recovery operation and its economy are adversely affected.

### *4.2. Questions*

How does the silica from the soil enter into the plant?

How is it deposited?
Which chemical structures are present?
How much of the silica is water soluble and/or alkali soluble?

UNIDO developed a desilication process whereby carbonisation silica from bamboo-bagasse black liquors can be precipitated.

Sometimes very fine, practically non-filterable sludges are formed, sometimes sand-gritty-like agglomerates. Why these differences?

Annual plants seem to absorb from the soils, and from the fertilisers which are applied, cations (sodium, potassium, magnesium, etc.) which, when in a black liquor smelt or in a fluidised bed combustion unit, influence the smelt temperature. Such variations in smelt temperature can result in either loosing chemicals through the stack or solidifying the fluidised bed thereby making chemical recovery units unworkable.

What is the chemistry involved? How can such a behaviour be predicted?

### *4.3. Vessel Picking*[9, 10]

In offset-papers or in coated papers this is a widely known problem when using hardwood pulps from moderate or tropical areas. It can also occur in bamboo and bagasse pulps. What are the causes? Are some vessels more hydrophobic than others? Or is it also the size of the different vessels? Or do the variations in the pulping technology create vessels that pick or do not pick? When you have pulps with vessels that pick, how must the pulps be treated in the stock preparation area to make them non-picking?

Or are there tree species which have vessels that must pick?

It is known that many non-woody fibrous materials are *brittle* and *hard to wet out* by nature, and here research on how to reduce these characteristics could help to have longer fibres and more flexible fibres in the finished pulps.[11,12]

And there is the big area of *storing such materials* because they are not available all year round.

*For example*: Bagasse storage: How to preserve fibre strength and brightness? There are several methods — a new one has just been published[13] — but where is the science of fermentations of alcohol in a bagasse pile or a bagasse bale? How should it be controlled?

### *4.4. Pulping*

Non-woody materials in general have less lignin, therefore, they are easier to pulp — one big advantage of their usage. Is the structure of their lignins different from wood lignins? Bamboo lignin is pink in colour. Why?[14,15]

The percentage of lignin and hemicelluloses in these materials is different from hardwood. It is well known that kraft — or soda black liquors upon concentrating have above 35 per cent solids/sharp increases in viscosity that make such black liquors difficult to handle. Which chemical substances are responsible for these viscosity increases? How can they be eliminated or chemically modified so that such black liquors can be handled easily above 55–60 per cent solids?

An answer must be found, because many pulp mills in developing countries do not have chemical recovery units because they are too expensive to run, or where they are installed bigger mills, excessive costs occur.

What is the effect of silica in the viscosity scenario? There are some conflicting publications either confirming that silica does increase the viscosities or does not influence the viscosities.[8]

Bleached chemical pulps have rather low yields, all efforts are welcome to make good pulps with higher yields, therefore research in soda/anthraquinone pulping of non-wood materials might even be more rewarding than with hardwoods.[16]

Do we really understand why it is practically impossible to make good mechanical pulps from such materials? Which chemical pre-treatments make such materials swell and wet out quickly? Are there latency problems with bamboo or bagasse CTMP pulps? Are they different from softwood and hardwood CTMP or CTMP pulps?[17,18]

Are bamboo or bagasse or straw pulps suitable for fluffing? Are their "other constituents" acceptable in hygienic products?

Why do such pulps when dried and then repulped, i.e. market pulps, lose far more strength than softwood or hardwood pulps? What can be done against it ? To ship them semi-dried, as done e.g. with hemp pulps, is not the answer for the future.

Is there a chance of using biopulping approaches while storing the bagasse to save chemicals in pulping and to get a better pulp at lower costs? Here is a real challenge to test the recently discovered ligninases.[19, 20]

And there is the new, but very challenging field involving the use of such non-woody materials for pulping and paper-making, but also for by-products in the pulp mill like bagasse screen rejects and pith for animal fodder or black liquors from unbleached straw pulp mills as fertilisers in rice fields.[21]

May I close by pointing out that the application of oxygen in pulping, and bleaching and treating black liquors of such materials, opens a vast area of new possibilities, where the small mill of the future in a developing country will eliminate chlorine and sulfur and still produce pulps in a manner which is far less polluting than the conventional methods.

UNIDO is confident that non-wood fibres have a great deal to offer. They have the advantage that they grow yearly, even sometimes thrice yearly, like rice, and that often parts of the plant are converted into food. There is a world-wide rediscovery at present that the priority activities in developing countries must be in agriculture and in food production to meet the needs of the fast growing populations in these countries. Often industrialisation has fallen back to second priority.

## REFERENCES

1. FAO Publication: "The Outlook for Pulp and Paper to 1995".
2. Atchison, J.E.: "Symposium International, EUCEPA, Madrid, May 1984".
3. Atchison, J.E.: "Non-wood Pulp's gradual Challenge", *PPI* — Dec. 83, 58-60.
4. Mc Govern, J.N.: *TAPPI*, 1975, 58(1): 82—86.
5. Carpenter, C.H.: "Paper-making Fibres" — State University College of Forestry at Syracuse University, Syracuse, New York, 1963.
6. Marcks, R. and Schildhauer, G.: "Trials prove Black Liquor System" *PPI* 86(11): 48—49.
7. Bleier, F.: "Desilication" — UNIDO Publication, UNIDO/10/629 p. 206—214
8. Kar, S.K. *et al.*: "Physico-Chemical Characteristics of Soda Black Liquor of Rice and Wheat Straw.
9. Colley, J. *et al.*: "Overcoming the Vessel-Picking of Coated Papers" *APPITA* vol. 39, No. 1, 26—30.
10. Ohsawa, J. *et al.*: "Prevention of Vessel-Picking Trouble in Tropical Hardwood Pulps" *J. Jpn. Wood Res. Soc.* Vol. 30 No. 9, 1984, 742—749 (several publications).
11. Tam Doo, P.A. and Kerekes, R.J.: "The Flexibility of Wet Pulp Fibres", Pulp and Paper Canada 83:2. T37—T41.
12. Salmen, L: "Thermal Softening of the Components of Paper, its Effect on Mechanical Properties", STFI-meddleland serie A No. 600.
13. Atchison, J.; "Controlled Fermentation is the Key", *PPI* 86 (11), 44—45.
14. Jianhao, Feng and Glasser, W.: "The Chemical Structure of Bagasse Lignin", *China Pulp and Paper*, Vol. 5, 3 (1986), 13—17.

15. Sabatier, J. *et. al.*: "Structural Changes" in Bagasse Lignin by Alkaline Peroxide II, *Cellulose Chem. Techn.* 20, 1986, 51—57.
16. Kuang Shijun: "Some Aspects of Soda and Soda/AG Pulping of Reed", *Cellulose Chem. Techn.* 20, 1986, 93—105.
17. Vikström, B. and Nelson, P.: "Mechanical Properties of Chemically Treated Wood and Chemimechanical Pulps", STFI meddelande serie A No. 640.
18. Vikström, B. and Hammar, L.: "Defibration in Chemimechanical Pulping Vicoelastic Properties of Kraft. Sulfide/Sulfite and Bisulfite Cooked Spruce Wood", STFI meddelande, Serie A No. 580.
19. Eriksson, K.E. and Kirk, T.K.: "Biopulping, Biobleaching and Treatment of Kraft Bleaching Effluents with White—Rot Fungi", STFI-meddelande Serie A No. 957, 986.
20. Kirk, T.K., Tien, Ming, Eriksson, K.E., Johnsrad, S.C.: "Lignin Degrading Activity of Phanerochaete Chrysoporium Burds, Comparison of Cellulose-Negative and other Strains", STFI-meddelande, Serie A No. 955, 1986.
21. Rajannan, G. *et. al.*: "Effect of Paper Factory Effluents on Soil and Crop Plants" *Indian J., Environmental Hlth.* Vol 21. No. 2, 1979, 120-130.
22. Judt. M.: "Research Problems in Developing Countries Using Non-Woody Fibres as seen by UNIDO", Transactions of the Fundamental Research Symposium, Cambridge, 1981, 829—849.

# 5

S. SRINIVASAN

# TECHNOLOGICAL INFORMATION PILOT SYSTEM

## Its Relevance for the Paper Industry

"ARE YOU aware that researchers at the Fibre Industry Development Authority (FIDA) in the Philippines have developed a process for extracting fibre from kenaf by retting an bacterial action?"
"Would you like to consider a Filipino technology offer for producing paper from rice straw?"
"Do you require aluminium sulfate, used for sizing paper?"
"Can you supply machinery and technology and provide finance for a paper recycling plant in Nicaragua?"
"A Pakistani company seeks technology for paper manufacture from agricultural waste materials. Can you help them?"
"Do you want to bid for supplying Nomex Armid paper and textbook paper?"

These are a few samples of the type of information disseminated by TIPS, a new service exclusively aimed at promoting technology exchange and trade among developing countries.

Let us be very clear about one point: TIPS is not solely devoted to pulp and paper mill technology. In fact, as of now, it touches this sector only obliquely: via post-harvest measures in agro-industries; bio-technology; general business opportunities; etc.

Its relevance, for that matter in any technology area in developing counties, arises from the dire need for a suitable information system: to create *an awareness of advances made, so that one can access, exchange and consolidate the work done, for fruitful use and further development*:

Sponsored by the United Nations Development Programme (UNDP), the DEVNET/TIPS has set up the Technological Information Pilot System (TIPS), an experimental project to assess the viability of such a service and eventually lead to a fully-fledged information network.

TIPS is initially being financed by a trust fund set up by the Government of Italy with the United Nations Fund for Science and Technology for Development (UNFSTD). The policy guidance is given by an Inter-Governmental Advisory Board (IGAB) consisting of representatives from participating and donor countries.

TIPS is run, managed and developed by a Rome-based non-profit, non-governmental organization, DEVNET, under a subcontract with UNDP. DEVNET/TIPS will become a subscription service in July 1988, with the ultimate objective of eventually becoming self-funding.

Currently, ten countries are participating in the pilot exercise: Brazil, China, Egypt, India, Kenya, Mexico, Pakistan, Peru, Philippines and Zimbabwe.

Several other developing countries, notably Algeria, Argentina, Bangladesh, Cuba, Colombia, Tanzania, Tunisia and Zambia have expressed interest in joining this unique South-South information system.

**1. TIPS Network and Operations**

TIPS is a network of national bureaus (NBs) linked through the International Operations Centre (IOC). The IOC, now in Rome, receives and transmits information to NBs through dedicated teleprinter circuits. At the country level, the NB packages and disseminates information to users by mail and other means.

In the first year of TIPS operation, some 2500 users from the participant nations have been receiving SOUTH TECH information bulletins in sectors of their interest. The user group includes Government agencies, R&D institutions, manufacturers, exporters, trade and professional associations, financing institutions, etc.

It may be pointed out that, through the various agencies and associations, many more users have access to the information provided by this service.

In developing countries currently not participating in TIPS,

SOUTH TECH is distributed, albeit on a very limited scale, through 120 UNDP offices and Chambers of Commerce and Industry, directly from IOC, Rome.

The information for publication through SOUTH TECH is collected from various development agencies — public/private productive sectors, professional organisations, and research, academic and training institutions.

TIPS disseminates information along the following lines:

* Offers and requests of technology/trade/investment
* Research and Development activities
* Technology and trade events, news, policies
* Training opportunities
* UN system's procurement and consultancy needs

TIPS endeavours to bring out only that information which has the potential of either leading to transfer or exchange of technology or trade among the developing countries.

## 2. SOUTH TECH Publications

The daily SOUTH TECH bulletins deal with specific sectors on agro-industries, electronics, energy (hydro-power, solar energy and biomass), food processing, machinery and machine tools and pharmaceuticals. Sectoral bulletins on textiles, fisheries and biotechnology are released on a weekly basis.

Another daily package entitled "Business Opportunities" covers trade and technology offers, requests from developing countries and global procurement and consultancy tenders of the UN system. As DEVNET/TIPS service develops, the coverage is likely to be expanded to include more sectors.

A typical SOUTH TECH bulletin consists of about 3 pages. Each page describes an item and contains data useful both to technical and business professionals. Incorporated in each item is a contact address for further information.

SOUTH TECH is released in English and Spanish. Further, it is available in Portuguese in Brazil and Arabic in Egypt. Plans are afoot to bring out the Chinese version for the benefit of users from China.

### 3. TIPS Usage —A Review

Since its start in May 1987 until the end of February 1988, TIPS has collected over 5000 items of information of which nearly 3000 have been processed and distributed through SOUTH TECH. In style and format, SOUTH TECH bulletins emphasise precision and readability, and include technical data as well as pricing/cost information where available.

In an independent survey last October, over 70 per cent of TIPS users sent their response on various aspects of TIPS services. Of these, nearly 97 per cent considered network's information "good to excellent" and a little over 94 per cent found the bulletins, in terms of content and style, effective.

The number of user-to-source queries resulting from DEVNET/TIPS to-date exceeds 1000. Through TIPS, many small or medium-scale entrepreneurs have got access to distant international markets, which otherwise would not have been conceivable due to limited resources and lack of information.

A Filipino veterinary drug manufacturing company has become an exporter for the first time. An Indian public sector institution is finalising an agreement with a Peruvian company. A Zimbabwe firm is seeking technology from Pakistan while an Egyptian company is negotiating for rights to produce drugs developed in Zimbabwe. Scores of other deals for technology transfer and trade are in the offing, involving Brazil, China, Nigeria, Zambia and many other developing countries.

DEVNET/TIPS is a dynamically evolving information system wherein the users of the service can contribute in many ways. Subscribers receiving SOUTH TECH are excepted to provide a feedback on how their needs are met, possible improvements in content, style and format, etc. The sources providing information for dissemination through TIPS can give their comments on the presentation, queries they receive, and on the resulting commercial exchanges.

TIPS is just a first step, and a very limited one at that, which has barely touched the surface of the vast information available in developing counties. Perhaps, by underlining their needs and capabilities, it might prompt them to establish and strengthen the necessary facilities paving the way for development through mutual cooperation.

For further information, please contact:

Project Co-ordinator
TIPS (IOC)
Via Panisperna, 203
00184 Rome, Italy
Tlx: 610574 IPSROM I
Cab: DEVTIPS ROMA

The Director
TIPS - NB India
158, Jor Bagh
New Delhi (India)
Phone: 618657/618667

**REFERENCE**

1. The work of the Technological Information Pilot System (TIPS) is described in detail in the following articles:

   Roberto Savio: "TIPS: An Information System for South-South Communication", in: *Transborder Data Flow and Development*, ed. by Jörg Becker, Bonn: Friedrich-Ebert-Foundation 1987, pp. 131-137; Narinder Aggarwala: "DEVNET/TIPS: A Bridge Across the South", in: *Co-operation South*, 1/1988, pp. 3-4; Werner E. Breede: "10-Staaten-Brücke über dem Süden. Das Technological Information Pilot System (TIPS)", in: *Cogito* (Darmstadt), 2/1989, pp. 9-14.

TWO

# THE GTZ PROJECT

# 6

JÖRG BECKER & ARTHUR W. WESTERN

# SMALL-SCALE PAPER MILLS IN FOUR DEVELOPING COUNTRIES
## Summary of the GTZ Project

### 1. Introduction

AS A part of the project "Small Paper Mills Using Non-wood Fibres in Developing Countries", five paper mills were examined between 1985 and 1987, all meeting the following basic conditions:

- Production of cultural paper,
- Annual production amounting to approx. 10,000 tonnes a year,
- Use of raw materials such as bagasse, straw, bamboo, reeds or waste-paper.

The following mills were examined:

- Shree Warana SSK Ltd. Paper Division in Warananagar, Kolhapur District, Maharashtra State, India (raw material bagasse),
- Rohit Pulp & Paper Mill, Bulsar District, South Gujarat, India (raw material rice straw),
- Qiong-Shan Paper Mill, Qiong Shan Xian District, Hainan Island, Guangdong Province, People's Republic of China (raw material rice straw),
- Bang Pa-In Paper Mill, Bang Pa-In, Ayuthaya Province, Thailand (raw material rice straw),
- Embilipitiya Pulp and Paper Mill, near Chandrika Wewa, Sri Lanka (raw material rice straw).

The following is an attempt to summarize the experiences gained during these five evaluations and thereby draw general conclusions for future practical work.

Whatever differences may exist between the various mills reported on, and there are differences in plant, scale, viability etc., they have something in common. By deliberate selection, each mill operates in a developing country and this leads to the most significant common factor; if the mills concerned were not producing at all, the total paper consumption would fall by that amount. There would be no substitute for the production lost, by import or from another mill; the alternative is nothing! When the consumption per capita is no more than between one fiftieth and one hundredth of that pertaining to the industrialised world, this must be the most telling comment. Paper is essential for education, industry and commercial development and its absence in sufficient quantity is a serious deterrent to progress. The market is not a problem; sales can be achieved even when the selling price has to be supported by a heavy duty on imports.

Adequate supply of basic fibre is a factor limiting production for most of the mills examined. The principal fibre source is straw from wheat or rice; the major exception is the Warana Mill in India which uses bagasse from an associated sugar mill plus some from non-associated mills in the district. Significantly the bagasse for the Warana Mill is surplus to the requirements of both the sugar mill and the paper mill for steam generation, and although the sugar mill surplus alone is insufficient to provide all that is necessary for paper production, it is notable as an indication that there can be a surplus after sugar production and it would be even more substantial if the paper mill was not dependent on the sugar mill for its steam supply. Bagasse as a paper fibre source has considerable advantages over straw, its only serious rival in developing countries. The paper is stronger, needing less of the scarce and expensive long fibre reinforcement; the yield is higher if the removed pith is burned for fuel, as it should be; there is very much less silica in the fibre, making chemical recovery a practical possibility though some difficulties remain; finally, quality standards are easier to achieve and maintain. The Warana Mill experience offers the promise that the cost and expense of sugar mill boiler conversion to alternative fuel need not be the deterrent to the use of bagasse for paper-making that it has for so long been assumed to be. It also suggests that there could be substantial advantages in improving the efficiency of raw bagasse combustion in sugar mills. The most obvious route to this must be that of reducing the moisture content and some research along these lines could be rewarding.

Straw as a source of fibre may not be ideal but its disadvantages are not insuperable. The collection of straw must be organised on a rational long-term basis with guarantees from all parties, but this is almost never done and there are other uses competing for surplus straw. If a paper mill is to have continuity of supply and sufficient confidence in regular availability in order to invest in reliable preparation and handling equipment, then something more than bargaining for surpluses is required; the farmer must be paid enough to give priority to the mill. The Rohit Pulp & Paper Mill, in India, and perhaps the mill in China have organised supply conditions but supply is still limited at the Indian mill and this in turn limits production. The Chinese mill operates under centralised government conditions which cannot apply where private ownership and smaller farms are involved.

The economic limitations to transport for straw and bagasse also limit the scale of operations for paper mills. Where the paper mill can take all the bagasse available from a sugar mill or mills, because alternative fuel is available and the boiler plant can be modified to burn it, the scale of operations can be relatively high but this is seldom the case in developing countries and was not the situation in any of the mills visited. The Warana Mill complex estimates that about 5 per cent of total bagasse could be considered surplus to sugar and paper mill fuel requirements, possibly 10 per cent if the paper mill has its own independent boiler plant. But taking this as a criterion a paper mill using bagasse could only regard it as a supplementary source of fibre to a relatively small mill. The Chinese mill can take 5,000 t/annum of bagasse from a total of 50,000 t/annum available from a local sugar mill, which seems to support this opinion. It supplements about 6,000 t/annum of straw from local farmers.

The Bang Pa-In Pulp & Paper Mill in Thailand has used Burma grass to supplement the rice straw used and prefers the pulp produced from it, but it is limited in availability, relatively expensive and bound to increase in cost with time because it is labour intensive. It is now almost axiomatic that the bulk of paper-making fibre source anywhere in the world must be of by-product nature because the industry cannot any longer afford to carry all the coasts of collection and handling. This is true today, even of wood-based paper mills; the trend is now towards integrated the trend is now towards integrated timber/pulp and paper operations. For the developing countries, therefore, straw from wheat or rice and bagasse are the chief sources for fibre and must remain so, and except for rare and unusual cases this must limit the scale of pulp and paper-making activities. It need not limit viability.

All of the mills reviewed, in common with practically every other mill of similar capacity in developing countries, have another common problem in relation to fibre supply; that of obtaining in sufficient quantity and at economic cost the long fibre component of total furnish which is essential for strength, in production and as finished paper. The quantity required varies from 20 per cent to 30 per cent of the total fibre involved according to the substance of the paper being produced. Bagasse-based papers need slightly less in proportion than straw-based paper but, for either grade of paper, supply is an acute problem. The chief source of long fibre supply internationally is from pine, and those countries where it grows in self-sustaining plantations dominate the paper industry. It is not available in developing countries; the climate is generally unsuitable and timber of any species is scarce and expensive. The problems of infrastructure and transport are also of a long-term nature, even where in rare situations, cultivation is possible. There are alternative long-fibre resources available in some locations; cotton-waste in India is regarded as the main long-fibre support by both the Rohit Pulp & Paper and Warana Mills, but supplies are restricted and processing expensive because the better grades of waste cotton are greatly in demand for the highest quality papers which normally are reserved by cost for art purposes.

There is nowhere near enough indigenous long-fibre resource to satisfy present needs for any of the mills visited or, indeed, developing country mills generally. All mills used imported long fiber, as pulp, which is very expensive, or waste-paper of suitable grade. As is indicated by the Rohit Pulp & Paper Mill in India the waste-paper import is most economic, providing good quality long fibre at a coast cheaper than that of converting rages. Only the U.S.A. or Canada can have waste of such quality to export and the declining exchange value of the $ U.S. must have further improved the overall economics. If long-term supply of such material could be

economy in fuel and chemical consumptions plus progress towards chemical recovery, for continuous pulping plant. Continuous digestion is commercially available for straw or bagasse but it is unsuited for production much less than 60 tonnes of pulp per day which is equivalent to 80 tonnes of paper per day and too great for most mills to sustain when based on straw from local farmers. The reason is that straw and bagasse cook very quickly compared with wood, less than 15 minutes is required at the pressures normally used for digestion. This is, or should be, an advantage but straw and bagasse are stringy materials which do not fall by gravity through a cooking zone, like wood chips. They have to be impelled by screw-type feeders and there is a lower limit to the size of digester which can operate at the 10/15 atmospheres pressure normally used. Units can now be obtained which operate at atmospheric pressure and have longer cooking times which give continuous digestion and enhance quality. All the mills inspected were using a multiplicity of rotating pressure vessels which have lengthy feeding and emptying periods, and uniformity of quality is difficult to ensure. Although they are relatively inexpensive when manufactured in India, the number required and the associated drives, piping and fittings with the accommodation requirements, make the full installation unnecessarily expensive compared with the alternative. When manufactured outside of India the units are prohibitively expensive. The continuous practical alternative with many years of successful operation with straw for unbleached semi-chemical pulping has yet to be confirmed as capable of equivalent performance with bleachable pulp digestion, although it is difficult to see how this could not be possible. Consequently, and in view of the transitional expense, progress in using the unit for bleached pulp production has been slow. It is understandable that a single mill would be reluctant to be involved in initial trials to develop the techniques which ultimately benefit competitors. Therefore, in this instance also, sponsoring could help.

### 4. Fibre and Water Recovery

Fibre is scarce for most small mills, and water in many areas is also difficult to obtain in sufficient quantity regularly throughout the year. In many mills, including most of those visited, the water consumption is excessive and the loss of fibre to drain seriously expensive. Unless it is checked, a burden of pollution to the neighbourhood results, which will ultimately also be a cause of expense as legislation is enforced. The Rohit Pulp & Paper Mill in India, has recognised these factors and is well advanced in installing a fibre and water recovery plant which pays for its initial cost in a very short period. The Warana Mill fibre losses were so substantial that the management were seriously considering purchase and installation of a plant to produce substandard boards from the fibre in the drains! The overall magnitude of the losses is difficult to quantify because of a general absence of metering, but a comparison over a period of materials purchased against paper sold is most revealing, when the exercise is carried out, but it seldom is. Water conservation and fibre recovery is a most rewarding exercise which is within the capability of the small mill, and it pays for the plant involved in a very short time. But there is widespread ignorance of the losses being sustained and how best to reduce them.

**5. Instrumentation**

All mills were lacking in metering and control instrumentation which would be considered essential in efficient mills. In particular, consistency regulators are either absent or not working. The Sri Lanka Mill, acknowledging the scarcity of instrumentation, claim that it is good enough for their mill (which is making a virtue out of poor maintenance) but elsewhere they express the desire to install the most complex and maintenance-needing instrumentation. There should be, available to small mills, a training centre to teach mill staff how to operate, calibrate and service fundamental instrumentation and how to establish an instrumentation department at the mill.

**6. Paper-making Plant**

In at least two of the mills, Sri Lanka and Thailand, the machines and supporting equipment were of reasonable design and capable of producing the specified output. The Warana machine was relatively new but there were shortcomings in design and ancillaries which made output difficult. The Rohit Pulp & Paper Mill machines were old, second-hand when installed and only the enthusiasm and abilities of the supervisory team enabled the mill to produce at the rates obtained and at a profitable level. The quality of staffing at this mill was high, reflecting sound management judgement, because their energies and dedication were overcoming obstacles and bringing about improvements at an impressive rate.

Most mills had problems with drying, associated mainly with uneven pressing, poor state of the stationary stearn nozzles with outworn inner bearings and rudimentary or absent steaming systems.

None of the mills visited possessed a roll grinder and none appeared to have made any arrangements to have press or calendar rolls ground regularly. Routine, planned maintenance has not yet become general practice as it is for established mills in industrialised countries, and in consequence the poor state of the plant is a limitation to production although this is seldom recognised. Most mills have difficulty in doctoring the composition press rolls which, because they can be manufactured and covered locally, have largely supplanted the granite rolls, originally standard to presses. In consequence the number of paper breaks experienced is phenomenal, more in one day than a well-serviced mill would suffer in a month. It is true that the non-wood based papers, particularly when straw is the medium, are low in wet-strength and more prone to breaks, but this should shows the need for better servicing and it has not; the weakness is too often accepted fatalistically as something which must be endured.

In relation to the references given above, and many others, mills of this type have much to learn, but there is little evidence that active steps are being taken to remedy the situation. Most of the learning which has been achieved in the industrialised paper-making world has come from the interchange of ideas and techniques with other mills. Much of the technical advance has equally come about through partnership between equipment manufacturers and mills, largely because there is seldom any practical way to test equipment other than under operating conditions in a mill. Working in the pulp and paper trade in non-developing countries was almost like belonging to a club. Inter-mill visits generally were actively encouraged because it was recognised that paper-manufacture is not an absolute science; there may be several ways to achieve an objective; all of them right because the objective is achieved, but one method, in the circumstances pertaining, more right than the others as more appropriate to the conditions.

There is little evidence of such an interchange of ideas in developing countries either between mills or between mills and suppliers. If a mill has problems the staff must find a solution themselves or live with it. Another mill operating under similar conditions will almost certainly have experienced the same problems and may have reached a solution, but the cure will not be passed on. Similarly, a mill purchasing new equipment ought to verify the bona-fides of the claims made for it by visiting another mill where it is operating, but this does not happen either. There is almost an atmosphere of suspicion although in fact there is seldom the competition which might conceivably justify such an attitude. Most small mills have a territorial market limited by transport costs, one of the small mills' major advantages. Some steps to remedy this situation would benefit all mills because the small mill based on non-wood fibres generally suffers from a reputation for low quality which is quite unnecessary. The best mills enjoy a reputation for high quality.

In the circumstances outlined above the mill most capably staffed with competent supervisors does best and for this reason, the Rohit Pulp & Paper Mill stands out amongst those visited. It is also noteworthy to point out that in this mill the management recently decided to make a substantial investment in a research and development department and staff, although it could be argued that the money could have been spent on new equipment. The profit record of this mill is a testimony to the foresight of its management in this and other respects.

**7. Concluding Remarks**

The developing world badly needs cheap paper, not paper at any price which limits its availability to the poor, who need it most. In substantial proportion it has to come from mills utilising indigenous materials, predominantly surplus straw or bagasse, and for this reason such mills must be located in rural or agricultural areas and, in the absence of special circumstances, the mills must be small in relation to industrialised country standards. This need not be a prohibiting handicap. There is evidence to show that although to date such mills are generally forced to operate under the economic burdens of no chemical recovery and other plant limitations, they can produce quality paper and be viable because the materials they are forced to use are not wholly without offsetting advantages. In terms of specific energy usage, chemical consumption for bleaching and unit labour costs, they can have positive incentives. In general, also, they can be installed with a significantly lower capital cost burden because they are not forced to the limits of performance in design. How much brighter would be their future and their growth if their present handicaps could be eased, or eliminated, and it is to these ends that sponsored aid should be directed because it will be a slow and uncertain path by any other route.

Apart from their prime function, that of producing paper where otherwise none could be expected, the small mills in agricultural areas provide benefits which cannot be over-estimated and may, indeed, be the chief contribution long-term. In terms of numbers required per unit quantity of paper produced, the small mill employs more, but labour costs per tonne of product are significantly less than those of the large mill because labour rates are lower. The mill becomes the social centre for the neighbourhood, supporting parallel business, providing good standard accommodation, subsidising education and sponsoring cultural pursuits generally. The Warana mill is perhaps the best example of what can be achieved, but owes a substantial proportion to the sugar mill for what is provided. All mills visited, however, have made their contribution to their locality and by their presence are reducing urban drift and improving earning potential which is so badly needed.

# 7

P.K. KAUPPI

# THE QIONG SHAN PAPER MILL IN THE PEOPLE'S REPUBLIC OF CHINA

## 1. Outline of Pulp and Paper Industry in China

CHINA'S total pulp production is presently over 9,000,000 t/year with a current rate of increase around 1,000,000 t/year. About 60 per cent of China's fibrous requirements for paper-making come from non-wood fibers, 25 per cent of wood and 15 per cent of waste-paper.

Straw represents about 70 per cent, reed 19.7 per cent, bagasse 6.9 per cent and bamboo 3.4 per cent of China's non-wood fiber requirements for pulp and paper making. Other non-wood fibers used in China are grasses, hemp, sisal, etc.

Guangdong and Fujian Provinces are leaders in sugarcane processing in China, making a strong bagasse-based pulp and paper industry possible. Hainan Island has a substantial sugarcane processing industry with 32 sugar mills, and the industry appears to be continuously expanding. Fledic Engineering Ltd. has conducted a feasibility study of a modern bagasse pulp and paper mill on Hainan Island. The mill is intended to produce 180 t/day of coating base paper and coated papers.

Paper represents up to 61.5 per cent of the total production, of which printing and writing papers cover 47 per cent. Paperboards represent 38.5 per cent of the production, of which packaging boards cover 85 per cent.

It is obvious that the non-wood fibers play a very important role in the pulp and paper industry of China. Writing and printing paper production is the dominating sector in the paper industry, for which non-wood fiber pulps are well suited.

The paper industry in China is composed of a large number of small and medium size paper and paperboard mills. Typical to many mills is that each of them produces a wide range of products sold within the province.

## 2. General Description and Outline of Operation

The Qiong Shan paper mill is located at Qiong Shan Xian, Hainan Island, about 14 km from Haikou, on the bank of the Nan Du river. The mill was established in 1940 in another location to produce hand-made cigarette paper from cotton. In 1960 the mill was moved to the present location, new equipment added, and the production started in 1964.

Rice straw is the main fiber raw material, and the use of bagasse was started in 1985. Conventional soda cooking process without chemical recovery is employed, and bleaching is by calcium hypochlorite system. There are three paper machines in the mill to provide total paper production of approximately 3500 t/annum, printing, typing and wrapping papers.

Process water is obtained from the Nan Du river and the untreated water effluent is discharged downstream into the same river. Power is supplied by the main hydropower station of Hainan Island, located near Haikou.

The total mill site area covers approximately 52,000 sq.m. The total building area is about 15,500 sq.m., of which production area covers 8,350 sq.m., personnel living area 5,500 sq.m., and the social activities area about 1,700 sq.m. The total work force is 335 persons, including the management and administration staff.

The living quarters and social facilities for the mill labour force and the management staff are provided in the area next to the mill. For the people living in these facilities the mill is naturally the central point of their every-day activities.

The equipment in the mill are all Chinese made, with spare parts provided by the mill maintenance shop and larger work shops in Haikou, and in the mainland of China. There are no instruments in the mill.

Environmental impact from the mill does not appear to be of significant concern, although the mill pays a fine for untreated process water effluent discharge into the Nan Du river. Fishing in the river was not observed during the mill visit.

### 3. Water Supply

The mill water is obtained from the Nan Du river. Four water pumps, each with a capacity of 260 cu.m./hour, are located approximately six meters below the river bank and about half-way between the river level and the mill site elevation. Two pumps are normally in use, and the other two pumps are spares.

Water is pumped into a 4m diameter concrete treatment tank with central intake, at which point alum is added. From the treatment tank water overflows by gravity into a rectangular water holding/settling basin with two sections in series.

From the end of the last settling basin section, water flows through stationary filters and into a clarified water basin to be pumped to the mill. There are four pumps at the treated water pumphouse, of which two pumps are normally in use, and the other two are spares. The capacity of each pump is 260 cu.m./hour.

The average water usage of the mill is 500-600 cu.m./tonnes, typical for a small pulp and paper mill without any water re-usage.

### 4. Effluent Disposal

The mill effluent is discharged untreated into the Nan Du river. There is a dark zone with some foam around the effluent outfall area. However, even during the dry season there is enough flow in the river to provide sufficient dilution to dispose the effluent.

The mill management would like to construct an effluent treatment/settling basin system to ease the impact of the effluent discharged into the river, but considers this too expensive to undertake. The government charges the mill a fine of 35,000 Yuan/year for the untreated effluent disposal into the Nan Du river. (U.S. $ 100 is equal to approximately 360 Yuan).

### 5. Steam Generation

Steam supply for the pulp and paper mill is provided by two Chinese made coal burning boilers, each with a capacity of 4 t/hour. The maximum steam generation pressure is 13 kg/sq.cm. The process steam pressures are 4 kg/sq.m. and 6 kg/sq.m.

Coal is fed to the boiler by a simple cable lift arrangement. The ash is collected by a screw conveyor and taken away manually.

The boiler feed water is obtained from the mill treated water basin and stored in a 12 sq.m. storage tank. Boiler feed water treatment is by ion exchange.

The paper machine condensate is returned to the boiler plant. Boiler cleaning is required twice a year.

The flue gas from the two boilers is discharged by I.D. fan into a common horizontal brick tunnel, equipped with a flue gas scrubbing arrangement to minimize dust discharge.

The mill is considering installation of a third boiler to generate more steam for the anticipated increase in the mill production.

**6. Power Supply**

Normally the mill power is provided by the main hydropower station of Hainan Island at 6,300 V. A 4,500 kW coal burning power station is located 2 km away and is used during the dry season. The mill power supply line is designed for 2,500 kW providing room for additional transformer capacity. The transformers at the mill are as follows:

1 - 320 kW for process
2 - 560 kW for process
1 - 100 kW for town site

Mill distribution voltage for electrical motors is 400 V.

The power cost is 0.11 Yuan/hWh for industrial use and 0.25 Yuan/kW for non-industrial use. The average power consumption for production of pulp is 450 kW/tonnes. Total power consumption (including pulping) for production of 60 g/sq.m. white paper is approximately 1,050 kWh/tonnes, and 1,450 kWh/tonnes for production of 28 g/sq.m. typing paper.

**7. Rice Straw Supply**

Rice straw is the main fibre raw material for the mill and is supplied by local farmers within a radius of about 100 km around the mill.

The annual use of rice straw is 6,000–8,000 tonnes of which 1,000–2,000 tonnes is purchased in May-June, and 5,000–6,000 tonnes in November-January during the main harvesting season.

The average cost of straw delivered to the mill at 20 per cent moisture content is 85 Yuan/tonnes, including transportation and handling fees. The handling fee is 2.5 Yuan/tonnes and the transportation cost is 0.50 Yuan/tonnes/kilometer.

Pile construction is the responsibility of the farmers. Payments of the handling fees to the farmers are made in two parts. First 2 Yuan/tonnes, and 20 days later 0.50 Yuan/tonne, provided that the pile construction is carried out to the satisfaction of the mill.

In the discussions with the mill personnel, no rice straw shortage was indicated. The supply would support even an increase in the mill capacity. The need of agricultural waste, such as rice straw, for cattle feed is naturally of concern. In the present situation, the amount of rice straw used for the pulp mill is not hampering the needs of agriculture in the region. The climate and terrain around Haikou are well suited for growing rice straw. Lack of forestry makes the use of non-wood fibers increasingly important on Hainan Island.

## 8. Rice Straw Preparation

There are two straw preparation lines of the same capacity, one for the old pulping line and one for the new pulping line. Straw is stored adjacent to the feed conveyors, and it is fed manually into the straw preparation lines.

From the feed conveyor straw enters into a cutter, and is fed by a conveyor into the straw dusting and screening system. After dusting and screening the straw is conveyed to the digester building and fed into three (3) spherical digesters in the old line, and two (2) in the new line.

The capacity of the straw lines is approximately 4 t/hour. It appears that the straw preparation for the new digesters system may have capacity limitations. Uniformity of the cut straw entering into the digester could be improved and would benefit from larger straw cutters, and the screening and dusting lines. It appears that the present lines are operating under heavy overloading conditions.

## 9. Bagasse Supply

There are four sugar mills in the area with a total sugarcane grinding capacity of 2,400 t/day. Total availability of the bagasse is estimated at 50,000 BDT/annum. The sugarcane harvesting season is approximately 150 days per season.

The paper mill started the use of bagasse in 1985. At the present, the mill uses only 5,000 tonnes of dry bagasse from one of the sugar mills located 7 km away. Bagasse is obtained free of charge, but the mill must pay for the transportation. The mill management estimates that during 1987 the bagasse cost will be approximately 60 Yuan/tonnes. Most of the sugar mills use bagasse as fuel and sometimes use wood as a supplementary fuel with bagasse. The local farmers use bagasse as a fertilizer substance in growing animal food. It appears that there is excess bagasse available from the sugar mills for pulping.

The depithed bagasse with 50 per cent moisture content is stored in loose piles at the sugar mill. The piles are managed manually. Fresh bagasse is of a light colour, but the bagasse stored for 10 months, and mostly used by the paper mills, is very dark.

It is considered that the storing of undepithed bagasse for long periods causes serious deterioration of the bagasse fiber. Storing bagasse on the ground without concrete protection may allow sand and other impurities enter into the system. The value of bagasse is determined as the fuel value equal to wood.

## 10. Bagasse Preparation

Bagasse is now pulped only in the new line consisting of two digesters, mainly because the old bagasse depithing line is inadequate for sufficient pitch removal, especially with high moisture content bagasse.

From the storage area at the pulp mill site the bagasse is loaded manually on a belt conveyor feeding a rotating drum depither with 6 mm screen perforation. Approximately 35-42 per cent of pith is removed and discharged into the mill sewer. The cleaned bagasse is conveyed to the upper digester floor for loading into the digesters. The digester feeding system is common for both the rice straw and bagasse. The new depithing line capacity is approximately 5 t/hour.

With high bagasse moisture content the depithing operation is having significant problems and therefore a by-pass is provided.

Cooking of the dark and undepithed bagasse is not considered feasible because of a high consumption of pulping and bleaching chemicals. In situations where the supply of rice straw is interrupted, the mill would be forced to use bagasse.

## 11. Cooking

The mill has two cooking lines. The old line consists of three spherical digesters, two with a volume of 14 cu.m. and one with a volume of 8 cu.m. In our description of the cooking process in this report, we concentrate on the new line consisting of two spherical digesters, each with a volume of 25 cu.m.

The total digester cycle is approximately 8 hours with the breakdown cycle as follows:

| | |
|---|---|
| Filling | 3.0 hours |
| Rotation | 0.5 hours |
| Steaming up to pressure (5.5 kg/sq.cm.) | 1.5 hours |
| At temperature | 2.5 hours |
| Blowing | 0.5 hours |
| | 8.0 hours |

Approximately 3,000 kg of BD bagasse is fed into a 25 cu.m. digester. Cooking takes place with liquor to wood ratio of 3:5:1, and with 12.5 per cent caustic soda on BD fiber. It is estimated that one cook yields approximately 1.2-1.35 BD tonnes of brown stock.

The new digesters are emptied by blowing through small cyclones into two 50 cu.m. open blow tanks. Each blow tank is equipped with a stock pump with a capacity of 28 cu.m./hour to pump the fiber slurry into the brown stock washing and screening department. The cooked pulp is reported to have a pH of 13-14.

## 12. Washing and Screening

The description herewith is related only to the new pulping line fed by the two new digesters.

From the two blow tanks (one for straw and one for bagasse pulp) the pulp is pumped into two slusher type drum washers equipped with a press roll. The washers are operated in series, and cold fresh water is used for washing. The washing efficiency with this type of low consistency washing is rather limited and the water consumption is high. Efficient washing of bagasse and straw pulp usually requires twice as much water as wood fiber pulp. The surface area of each washer is 7 sq.m. Washing filtrate is discharged into the mill effluent system.

From the washers the pulp enters into a vibrating screen with capacity of 10 t/day. The accepts from the vibrating screen enter into a Cowan screen with an estimated capacity of 20 t/day. Rejects from both the vibrating screen and the Cowan screen are led out from the system and used in the corrugating medium (wrapping paper) line in the paper mill. The exact amount of rejects is not known but it is estimated at approximately 2-3 t/day.

The accepts from the Cowan screen are fed into a 30-unit centrifugal cleaning system, and further, to two 2 cu.m. vibrating screens fitted with a fine mesh wire for dewatering. From the vibrating screens the pulp is directed into two 1.5 m diameter rotating slushers for further thickening before being discharged into the storage chests, one with 42 sq.m. volume for bagasse pulp, and the other with 38 sq.m. volume for straw pulp. The rejects from the centrifugal cleaners, and the filtrate from the dewatering screens and slushers are discharged into the sewer.

**13. Bleaching**

The pulp is bleached as a blend containing 70 per cent rice straw pulp and 30 per cent bagasse pulp. The bleaching is calcium hypochlorite system, and it is carried out in six bleaching machines with a total volume of 132 cu.m. There are two bleaching machines with a volume of 35 cu.m., three with a volume of 14 cu.m., and one with a volume of 20 cu.m.

The bleaching machines are of concrete construction with a re-circulator in one end and a baffle in the middle to direct the stock flow. There is a rotating dewatering drum provided in each machine to facilitate thickening and washing of the pulp.

The washed and screened rice straw and bagasse pulps are pumped from the respective storage tanks to the bleaching machines. Before bleaching the pulp caustic soda is added to maintain pH at about 8.5.

Bleaching is carried out in two steps in each bleaching machine. In the first step approximately 5 per cent of chlorine is mixed with milk of lime in a ratio of 1:2.2. The milk of lime is prepared by mixing 1 tonne of lime in 8 tonnes of water. After one hour 4 per cent chlorine with the milk of lime is added.

There is no washing of pulp between the two bleaching steps. However, after the first bleaching step the pulp concentration is

plates are used.

*14.4. Manufacturing Costs*

The following data on the costs to manufacture one tonne of bleached pulp were provided by the mill management.

| Item | Rice Straw Pulp | | Bagasse Pulp | |
|---|---|---|---|---|
| | Amount | Cost-Yuan | Amount | Cost-Yuan |
| Rice Straw | 4.1 tonnes | 348.5 | — | — |
| Bagasse | — | — | 3.5 tonnes | 210 |
| Caustic Soda | 0.3 tonnes | 346.5 | 0.35 tonnes | 404.3 |
| Chlorine | 0.09 tonnes | 73.35 | 0.1 tonnes | 81.50 |
| Lime | 0.2 tonnes | 31.0 | 0.22 tonnes | 34.10 |
| Coal | 1.1 tonnes | 115.5 | 1.1 tonnes | 115.5 |
| Power | 450 kWh | 49.5 | 450 kWh | 49.5 |
| Steam | — | 2.5 | — | 2.5 |
| Salary | — | 40 | — | 40 |
| Departmental Expenses* | — | 85 | — | 85 |
| Total Cost/BDT | | 1114.35 Yuan | | 1044.85 Yuan |

*Note:* * Includes depreciation, repair expenses and miscellaneous services.

In discussions with the management it became clear that the mill would prefer 60 g/sq.m. writing paper and 28 g/sq.m. typing paper production. Production of 70 per cent of the 60 g/sq.m. paper, and 30 per cent of 28 g/sq.m. paper would fit well into the present configuration of the mill. Production of the 28 g/sq.m. paper has been low due to the low quality of the rice straw pulp and the shortage of a good quality long fiber wood pulp, usually obtained from Canada and New Zealand.

The following manufacturing cost calculation for 60 g/sq.m. and 28 g/sq.m., was kindly provided by the mill management.

| Item | 60 g/sq.m. | | 28 g/sq.m. | |
|---|---|---|---|---|
| | Amount | Cost-Yuan | Amount | Cost-Yuan |
| Straw Pulp | 0.7 tonnes | 780.05 | 0.8 tonnes | 891.48 |
| Bagasse Pulp | 0.3 tonnes | 313.46 | — | — |
| Wood Pulp | — | — | 0.3 tonnes | 480 |

*Contd.*

*Contd.*

| Item | 60 g/sq.m. | | 28 g/sq.m. | |
|---|---|---|---|---|
| | Amount | Cost-Yuan | Amount | Cost-Yuan |
| Resin | 0.015 tonnes | 22.95 | 0.02 tonnes | 30.6 |
| Alum | 0.12 tonnes | 48.2 | 0.1 tonnes | 41 |
| Talc | 0.22 tonnes | 41.8 | 0.18 tonnes | 34.2 |
| Dye | 0.4 kg | 10 | 0.4 kg | 10 |
| Calcium Carbonate | 1 kg | 20 | 1.5 kg | 30 |
| Felt | 0.4 kg | 22 | 0.8 kg | 44 |
| Wires, etc. | 0.2 cu.m. | 15 | 0.5 cu.m. | 37.5 |
| Coal | 0.5 tonnes | 52.5 | 1 tonne | 105 |
| Power | 600 kWh | 66 | 1000 kWh | 110 |
| Packaging | — | 45 | — | 45 |
| Steam | — | 15 | — | 20 |
| Salary** | — | 30 | — | 40 |
| Departmental Expenses* | — | 50 | — | 70 |
| Management Expenses^ | — | 80 | — | 80 |
| Miscellaneous^^ | — | 40 | — | 40 |
| Manufacturing Cost-tonnes | | 1652.96 Yuan | | 2108.75 Yuan |
| Tax | | 185 Yuan | | 250 Yuan |
| Selling Price | | 1850 Yuan | | 2500 Yuan |
| Profit/tonnes | | 12.04 Yuan | | 114.22 Yuan |

* Depreciation, repair expenses and miscellaneous material expenses

** 11 per cent labour, welfare and 2 per cent social activities allowance included

^ Retired labour salaries, effluent disposal fine, some social assistance for children

^^ Loan interest charge, management salaries, housing depreciation and miscellaneous

It is obvious from the above that the fiber cost for the mill is high. This should be one of the first matters to be investigated when studying improvements to the profitability of the operation.

## 15. Conclusions

The mill location is good with reliable power, water, raw material supply and transportation facilities. The effluent disposal to the Nan Du river is convenient, but may require some treatment, especially if the mill production is increased.

Availability of rice straw and bagasse is sufficient for an increase in the production up to 10,000 t/year.

Should the mill increase its production level, then the usage of more bagasse should be studied. To prevent deterioration of the bagasse fiber, and to preserve the bagasse brightness, an adaption of the pith removal system should be examined.

In summary, to improve the mill operation and profitability, the following could be listed for potential improvements:

- Minimize bagasse and rice straw losses in handling and in storage;
- Optimize cooking and the cooking chemical usage;
- Improve fiber preparation before cooking to obtain more uniform cooks (straw cutting, screening, dusting, bagasse pith removal and washing);
- Improve pulp washing to minimize bleaching chemical usage;
- Optimize unbleached pulp screening operation to use maximum amount of fiber in the white paper line (to minimize fiber discharge to the corrugating medium line);
- Study bleaching system for improvements;
- Minimize fiber losses to sewer from the pulp mill, and the paper mill;
- Re-circulate water, where possible, to use less water and minimize fiber losses;
- Study improvement to the stock preparation line, paper machines and the finishing line of white papers; and
- Review requirements for water effluent treatment.

It is clear that the mill's biggest cost items, at present, in the manufacturing of a tonnes of paper are:

- Cost of fiber;
- Cost of cooking chemicals;
- Cost of bleaching chemicals;
- Cost of fuel.

Our recommendation, on a long-term basis, would include installation of a more modern type paper machine for writing and printing paper with a capacity not less than 10,000 t/annum. This type of machine could be purchased as a second-hand machine, either from Scandinavia, Europe or North America. The cost of such a machine would be substantially lower than that of a new machine.

To supply pulp for the increased capacity with the new paper machine, three alternatives could be considered and are as follows:

- Increase pulp mill capacity;
- Keep pulp mill capacity as it is, and purchase pulp from the mainland of China;
- Obtain bleached bagasse pulp 20-30 t/day from the new planned bagasse pulp and paper mill on Hainan Island.

8

Y.R. AMARASINGHE

# THE EMBILIPITIYA MILLS IN SRI LANKA

THE DEVELOPMENT of paper a industry in Sri Lanka is closely linked with the industrial policies adopted by successive governments in the country. The first paper factory — which was a semi-mechanised factory designed to convert waste-paper into wrapping paper — was established during the Second World War period. This did not function properly and was closed down within a couple of years. The first modern paper factory was established in 1956 at Valachchanai, and this was followed over twenty years later by the second one, the Embilipitiya factory.

Both the paper mills in Sri Lanka are government owned enterprises and are managed by the publicly owned National Paper Corporation. "Public Corporation" is an organisational device created in the mid 1950s with the dual objective of allowing the flexibility needed for a commercial undertaking while at the same time retaining the control by the government.

## 1. The Pulp Mill and the Paper Machine

The Embilipitiya Pulp and Paper Mills was established in 1978 with a rated capacity of 15,000 M/T. The Pulp Mill has capacity to produce 36 t/day of pulp from rice straw by the soda process. It has been specially designed to use rice straw as raw material but it has been able to do mill trials with Gini Grass, Bagasse etc. A small chipper plant, which can handle about 90 tonnes wood, has been installed, and wood pulping it done now quite frequently. The paper machine is a Fourdrinier type with 50 M/T/day capacity to produce fine printings and writings with basis weight in the range 30 — 120 gsm. The paper mill has been designed to use rice straw pulp with admixing of bleached kraft long-fibred pulp. Two pulpers, each having a capacity of handling 30 tonnes of pulp, have been installed to dissolve long-fibred pulp and broke from the finishing house.

The pulp mill has not been running at full capacity since 1983 due to rice straw supply problems, and naturally under capacity utilisation has caused the cost of production to rise. Chlorine consumption is fairly high (8%) and this is mainly due to low washing efficiency of rice straw pulp with high SR value. The consumption figures for water and steam are high and could be reduced further by running the mill at full capacity.

In general the performance of the paper machine is very good. The machine has been able to produce even 75 t/day without difficulty when making grades such as 64 gsm. As the machine sometimes uses up to 50 per cent of waste-paper in the furnish it is very essential that a waste-paper treatment plant is added. Since inception the mill has been using phosphor bronze wires on the machine and recently some plastic wires have been tried. The results are encouraging, according to the mill staff, except for high rate of wear on foil boxes and suction box tips. Full advantage of the size press is being not taken. Size press is bypassed when low grade printing and duplicating are made, in order to cut down specific steam consumption. The production programme consists of about 60 per cent of ordinary white printing paper, which is being used for printing of school books, etc. The quality problems of mill's products are mainly due to variations in basis weight, moisture, thickness, colour, and inconsistent furnish. Most of the variation problems are thought to be possibly avoidable by the installation of a B/M gauge and control system. Non-uniformity of raw material usage is also another reason for quality problems.

## 2. Capacity Utilisation

The capacity utilisation of the mill has been very poor. Between 1980-85 the capacity utilisation varied between 30 per cent to 50 per cent. This rose to 67.4 per cent in 1986 and has remained around that range since. The excess capacity in recent years has been caused mainly by (a) competition from cheaper imported varieties, (b) increasing cost of production, and (c) inadequate raw material supply. All these factors have affected the profitability of the industry. Right up to 1985 Embilipitiya has been running at a loss. Since then there has been considerable improvement due to cost reduction measures and increased utilisation of capacity. At Embilipitiya one can see a close link between the rate of profit and capacity utilisation. Capacity utilisation is constrained by raw material supply problems and the market.

**3. Raw Material Supply and Usage**

The Embilipitiya mill is designed to use rice straw. The very location of the mill in the vast irrigated paddy growing area of Southern Sri Lanka was determined by this. The total annual requirement of rice straw in order to run the mill at capacity is 30,000 M/T. However, in its history the mill never succeeded in approximating this target. The straw collection has been going down gradually and now the mill expects to collect only about 10,000 M/T. Regular supply short-falls (among other reasons) have caused the mill to use imported pulps in increasing quantities. In 1986, 10,537 M/T of various types of pulps were used; out of this only 2895 M/T were straw pulp. The proportion declined further in 1987. This shows very clearly the reduction of the importance of straw as the raw material base. More importantly, except for the straw and a further 124 M/T of waste-paper the rest of the pulps were all imported. Considering the fact that most of the additives used are also imported (alum, rosin, starch, dyes etc.), the imported component of the material used in the paper-making is very high indeed. The increasing in price of the imported items leads to increases in the cost of production thereby causing adverse effects on the market share of the local production.

One problem with regard to rice straw as a raw material is related to supply. This really has more to do with procurement of straw rather than its actual production, as some have attempted to show. The mill at present is dependent on intermediaries for its straw supply. Their mediation prevents the actual producers of straw — the farmers — from getting a satisfactory price. Measures to motivate the farmers — through price and other incentives — to supply to the mill, and the reorganisation of the straw procurement arrangements would cause the supply level to increase. The mill needs to involve itself more positively in the collection of straw. Any returns for the supply of straw will also help to strengthen the economic position of the farmers.

Of late, the mill has been resorting to wood pulping. Eucaliptus plantations located over 100 km away in the hill country are used for this. From the point of view of cost of production, straw pulp costs much less than wood pulping. In 1985 the cost of bleached straw pulp tonnes was Rs. 14,631.18, while that of wood was Rs. 22,310.66. Of course both these are costlier than imported bleached pulp, but the entire cost of imported items have to be borne through foreign exchange which the country can ill afford as it is. The second problem with regard to using rice straw as a raw material is the failure of the chemical recovery system to process rice straw black liquor.

### 4. The Chemical Recovery System and Related Problems

The CRS at Embilipitiya was erected in 1979 but the holding of the first performance trial was delayed till February 1982 due to certain necessary modifications to the process and equipment. The objective of the system was to eliminate the polluting effluent black liquor and to recover at least 75 per cent of the pulping chemicals. Even after the first trial-run further modifications were added and the final tests done in October 1983.

During the trial-run many problems were encountered. Most of these problems were related or associated with the high silica content of the rice straw black liquor. The lime mud could not be burnt as a result of high silica content. A constant supply of furnace oil became necessary due to low solids in heavy black liquor and low calorific value of rice straw black liquor. High silica content caused scaling and the evaporator had to be cleaned very frequently. On the whole, the recovery process turned out to be extremely expensive and the recovery efficiency very low. The cost of caustic soda recovered during the trial run was about 4½ times the locally purchased caustic soda. Consequently, the CR has not been put into use, although several more millions of rupees have been spent since on further modifications and maintenance.

The failure of the CR system is definitely one of the most pressing problems confronted by the Embilipitiya factory. It has serious implications for the cost of production, raw material usage, and the environmental situation. The factory has to bear the cost of an investment of Rs. 175 million (on CR system), without having had any contribution to the production system. A staff of 75 recruited for CR work is being maintained.

Moreover, as a result of the non-operation of the CR system, the full benefits of using the locally available cheap raw material — rice straw — cannot be obtained in full measure at Embilipitiya. To avoid the problem of increased accumulation of black liquor which can neither be processed nor disposed of without creating serious environmental problems, the mill authorities have resorted to using imported pulps and waste-paper to an increasing degree.

Needless to say, with a properly functioning CR system all these problems could be averted and the cost of production be reduced and mill viability increased.

Even for partial recovery — i.e. recovering soda ash only — there are serious problems. The evaporation of rice straw black liquor remains a serious problem. The drying of soda ash will be a considerable difficulty. Even if it is possible to recover soda ash, the market for it in Sri Lanka is very limited and a costly distance away from the factory. If desilication of rice straw black liquor at Embilipitiya is either not practicable or not economical, the only alternative open to the Mills is to shift the raw material base. The currently practiced method of using imported raw material like waste-paper or using imported pulp, is really no alternative at all. It is only a very costly way of evading a major problem. The full scale adoption of such an option will preclude the country from gaining the maximum benefit from the establishment of the Pulp and Paper Mill. The employment opportunities available in activities related to straw supply, collection, baling and pulping would be eliminated. Most valuable foreign exchange will be drained to pay for these imports, and a chance to utilise an abundantly available agricultural by-product, that is going to waste, for a local industry will be lost.

Using wood for pulping, which is being practiced to a limited extent now with the help of a chipper plant, is another alternative. At present limited amount of wood is available and this is expected to increase in the future. But wood, unlike straw, has a wide variety of alternative uses. And the cost of wood pulping is much greater. Moreover, the feasibility of chemical recovery on wood black liquor has yet to be tested.

At third alternative, i.e. using bagasse, appears to be more promising than the other two. The mill authorities themselves are favourable to this idea. If bagasse is purchased at fuel equivalent value, the total cost of a tonne of bleached bagasse pulp is estimated to be about Rs. 12,262, a figure which is much lower than the price of any imported (short — C.T.M.P.) variety of pulp. However, the problem with regard to bagasse is one of availability. At the moment sugar factories in Sri Lanka are using their bagasse as fuel and there is no excess bagasse available for pulping. Moreover, except for one of the sugar factories — that of Sevenagala — all the others are located a fair distance away from Embilipitiya. Right now, Sevenagala is working much below capacity, and once it reaches capacity production in its stage II, approximately 37,000 MT of bagasse would be available at fuel equivalent value for pulping. This amount, of course, is sufficient to produce about 11,000 MT of bleached pulp per year, quite adequate for the needs of Embilipitiya. However, whether stage II of Sevenagala will get off the ground as scheduled is very much in doubt. In the long run, with the expansion expected in the sugarcane industry, under the new irrigation schemes, the availability problem of bagasse will most certainly be eliminated.

Another problem with regard to bagasse is again whether the recovery system as it exists now is capable of recovering bagasse black liquor. At the moment the mills management is not inclined to increase its capital outlay on the CR plant any more, but if the bagasse is available in adequate quantities the obtaining of capital provision for any modifications needed may be possible.

**5. Affluent Disposal and the Environment**

The arrangement for the disposal of effluent at Embilipitiya has led to some problems. Non-black liquor effluent is channelled through a pipe-line to the nearby river, after collecting in a settling-pond and an aeration lagoon. Most of this effluent is utilised profitably by cultivators living on high ground along the path of the pipe-line. Agricultural authorities do not sanction this; nevertheless the practice continues. As yet, no one has studied the possible adverse effects of this practice.

The black liquor effluent, which is also emptied to the river from the two collecting ponds from time to time, is not so acceptable. Its disposal causes protests from the locals and the National Environmental Authority. It is alleged that the disposal of black liquor to the river affects fish and disrupts water intakes down river. The National Paper Corporation has reacted to these protests by directing the mill to use less of black liquor producing raw materials or resort to imported pulps.

The black liquor effluent disposal problem is held up as a factor

9

AROON AUANSAKUL

# THE BANG-PA-IN PULP AND PAPER MILL IN THAILAND

THE OBJECTIVE of this report is twofold: (1) To present a thorough review of some aspects of the current pulp and paper industry in Thailand. The presentation includes a review of major constraints/limitations to the development and growth of the industry. (2) To report on the results of critical evaluation, with respect to technical and financial performance, of one of the small pulp and paper mills using rice straw and Burma grass as major raw material, i.e., *the Bang-Pa-In Pulp and Paper Mill.* The Bang-Pa-In mill is a government-owned mill, erected in 1955. It is considered to be a small mill based on its size, and also employs a very simple production technique, i.e., the mill's production control system is still done by man and experience, not by computer. It is now under a government privatisation scheme.

## 1. Markets of Pulp and Paper Products in Thailand

### *1.1. Demand*

#### *1.1.1. Paper and Boards*

(a) Average annual tonnages of paper and board consumed in Thailand during 1974-1984 is 430,105 t/annum.
(b) Various paper types are consumed but kraft occupied the highest share since it represented as much as 36 per cent of the total paper and board consumption.
(c) The total consumption increased more than twofold, from

262,430 tonnes to 605,332 t/annum, or grew at 9.3 per cent p.a. during 1974-1984.

TABLE 1: Average Annual Tonnages of Paper and Board Consumed in Thailand 1974–1984

| Paper Types | Tonnes p.a. | % |
|---|---|---|
| Krafts | 155,861 | 36 |
| Newsprints | 91,355 | 21 |
| Writing-Printing | 80,868 | 19 |
| Paperboard | 76,327 | 18 |
| Sanitary | 16,109 | 4 |
| Other | 9,585 | 2 |
| Total | 430,105 | 100 |

### *1.1.2. Pulp*

TABLE 2: Average Annual Tonnages of Pulp Consumed in Thailand from 1974–1984

| Pulp | Tonnes p.a. | % |
|---|---|---|
| Short-fibre | 64,577 | 51.8 |
| Long-fibre | 55,301 | 44.4 |
| Other types | 4,752 | 3.8 |
| Total | 124,630 | 100.0 |

(a) Average annual tonnages of pulp consumed in Thailand during 1974–1984 is 124,630 t/annum.
(b) Both short- and long-fibres are important inputs for making-paper and board products though the former contributed a larger share of 51.8 per cent of the total pulp consumption p.a.
(c) The total pulp consumption increased about 1.4-fold from 100,052 tonnes to 145,005 t/annum, or grew at about 11.8 per cent p.a. during 1974-1984.

### *1.1.3. Used Paper*

(a) Total industrial used-paper comes from domestic collection and import where data is available only for imported quantities.
(b) From 1974–1984, Thailand imported an average of 106,462

tonnes of used-paper p.a., valued at 329 million Bath, with an annual growth rat of 5.4 per cent p.a.

### *1.2. Supply*

#### *1.2.1. Paper and Board*

TABLE 3: Average Annual Tonnages of Paper Types Supplied by Sources from 1974–1984

| Paper Types | Own Production | | Net Import | | Total | |
|---|---|---|---|---|---|---|
| | tonnes p.a. | % | tonnes p.a. | % | tonnes p.a. | % |
| Newsprints | – | – | 91,355 | 72.4 | 91,355 | 21.2 |
| Writing-Printing | 69,588 | 23.0 | 11,280 | 8.9 | 80,868 | 18.6 |
| Sanitary | 18,536 | 6.1 | −2,427 | −1.9 | 16,109 | 3.8 |
| Krafts | 154,377 | 50.8 | 1,484 | 1.2 | 155,861 | 36.2 |
| Paperboard | 58,129 | 19.1 | 18,198 | 14.4 | 76,327 | 17.8 |
| Other | 3,236 | 1.1 | 6,349 | 5.0 | 9,585 | 2.2 |
| Total | 303,866 | 100 | 126,239 | 100 | 430,150 | 100 |
| % | (70.6) | | (29.4) | | (100) | |

(a) About 71 per cent of total paper and board consumption is supplied by own production whereas the remainder is imported, valued at 1,621 million Bath p.a.

(b) Except for newsprints, all other types are manufactured in Thailand. And except for sanitary papers, all others are not produced sufficiently for home consumption and, thereby, more than a hundred thousand tonnes per annum. are imported.

#### *1.2.2. Pulp*

TABLE 4: Production and Import of Pulp: Average Annual Tonnage from 1974-1984

| | tonnes p.a. | % |
|---|---|---|
| *Production* | | |
| Short-fibre | 36,917 | 28.6 |
| *Net Import* | | |
| Short-fibre | 27,660 | 22.2 |
| Long-fibre | 55,301 | 44.4 |
| Others | 4,752 | 3.8 |
| Total | 124,630 | 100 |

(a) Only short-fibre pulp is produced by local manufacturers and shares about 30 per cent of total domestic demand.
(b) Among imported items, long-fibre shares the highest, i.e., about 44 per cent of the total domestic pulp demand and use.

*1.3. Product Price Situation*

This study concluded that in the past imported prices of paper products, pulp and used papers were relatively unstable, and nominal price levels of imported pulp were relatively lower than that of the domestically produced pulps. This price instability has direct impacts on the domestically produced pulps, since as much as 70 per cent of the total pulp consumption were still imported.

To help protect domestic pulp manufacturers, the government, therefore, imposed variable tax rates on imported pulps so that the resulting c.i.f. + tax prices were about 20 per cent higher than those of the domestically-produced pulps.

*1.4. Number of Mills and Production Capacity*

There is a total of 36 pulp and paper mills with a total production capacity of 107,000 tonnes pulp per annum. and of 617,950 tonnes paper per annum.

Out of these 36 mills; 33 are paper mills, 2 are pulp mills and only one is an integrated mill producing both pulp and printing-writing papers.

*1.5. Demand Projection*

Paper and board products per capita consumption increased twice from 6 to 12 kg./cap./year from 1974 to 1984.

Future demand is expected to increase more due to the technological advance and the economic and social development of this nation which will demand more paper and products. Average annual growth rates of consumption for paper products, pulps and used papers during the next 5 years are estimated at 9.3 per cent, 11.8 per cent and 5.4 per cent p.a. respectively.

**2. Raw Materials for Pulp Production in Thailand**

Kenaf, straw, bagasse, Burma grass, bamboo and eucalyptus are types of raw materials that are currently used to produce short-fibre pulps in Thailand.

Three domestic pulp mills are using different types and quantities of raw materials, i.e., the Phoenix Pulp Co. is presently the largest pulp mill (70,000 tonnes pulp per annum capacity) using kenaf, bamboo and eucalyptus as fibrous raw materials. The Siam Pulp Co. (28,000 tonnes pulp per annum capacity) uses bagasse with a total demand of 120,000 t/annum. And the Bang Pa-In Paper mill (9,000 tonnes pulp per annum capacity) utilises straw and Burma grass as raw materials in their pulp production process, with annual uses of approx. 24,000 and A.D. 2,000 t/annum, respectively,

Production rate of all three mills combined is presently about 73 per cent of total installed capacity.

All of these raw materials are domestically collected by the mills, mostly via private collectors under contract. The Phoenix and Siam Pulp mills have sometimes faced problem of insecurity in their raw material supply source due to, e.g., highly competitive demand by other users, government production/supply control programme, weather variability and world price situation, etc., resulting in limited raw materials available to the mills. For the Bang Pa-In Paper mill, the problem of raw material collection, especially for rice straw, is almost non-existent.

## 3. Limitation to Growth of the Industry in Thailand

### *3.1. High-Unit Cost of Pulp Production*

Presently, the average variable cost of short-fibre pulp production in Thailand is about 8,000 – 9,000 Bath/tonnes, which is twice as much as that of hardwood short-fibre pulp produced in Brazil. High-unit cost has been due to disadvantages in prices of raw materials, energy and chemical inputs, which are comparatively higher, and low operating efficiency of the mills. Therefore, domestic produced pulps cannot compete well with the imported ones.

### *3.2. Low and Unstable World Price of Pulp and Paper*

Low and unstable world price of pulp and paper c.i.f. price levels of imported pulp and paper are generally varied and lower than those of domestically manufactured products. Without the government tax programme, low and unstable prices of imported products would have provided disincentives to investment in production. Nevertheless, uncertainty whether the tax policy would prevail in the long-run, has provided disincentives to the mills to expand production.

### *3.3. Dumping Problems*

In recent years, long-fibre pulp from abroad was dumped in Thailand and the relatively lower price was one of the factors limiting growth of the domestic pulp industry.

### *3.4. Raw Material Problem*

This problem exists for some pulp mills utilising kenaf and bagasse from sugarcane as major raw material, since their production are subjected to weather variability, crop prices and government crop restriction/control programme, etc. In addition, some mills have to compete with other users of the same, limited amount of raw material. Thus uncertainty in supply sources, implied risky investment in pulp and paper production.

### *3.5. Tax Disincentives*

The current government tax programme is claimed to have advantages only for an established integrated mill but not for an individual pulp or paper-making mill, since the former relatively lower tax burden. The present tax scheme thus provides disincentives for the establishment of a separated mill.

## 4. The Bang Pa-In Paper Mill

### *4.1. Background*

The Bang Pa-In Paper Mill was initially established as a state-owned mill by the National Economic Development Corporation. The mill is situated at Bang Pa-In, Ayuthaya province, about 70 kilometers north of Bangkok, Thailand. The prime objective in establishing the mill was threefold:

- To develop and promote pulp and paper industry in Thailand with an economically sound status, and to meet domestic demand for paper.
- To save a substantial amount of foreign exchange used in importing both industrial and cultural paper.
- To financially help farmers in the Central Plain, where most of the rice crops are grown. The farmers could increase their income considerably by selling surplus rice straw to the mill.

The construction of the buildings and the installation of the machinery and equipment for integrated operations was completed in 1961. Full-scale operation was on stream the year after. The mill was designed according to produce 40 t/day writing and printing paper based on 60 gm/m$^2$ weight. The furnish is 80 per cent rice straw pulp and 20 per cent imported pulp.

The 1965 the mill decided to a search for some fiber resources and to assess the availability and technical suitability for the manufacture of pulp. Samples of certain grass (which could be classified as a reed) widely grown in the high lands in the provinces of Saraburi, Lopburi, Nakornrajsima (Korat) and Petchaboon, were tested in the mill's laboratory. The pulping was done by the Neutral Monosulphite Process and the bleaching by conventional CEHH sequence. The conclusions reached from studies and a number of tests conducted, were that the grass pulp is very suitable for paper-making and could be substituted to some extant for BKP in the furnish. The paper produced from either 100 per cent grass pulp or from a furnish of 70 per cent grass pulp and 30 per cent BKP possesses a superior quality to the paper produced from conventional furnish (rice straw and BK). As previously mentioned, the mill was initially designed and equipped to process the pulp from rice straw. Though some pieces of machinery and equipment could be applicable to the grass pulping by the same Neutral Monosulphite Process, the mill eventually meets some difficulties, particularly in the pre-treatment operations before bleaching operations. Modifications of existing equipment are to be made. To cite an example, the screen equipped with lots specially designed for rice straw processing does not work well for the grass pulp.

From the production record it can be seen that from the year 1983 onward, the mill could produce some 12,000 metric tonnes paper per year, which is within the range of the target established.

### *4.2. Raw Material: Sources and Problems*

(1) *Rice Straw*. Thailand is a large producer of rice, consequently large quantities of rice straw are available. One acre of rice land produces one tonne of straw when a high cutting is carried out, i.e. with an 18 inch stubble remaining. With low cutting, leaving a stubble of only a few inches above the ground, two tonnes of straw per acre are available for use.

From an acreage of 700,000 in the large central plain of Thailand, (Ayudthaya province, Singburi, Lopburi, Chainath, Pathumthani, Saraburi, Suphanburi), it is estimated that between 7,000,000 and 14,000,000 tonnes of straw are available annually, depending on the height of cutting. Bang Pa-In Paper mill, located in Ayudthaya province, needs rice straw for pulp amounting about 24,000 t/year.

(2) *Burma Grass*. This grass grows naturally in Saraburi Province, Nakorn Rachasima, and in some provinces of North-Eastern Thailand. Cropping areas are approximately 5,000 ha., with a 25,000 t/year volume. The harvesting period is about 3 months, in December, January, and February. The quantity needed for pulp making at Bang Pa-In Paper mill is about 2,000 t/year. Scientific name of Burma grass: Pannisatum pedicallatum polystachyon.

(3) During the past 18 years of operations, the mill has faced no critical shortage of supply of rice straw. For Burma grass, the cropping area around the mill may be quite limited, but the mill never had any problem with their supply sources. The location where the grass is cut, bundled and collected, is at a distance of 100–200 km from the site along the Saraburi-Nakornrajsima and Saraburi-Petchaboon Highways. Collection work and delivery to the mill is done by the contractors at agreed prices, and the volume supplied usually does not exceed 500 metric tonnes per contract.

(4) The mill's problem is with storage losses due to rain or flood. Water seeps from the ground into the first layer of the bales under which stocks are piled. Also limited space area of the stock yard and the temporary nature of the stock building are a problem. An average loss of 10 per cent is thus accounted for. To minimize loss, the following are recommended:

- Acquisition of a number of baling presses specially constructed for working with the grass and installed at each depot. The grass delivered by the contractor in bundles is to be baled and stored in such buildings. In this manner, not only can you save the storage space but also preserve the quality of the grass in good conditions.

- Construction of semi-permanent or permanent buildings at the site, also at the depots.

### *4.3. Pulp and Paper Production: Selected Information*

#### *4.3.1. Raw Material Preparation*

Actual Consumption of raw material in 1986

| | | |
|---|---|---|
| Rice Straw | 24,000 A.D. Tonne | 92.3% |
| Burma Grass | 2,000 | 7.7% |
| Total | 26,000 | 100% |

#### *4.3.2. Cooking*

(a) Process — Neutral Sulphite Process
(b) System — Batch System
(c) Digester — Clobe Digester (45 m$^3$/ 6 sets)

| | *Straw* | *Straw + Burma grass* |
|---|---|---|
| (d) Cooking Cycle Feeding | (1) | 1.5 hr. |
| Heating up (40–165°C) | (1) | 1.0 |
| Keeping (at 165°C) | (2) | 4.5 |
| Blow | (1) | 1.0 |
| Total | (5) | 8.0 |

(e) Max, Temp, Pressure 165°C–B - 9 kg/cm$^2$
(f) Liquor Ratio 1 : 3.2
(g) Cooking Chemical
Rice straw only $Na_2SO_3$ 8% NaDH 2.5%
Rice straw + Burma grass $Na_2SO_3$ 9% NaDH 3.5%
(h) Feeding Amount of Raw Material — 5t/Batch (Bone-dry weight)

(i) Annual performance
in 1986 No. of Batch 4,815
pulp production 8,936 A.D. tonne.

### *4.3.3. Stock Preparation*

Stock preparation equipment composed of :

- 1 Hydropulper 7 m$^3$ for import pulp
- 5 Conical Refiner 100 H.P. each
- 2 circulating staff chest, each volume 30 m$^3$
- 3 60 m$^3$ chest for mixing chest, reserved chest and machine chest
- 1 Deflaker for broke pulper

### *4.3.4. Paper Machine*

| | |
|---|---|
| Wet part | Fourdrinier type (3,750 mm wire width) |
| Press part | Suction press (No. 1) |
| | Suction (No. 2) Reverse (No. 3) |
| Dry part | Multi Dryer Type (24 + 2 cooling pcs) |
| | Machine calendar 8 rolls |

### *4.4. Modification Plan*

The mill is planning to modify the existing machines and production process, to produce 60 t/day writing and printing paper, as following:

*4.4.1. Raw Materials* (Rice straw and Burma grass)

The raw material cropping areas are situated within a 150 km. range from the mill, of which the rice straw cropping areas cover approx. 20,000 ha giving an available total crop volume of 50,000 t/year, in terms of self produced pulp, required after completion of the modification plan.

As for the Burma grass, the harvesting period is likely to be for three month, the supply of the grass not more than 2,000 metric tonne/year, because the Burma grass around their cropping area may be limited.

### *4.4.2. Pulping*

The existing six sets of globe type digesters, 45 m$^3$ per each, could be replaced by a continuous digester of the pandie type. The capacity of about 50 t/day will be required for making self-produced pulp, after completion of the modification plan.

The capacity at each stage is to be 50 tonnes bleached pulp per day. The bleaching is to have 4 stages, i.e. chlorine, caustic soda, hypochloride 1 and 2, which is the same as the current sequence. The extraction stage caustic soda is converted into a downflow system instead of the existing upflow one; an attempt to increase the pulp consistency to be produced.

### *4.4.3. Chemical Preparation*

The electrolysis plant for $Cl_2$ and NaDH bleaching chemical, and an additional electrolysis plant of 4 tonnes for $Cl_2$ using a diaphram method and ion exchange diaphram, have been studied to supplement the expected shortage, but it was found to be uneconomical, and it is planned to rely totally an purchase for the time being.

An additional electrolysis plant using a diaphram method or ion exchange diaphram should be reconsidered, if in the future its erection costs can be reduced.

### *4.4.4. Stock Preparation*

The refining lines will be divided strictly into two groups. One for purchased pulp and another for self-produced pulp, and five sets of double disk refiners are planned for installation.

### *4.4.5. Paper Machine*

The wire part is fitted with a formation board and foils to improve quality and production performance. The marginal nature of the first, second and the third press is due mainly to the fact that it cannot be loaded above the first, second and the third press loading. Therefore, the sheet is not being sufficiently compressed for optimum water removal.

A picked-up system will be adopted for the press part and a size press is also to be installed, for both operation and product quality.

A sectional drive system will be adopted, and a thyrister system for the electricity.

### *4.4.6. Finishing*

The product in roll form is to be not more than 10 per cent of the total product and no radical change in this rate may be expected even in the future, so that no addition of a rewinder is considered necessary. An additional double cutter and guillotine cutter are planned for installation, in providing for an increase of sheet products.

No addition of a product warehouse is planned, as the existing one has sufficient capacity.

### *4.4.7. Utilities*

An additional transformer of 6,000 KVA capacity is planned for the electric power line of the mill. The substations are to be centralised to facilitate control, when adding the transformer. There are currently two boilers of 35 t/hour capacity each under normal operation. An additional coagulator and sand filter with a capacity of 25,000 $m^3$/day are planned because of the insufficient water intake.

### *4.4.8. Pollution Control*

While the current effluent treatment system is quite simple just to make effluent pass through the lagoon, it is planned that the black liquor derived from the cooking process be condensed in the evaporator and burnt out in the incinerator, and the effluent derived from the bleaching process be treated through the coagulater, including the current effluent, all of which then should be discharged into the lagoon through the canal.

The estimated investment cost for above facility is estimated to be about 15 per cent of the total investment cost.

# THREE

# DIFFERENT COUNTRY REPORTS

10

TIRATH GUPTA & VINOD AHUJA

# BAGASSE BASED PAPER PRODUCTION IN INDIA

## Economic, Managemental and Policy Issues

THE PAPER and paperboards industry in India has had a chequered history. Around 1910, the annual output of seven units was 25,000 tonnes. The fibrous raw materials were *Eulopsis binata* (Sabai grass), hemp, rags, jute, and imported spruce and wood pulp. The first paper mill which used bamboo as a source of cellulose went into production in 1918, and almost all the mills established during the next forty years were bamboo based. That was encouraged through policy interventions including levy of import duties on selected varieties of paper in 1925, and enactment of the Bamboo Paper Industry (Protection) Act in 1932 (Ahuja, 1980, pp. 36-37).

It can, therefore, be said that bamboo's inherent properties for pulping, its wide occurrence in natural forests, extremely low royalty charged for its use, and protection granted to the bamboo based paper industry were important factors responsible for the rapid growth of the paper and paperboards industry in India. The number of units rose from 17 in 1951 to 136 in 1981 and to 288 in 1987. Around 240 of these units were classified as small scale, i.e., with installed capacity up to 10,000 t/annum (Table 1). Similarly, the output of paper and paperboards increased from 135,000 tonnes in 1951 to 1,232,000 tonnes in 1981 and to around 1,570,000 tonnes in 1987.

This growth of a capital intensive industry should normally indicate its good health, but that does not appear to be the case as :

- Average annual installed capacity per paper mill increased from 8,100 tonnes in 1951 to 19,600 tonnes in 1971 but declined continuously thereafter to reach 9,600 tonnes in 1971 but declined continuously thereafter to reach 9,600 tonnes in 1987 (Table 1).

- Capacity utilisation in the paper industry declined continually from 98 per cent in 1951 to around 58 per cent in 1987.
- The compound annual growth rate of the output of paper and paperboards declined continuously from nearly 10.5 per cent during 1951-61 to a little over 4.0 per cent during 1981-87.
- Compound annual growth rate in the total availability of paper and paperboards declined continuously from 8.2 per cent during 1951-61 to around 0.6 per cent during 1981-85.
- Common varieties of paper and paperboards have not been imported since 1983 and the share of all types of paper and paperboards imports to their total availability in the country also declined continuously from 38 per cent in 1951 to nearly two per cent in 1986.
- There have been no felt scarcities in the paper market during the 1980s.
- In line with the industry's demand, restrictions on exports of paper and paperboards have recently been removed.

These trends are difficult to understand as an unprecedented increase in demand for paper and paperboards was anticipated for a number of reasons : rising income, development of industry and commerce, heavy emphasis on education and adult literacy, etc. Let us examine in some detail.

(i) the demand situation, and
(ii) the growth of small scale paper-making units in India.

**1. Demand Forecasts**

The Planning Commission of India and a number of other government and industry sponsored studies have been continually forecasting the demand for paper and paperboards. A review of the literature reveals that demand has been substantially overestimated and the demand forecasts for A.D. 2000 have varied from 3.25 to 4.40 million tonnes (Table 2). Moreover, qualitative observations on the state of the market for paper and paperboards, and discussions with knowledgeable people indicated that the demand in the foreseeable future could increase by 3.5 per cent a year. Thus, without imports and without attempts at *demand management*, the market for paper and paperboards could be in equilibrium with a gradual rise in production to 2.5 million tonnes by the turn of the century. But, in view of the installed capacity at 2.8 million tonnes, additional production capacity in the pipeline, the recent policy interventions to encourage the consumption of paper and paperboards, and the possibility of some exports, India may plan to meet a growth rate of 4.0 per cent a year. That would entail an output of 2.7 million tonnes by A.D. 2000 (Gupta, 1988).

TABLE 1: Number of Integrated Pulp and Paper Mills in India by Size Groups of Annual Installed Capacity: 1951 to 1987

*('000 tonnes)*

| Year | Annual installed capacity | | | | | Total | | Average annual installed capacity |
|---|---|---|---|---|---|---|---|---|
| | Above 20 | 10 to 20 | 5 to 10 | 2 to 5 | Below 2 | Number of mills | Installed capacity | |
| 1951 | 2 | 3 | 2 | 5 | 5 | 17 | 137 | 8.1 |
| 1961 | 6 | 4 | 3 | 8 | 6 | 27 | 410 | 15.2 |
| 1971 | 14 | 3 | 7 | 12 | 10 | 46 | 901 | 19.6 |
| 1979 | 19 | 6 | 23 | 27 | 31 | 106 | 1,530 | 14.4 |
| 1980 | 21 | 8 | 24 | 31 | 37 | 121 | 1,538 | 12.7 |
| 1981 | 22 | 9 | 31 | 33 | 41 | 136 | 1,657 | 12.2 |
| 1982 | 22 | 10 | 40 | 41 | 44 | 157 | 1,816 | 11.6 |
| 1983 | 23 | 11 | 41 | 49 | 51 | 175 | 1,907 | 10.9 |
| 1984 | 23 | 11 | 60 | 65 | 61 | 220 | 2,165 | 9.8 |
| 1985 | 23 | 15 | 68 | 80 | 63 | 240 | 2,350 | 9.4 |
| 1986 | 29 | 18 | 75 | 93 | 56 | 271 | 2,655 | 9.8 |
| 1987 | 29 | 22 | 82 | 97 | 58 | 288 | 2,760 | 9.6 |

*Sources*: 1. Gupta and Shah, 1987, p. 8 (up to 1985).
2. CMIE, 1987b, (for 1986).
3. CMIE, 1987c, (for 1987)

In addition, the demand for newsprint by the turn of the century has been estimated at 0.9 million tonnes.[1] Thus, to avoid continued dependence on newsprint imports and be able to export small quantities of paper and paperboards, the country should be producing 3.6 million tonnes to paper and paperboards and newsprint by A.D. 2000.

## 2. Potential Availability of Forest Based Cellulosic Materials

Concern has been voiced at depleting forest resources which, in turn, could have a perceptible effect on the supply of the raw materials for the industry. At the same time, it has been estimated that the production of *at least* 0.75 million tonnes of paper and paperboards by the turn of the century would be based on indigenous waste-paper as raw material (Gupta, 1988). Thus, the main issue is to ensure supply of cellulosic materials to produce 2.85 million tonnes of paper

TABLE 2: Demand Forecasts for Paper and Paper Boards in India

*('000 Tonnes)*

| Studies and methodologies used | Assumed annual growth rate in per capita income/GNP (%) | Years | | | | | | | |
|---|---|---|---|---|---|---|---|---|---|
| | | 1965 | 1971 | 1975 | 1981 | 1985 | 1990 | 1995 | 2000 |
| 1. Five Years Plan | — | 700 | — | — | — | — | 1,540 | — | — |
| 2. FAO, 1960 | 2.0 | 523 | — | 998 | — | — | — | — | — |
| (Log normal | 2.5 | 585 | — | 1,238 | — | — | — | — | — |
| distribution) | 3.0 | 649 | — | 1,519 | — | — | — | — | — |
| 3. ESRF, 1969 (Log-log distribution) | — | — | — | 1,563 | — | — | — | — | — |
| 4. IIPO, 1969 | — | — | 837 | — | 2,259 | — | — | — | — |
| 5. NCAER, 1972 | 4 | — | — | 930 | 1,342 | — | — | — | — |
| (Log normal | 5 | — | — | 1,012 | 1,701 | — | — | — | — |
| distribution) | 6 | — | — | 1,201 | 2,192 | — | — | — | — |
| 6. NCAER, 1972 | 4 | — | — | 1,040 | 1,462 | — | — | — | — |
| (Linear | 5 | — | — | 1,121 | 1,751 | — | — | — | — |
| regression) | 6 | — | — | 1,298 | 2,109 | — | — | — | — |
| 7. NCA, 1976 | Low | — | — | — | 1,307 | 1,667 | — | — | 3,254 |
| (Linear regression) | High | — | — | — | 1,486 | 2,118 | — | — | 6,564 |
| 8. Sharma, 1978* (Income elasticity) | — | — | — | — | — | 1,421 | 2,090 | 3,071 | — |
| 9. Sharma, 1978* (Semilog trend) | — | — | — | — | — | 1,391 | 1,781 | 2,461 | — |
| 10. DCPPI, 1983 (Time trend) | — | — | — | — | — | 1,440 | 1,839 | 2,349 | 3,001 |
| 11. DCPPI, 1983 | 4 | — | — | — | — | 1,348 | 1,897 | 2,503 | 3,302 |
| (Log-log regression) | 5 | — | — | — | — | 1,560 | 2,202 | 3,108 | 4,386 |
| Observed consumption | | 566** | 787** | 840** | 1,144** | 1,255*** | — | — | — |

* The forecasts pertained to the years 1983, 1988, and 1993 but have been taken as 1985, 1990 and 1995, respectively.

** Assumed equivalent to availability including imports but without considering exports.

*** There have been no imports in India since 1983. Output at home in 1985 estimated at 1.5 million tonnes of which at least 2,00,000 tonnes exported and another 15 per cent reported as inventories.

*Source*: Gupta and Shah, 1987, pp. 60-61.

and paperboards and newsprint by A.D. 2000. The mix of bamboo and hardwoods is expected to be 40:60 by the turn of the century. Thus, if the whole of 2.85 million tonnes of paper and newsprint output has to be based on bamboo and hardwoods, and if the requirement of these materials per tonne of pulp is placed at 2.5 and 2.7 tonnes, respectively, the industry's demand for them could be a maximum of 2.85 and 4.6 million tonnes, with chemical pulp process.[2]

A very conservative estimate of the potential output of bamboo has been placed at five million tonnes. It has also been reasoned that the output can be considerably enhanced without heavy capital investments and possibly at lower marginal cost per unit of output with scientific management of the land resource (Chugh, 1982, p. 621). Thus, the industry's demand for bamboo could be around 50 per cent of the annual output against 80 per cent till recently. About 2.2 million tonnes of bamboo could, thus, be available for other uses against less than one million tonnes in the past. Similarly, technically and managerially feasible potential output of mixed woods by the turn of the century can be at least 40 million cubic metres (Gupta, 1988). Thus, the paper and newsprint industry's estimated demand for raw material of 4.6 million tonnes or 3.7 million cubic metres would be less than 10 per cent of the potential output.

On the contrary, perceptions of *absolute* scarcities of forest based cellulosic materials, and substantially overestimated demand forecasts for paper and paperboards seem to have resulted in less than objective choices amongst policy and technological alternatives, including encouragement of small scale pulp and paper-making units to enhance the use of unconventional raw materials such as bagasse, cereal straw, waste-paper, hemp and gunny cuttings, cotton waste.[3]

### 3. Potential Availability of Bagasse for Pulping

Amongst the unconventional materials, bagasse has been the most emphasised. Paper produced with 75 per cent or more of bagasse content has been fully exempted from excise duties which, at the 1987-88 rates, amounted to approximately Rs. 1,500 and Rs. 2,500 per tonne of writing/printing paper and kraft paper, respectively. In spite of that, a number of paper mills which started with bagasse as the main source of cellulose shifted to other raw materials within a short span of 2-3 years. An analysis of bagasse availability for pulping could, therefore, be of interest.

On average, 70 million tonnes of sugarcane was crushed annually in the organised section during 1981 to 1987. The annual bagasse output must have been around 23 million tonnes (Table 3). To analyse the potential supply of this material for pulping, three scenarios could be envisaged:

- bagasse which is surplus with sugar mills
- enhancing the surplus by improving the thermal efficiency of the existing energy systems at sugar mills.
- enhancing the surplus by replacing bagasse fired boilers with coal fired boilers.

TABLE 3: Production of Sugarcane and the Quantities Crushed in the Organised Sector by States in India: 1981 to 1987 averages

| States | Sugarcane | | Per cent sugarcane crushed in the organised sector |
|---|---|---|---|
| | Production ('000 tonnes) | Processed in organised sector ('000 tonnes) | |
| Assam | 2,127 (1.2) | 74 (0.1) | 3.5 |
| Andhra Pradesh | 10,808 (6.1) | 4,506 (6.4 | 41.7 |
| Bihar | 3,908 (2.2) | 2,890 (4.1) | 74.0 |
| Gujarat | 6,220 (3.5) | 4,548 (6.4) | 73.1 |
| Haryana | 5,573 (3.2) | 1,874 (2.6) | 33.6 |
| Kerala | 557 (0.3) | 150 (0.2) | 27.0 |
| Karnataka | 13,666 (7.8) | 5,007 (7.1) | 36.6 |
| Maharashtra | 25,892 (14.7) | 22,382 (31.7) | 86.4 |
| Madhya Pradesh | 1,356 (0.8) | 595 (0.8) | 44.0 |
| Orissa | 3,223 (1.8) | 256 (0.4) | 8.0 |
| Punjab | 5,427 (3.1) | 1,454 (2.1) | 26.8 |
| Pondicherry | 189 (0.1) | 311 (0.4) | 164.5 |
| Rajasthan | 1,312 (0.7) | 211 (0.3) | 16.1 |
| Tamil Nadu | 18,070 (10.3) | 6,945 (9.8) | 38.4 |
| Uttar Pradesh | 75,633 (43.0) | 19,305 (27.3) | 25.5 |
| West Bengal | 1,034 (0.6) | 53 (0.07) | 5.1 |
| Others | 900 (0.5) | 130 (0.2) | 14.4 |
| All India | 175,895 (100) | 70,691 (100) | 40.2 |

*Note:* Figures in parentheses are percentages to column totals.
*Source*: Anon., various years.

Due to economies of scale in energy use per unit of sugar output (Fig. 10.1) the size of sugar factories has to be an important factor for the first alternative. Factories with cane crushing capacity up to 1,200–1,300 t/day have not only been incapable of generating any surplus bagasse but also purchased the material from larger mills to meet their fuel requirements.

Estimates of surplus bagasse with larger sugar factories have varied widely, but these could save four per cent of the total without using coal or other fuels to fire their boilers. Less than 40 per cent of the sugar factories which handled 54 per cent of the cane crushed in the organised sector belonged to this category (Table 4). Assuming that (i) there were no significant variations in capacity utilisation amongst these factories, (ii) 80 per cent of the surplus bagasse could reach the paper and newsprint factories, and (iii) cane crushed in the organised sector would gradually rise from 70 million tonnes to nearly 100 million tonnes by A.D. 2000; around 0.6 million tonnes of bagasse could be available for pulping.[4] If the ratio of bagasse and other cellulosic materials is 80:20, this could support a production of about 125,000 tonnes of chemical pulp, i.e., around 3.5 per cent of the estimated demand for paper and paperboards and newsprint by the turn of the century.

The second scenario would necessitate installing waste heat recovery units, air-preheaters, recycling the flue gases, etc. and partial drying of bagasse to enhance its calorific value. It has, for instance, been estimated that a 10 to 20 per cent reduction in the moisture in fresh bagasse would save around 7.5 to 10.5 per cent[5] of the material (Fig. 10.2). At the turn of the century, that could give 0.5 to 0.7 million tonnes of chemical pulp with 80 per cent bagasse content. The surplus could be further enhanced by depithing bagasse at sugar mills and using the pith in the boilers.[6]

In the context of the third scenario, it can be said that if bagasse fired boilers were replaced with coal fired boilers for all the sugar factories, and if other assumptions were valid, nearly 27 million tonnes of the material could be available for pulping by A.D. 2000. With 80 per cent bagasse in the furnish, production of nearly 4.5 million tonnes (or more than the estimated demand for paper and paperboards and newsprint by the turn of the century) can be sustained.

### 4. Cost of Bagasse Used for Pulping

In spite of the emphasis of bagasse for paper and newsprint production, comparative private and societal costs and managemental feasibilities of these alternatives have not been adequately studied. The paper and newsprint industry in India has had the experience of using bagasse. We have attempted to study the costs of these materials at eight existing or proposed bagasse based paper and newsprint manufacturing plants which could be categorised into four groups:

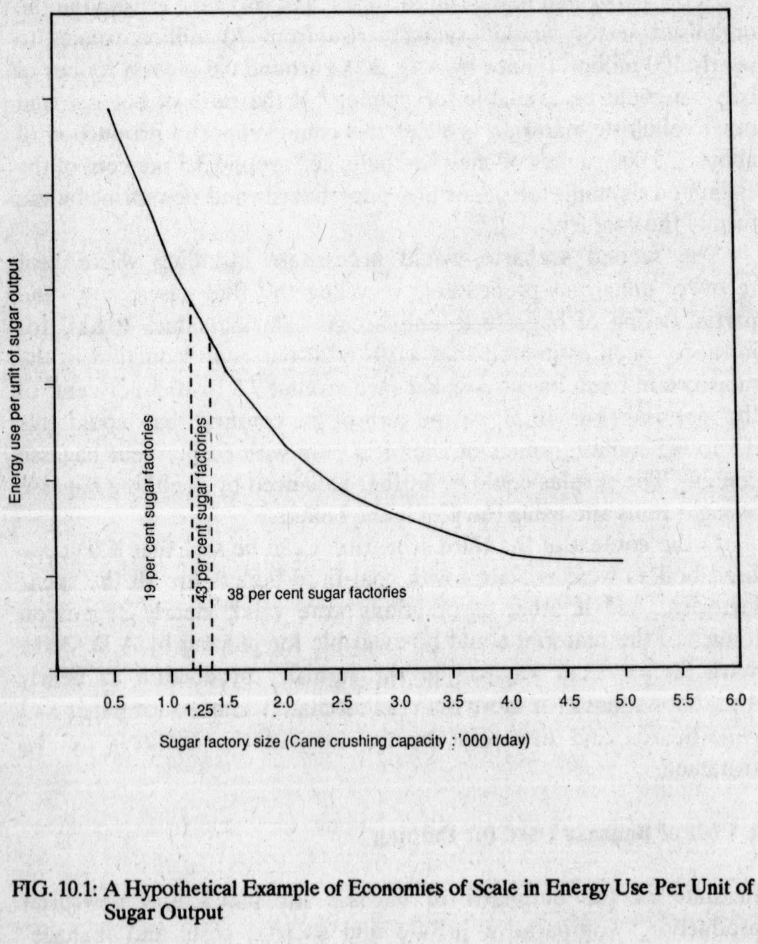


**FIG. 10.1: A Hypothetical Example of Economies of Scale in Energy Use Per Unit of Sugar Output**

TABLE 4: Distribution of Sugar Factories and Installed Cane Crushing Capacity by States in India: 1984-85

| States | Number of factories | Installed cane crushing capacity ('000 t/day) | |
|---|---|---|---|
| | | Total | Factories at or below 1,250 t/day |
| Assam | 2 (2) | 2.1 | 2.1 |
| Andhra Pradesh | 32 (22) | 53.4 | 25.2 |
| Bihar | 29 (19) | 35.6 | 18.5 |
| Gujarat | 15 (8) | 33.2 | 10.0 |
| Haryana | 8 (5) | 16.3 | 6.3 |
| Kerala | 3 (3) | 2.9 | 2.9 |
| Karnataka | 27 (15) | 51.5 | 18.5 |
| Maharashtra | 89 (56) | 146.6 | 67.2 |
| Madhya Pradesh | 8 (7) | 17.4 | 15.9 |
| Orissa | 3 (3) | 2.9 | 2.9 |
| Punjab | 8 (7) | 10.0 | 7.8 |
| Pondicherry | 2 (1) | 2.7 | 1.3 |
| Rajasthan | 3 (2) | 3.7 | 2.3 |
| Tamil Nadu | 23 (10) | 44.9 | 12.3 |
| Uttar Pradesh | 100 (55) | 161.0 | 59.2 |
| West Bengal | 2 (2) | 1.8 | 1.8 |
| Others | 2 (2) | 2.2 | 2.2 |
| All India | 356 (219) | 588.3 | 256.5 |

*Note:* The figures in parentheses are the number of sugar factories with crushing capacity at or below 1,250 t/day.
*Source*: Anon, 1985.

(i) small scale paper mills using surplus bagasse without any long term contracts with sugar factories, such that the quantity of bagasse received and the price payable by them were negotiated during each sugarcane crushing season,

(ii) small scale paper mills based on surplus bagasse generated by sugar mills with integrated management but not necessarily at the same site,

(iii) paper mills working on bagasse released as a result of steam economy and bagasse drying measures introduced at sugar mills in their proximity, and

(iv) paper/newsprint mills which had installed or propose to instal coal fired boilers at selected sugar mills and had agreed to pay for the bagasse on the basis of the landed cost of coal and the ratio of substitution between coal and bagasse.

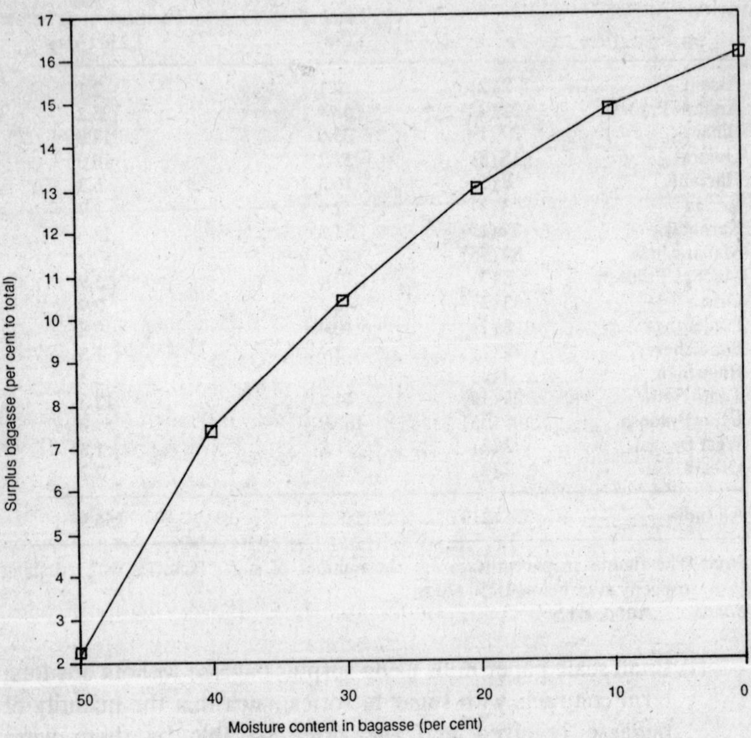


FIG. 10.2: Estimated Surplus Bagasse with Varying Moisture Levels before Burning

The sample included respectively three, two, one and two units in our study. Landed cost of bagasse in these cases varied between Rs. 225 and Rs. 545 per tonne. Assuming the bagasse-pulp ratio at 6:1 the bagasse cost per tonne of pulp ranged between Rs. 1,350 and Rs. 3,270. Further assuming the requirements of bamboo and mixed hardwoods per tonne of pulp at 2.5 and 2.7 tonnes, respectively, these units could afford to pay Rs. 540 to Rs. 1,300 for a tonne of bamboo, and Rs. 500 to Rs. 1,200 for a tonne of hardwoods, without considering the excise concessions on bagasse based paper. Some of these units also used or proposed to use or could use varying proportions of bamboo and eucalyptus wood in the furnish, and the landed costs have been substantially lower than these. During the last one or two years, there has also been at least a marginal fall in the market price of eucalyptus wood.

This situation must raise a few issues:

- Have the potentials of natural forests and of industrial plantations of forest land to supply the cellulosic materials at financially and economically feasible costs to the paper and newsprint industry been adequately assessed and exhausted?
- Have the complementarities between production of bamboo, industrial wood, and fuel wood on non-forest wastelands been studied and found unsuitable?
- Did bagasse-based pulp enjoy some intrinsic superiority over the pulp made from conventional materials of forest origin?
- Did bagasse-based pulp offer some managerial and technical advantages such as ease in acquiring and storing the base material, and lower quantity of other critical inputs like chemicals, water, power?
- Have the comparative economic costs of pulping bagasse for paper and newsprint *vis-a-vis* its alternative uses been objectively studied?
- Could enhanced use of bagasse and other agricultural and agro-industrial residues be sustained in the long-run without the policy interventions such as concessions in or exemptions from excise duty?
- Did small scale paper mills which were primarily based on bagasse enjoy comparative private and societal advantages: lower production costs for comparable quality of the outputs, lower stress on the bio-physical environment, etc.?

## NOTES

1. We cannot comment on this for want of literature and the methodology used.
2. That should, however, not be necessary. A considerable portion of paper and newsprint production capacity has already been based on unconventional materials. There were also the prospects of enhanced use of mechanical and chemo-mechanical pulping processes Such variables have, however, not been considered in this study.
3. Some of these materials were used at the dawn of the paper industry in India.
4. This assumed (i) two per cent compound annual growth rate in sugarcane output, and (ii) 45 per cent cane crushing in the organised sector.

5. Estimates based on the technical data provided by Hougot, 1960.
6. Cases have been observed where bagasse was depithed at the paper mills and the pith was used in their multi-fuel boilers.

## REFERENCES


Ahuja, S.P. (Ed.). 1980: *Paper Industry in India: Retrospect and Prospects*, Institute of Economic and Marketing Research, New Delhi.

Anonymous: Various Years. *Indian Sugar*, various issues.

———. 1985: *List of Sugar Mills in India, Bangladesh and Pakistan: Working and Projected*, Indian Sugar Mills Association, New Delhi.

Chugh, K.L. 1982: "Rejuvenation of Bamboo Forests", in *Papers Presented at the Seminar on Raw Materials for the Paper Industry*, Indian Paper-Makers Association, Calcutta, pp. 63-71.

CMIE (Centre for Monitoring Indian Economy) 1987a: *Production and Capacity Utilisation in 600 Industries: 1970 to 1986*, CMIE, Bombay.

———. 1987b: *Economic Outlook: June 1987*, CMIE, Bombay.

———. 1987c: *Economic Outlook: December 1987*, CMIE, Bombay.

GOI (Government of India). 1963: *Survey and Utilisation of Agricultural and Industrial By-products and Wastes*, Committee on Natural Resources, Planning Commission, New Delhi.

Gupta, Tirath. 1988: *Forest Based Cellulosic Materials for the Paper Industry in India: Demand-Supply Management and Pricing Policy*, Oxford-IBH, New Delhi.

Gupta, Tirath and Ahuja, Vinod. 1990: *Economic and Policy Issues for Bagasse-based Paper and Newsprint in India*, Oxford-IBH, New Delhi.

Gupta, Tirath and Shah, Nitin. 1987: *Paper and Paperboards in India: Demand Forecasts and Policy Implications*, Oxford-IBH, New Delhi.

Hougot, E. 1960: *Handbook of Cane Sugar Engineering*, Elsevier, New York.

Keswani, S.L. and Verma, Sudhir. 1983: "Scope of Bagasse Based Paper Mills in Uttar Pradesh", in *Papers Presented at the Seminar on Management of Small Paper Plants Based on Agricultural and Secondary Raw Materials*, Development Banking Centre (DBC), New Delhi.

Lonkar, M.Y. and A.A. Ansari. 1987: "Energy Conservations by Bagasse Drying", *Indian Sugar*, 27(5):265-268.

Manohar Rao, P.J. 1983: "Bagasse: The Promising Raw Material for the Paper Industry", *Indian Sugar*, 32(10):651-655.

Pundir, K.R. 1969: "Bagasse Saving", *Indian Sugar*, 19(7): 515-524.

Rangan, S.G. 1986: "Bagasse - India's Future Fibre for Paper Industry", *Indian Pulp and Paper Technical Association (IPPTA) Journal*, 23(4):1-6.

Rao, N.V. *et. al.* 1969: "Burning Bagasse on the Step Grate Furnace and the Importance of Air Fuel Ratio", *Indian Sugar*, 18(10):745-747.

Ramalinga Setty, T.K. 1985: "Bagasse Based Paper Mills: Some Indian Experiences and Financial Aspects", *IPPTA Journal*, 22(3):62-76.

Vishwanath, G.K. *et. al.* 1983: "Indian Paper Industry: A Case of Bagasse", paper presented at the *Seminar on Management of Small Paper Plants Based on Agricultural and Secondary Raw Materials*, DBC, New Delhi.

### *5.3.5. Auxiliary Equipment*

Apart from the major equipment and machinery for the operation of the Pulp and Paper Pilot Plant, there is auxiliary equipment for supplying power, steam and water.

The electric power is distributed from the main incoming transformer bank to a sub-station near the Pulp and Paper Pilot Plant. 33 kv high tension transmission line is connected to the outdoor type 630 ampere disconnecting switch and then step-down to 6.6 kv at 2500 kva transformer. The 6.6 kv is then stepped down to 415V at the 1000 kva transformer which is located near the plant.

The steam required for the Pulp and Paper Pilot Plant is generated by a package boiler with a capacity of 5 t/hour saturated steam. It is a fire tube type, three-pass design boiler, complete with protection and metering devices. Its maximum pressure is 19 bar, oil firing with a 22.4 kW F.O. preheater. Facilities for treating boiler feed water, like sand filter and an ion exchanger, are also provided.

The process water necessary for the operation of the Pulp and Paper Pilot Plant is supplied from 4 tubewells, each having an average capacity of about 2000 gallons/hour. Water from these tube wells are pumped directly into an underground storage tank with a capacity of 50,000 gallons, from which it is pumped to an overhead tank, 20 meter high. Water from this overhead tank is then distributed to the various sections of the plant as required. Two pumps are installed in the pump station, which works alternatively, with one unit as a standby while the other is in operation.

## 6. Cottage Industries

There are a number of cottage industries in the private sector engaged in producing paper and paper products. They are of the nature of small pulp and paper mills manufactured locally by themselves and mostly using waste-paper as raw materials. Data on the number of production units and the production capacities are not available at present.

But cottage industries engaged in the private sector for producing pulp and paper can be divided into two categories:

(a) Paper and Pulp from plants
(b) Paper and Board from waste-paper

Cottage industries engaged in the former category usually produce special type of hand-made paper namely:

(1) Thin wrapper tea packing made of bast fibres of paper mulberry plant
(2) Paper made from straw-pulp
(3) Gold foil forgoing paper
(4) Gold foil packing paper

Cottage industries engaged in the latter category produce boards from waste-paper in the form of recycling.

*6.1. Classification of Waste-paper*

In Burma, waste-paper can be utilised as follows:

1. Direct reuse of waste-paper, in which waste-paper is collected to be reused directly for packing and wrapping of materials.
2. Indirect reuse of waste-paper, in which waste-paper is collected for delivery to the cottage industries or to artisans who practise the manufacture of "PAPER MACHE" articles.

*6.2. Technical Aspect of Paper Recycling*

Indirect recycling of waste-paper is in fact, a source of prepared fibre which needs only to be converted into suspension in water to obtain pulp, which is then formed into sheets and paper board.

It is anticipated that proper treatment of waste-paper, cleaning, de-inking, and bleaching technology will have to be developed in the near future for the effective utilisation of waste-paper. From the environmental stand-point, and the country's economy, further intensive utilisation of waste-paper will constitute a major contribution to the country's economy and to the preservation of natural resources.

12

HU SHOUZU

# SMALL-SCALE PAPER MILLS IN THE PEOPLE'S REPUBLIC OF CHINA

## 1. Introduction

THE PAPER industry is one of the major components of the Chinese national economy. The products of this industry are either productive materials, or of necessity for the livelihood of the people. The industry is related to the cultural and ideological process, as well as to its material progress. Hence the conditions for the development of the paper industry are one of the principal signs of the country's modernisation.

During the 39 years since the foundation of the New China, the paper industry has grown at an impressive rate. The total output of paper and board in 1987 was 11,41 million tonnes or 102 times what it was in 1949. Of that quantity, the output of paper was 6,62 million tonnes while that of board was 4,7 million tonnes. Between 1980-1987 the average annual growth rate was more than 10 per cent, thus China ranked among the fast growing countries in the world. Even though the industry is developing steadily and quickly, China has a vast population and the supply of paper products is still behind the demand. The average per capita consumption of paper and board was about 11 kg, the consumption rate between the urban and rural areas being quite different. In urban areas the per capita consumption may reach 30-40 kg, with Beijing possibly reaching 70 kg, while in the rural areas it may be as low as 3 kg. However, the tendency in rural areas is gradually growing due to the successful agricultural policy being implemented there.

## 2. Fibrous Raw Materials

China covers an aggregate area of 115 million hectares, which is about 12 per cent of the total state area and about 4 per cent of the total forest area of the world. However, the total forest area of China is less than 3 per cent of the total world forest area. Thus wood resources in China are inadequate and the wood supply cannot meet the demand of the industry. However, non-wood plant fibrous raw materials are quite ample. Under such conditions, the industry has to rely on non-wood fibre raw material, using wood fibre as a subsidiary material. Table 1 shows wood pulp as 16.9 per cent of the total pulp production, and non-wood pulp as waste-paper pulp at 60 per cent and 24.1 per cent respectively.

TABLE 1: Percentage of Various Grades of Pulp Production of the Total Production

*(1000 tonnes)*

| Production of pulps | | % to total pulp production | % to machine-made pulp production |
|---|---|---|---|
| Total pulps | 8920 | | |
| Machine-made pulp | 6790 | 76 | |
| Uncooked pulp | 2130 | 24 | |
| 1. Chem. wood pulp | 1020 | 11.4 | 15 |
| 2. Me-ch. pulp | 400 | 4.5 | 4.9 |
| 3. Reed pulp | 710 | 8.0 | 10.5 |
| 4. Bagasse pulp | 260 | 2.9 | 3.8 |
| 5. Bamboo pulp | 110 | 1.2 | 1.7 |
| 6. Cotton, Jute pulp | 410 | 4.6 | 6.1 |
| 7. Straw pulp | 3860 | 43.3 | 57.0 |
| 8. Waste-paper pulp | 2150 | 24.1 | |

The main species of wood used in the north-east of China for the pulp and paper industry are red pine, larch, spruce, poplar birch, while massoniana pine, a kind of southern pine, is almost the only species used in the south, in places such as the Fujian, Guangdong, Gwangxi, Hunan, Sichuan and the Jianxi provinces (see Appendix).

There are more than thirty varieties of non-wood fibre raw materials being used in China's paper industry. The main varieties are rice straw, wheat straw, cotton stalks, corn stalks, sorghum stalks, bagasse, reed, Amur silver grass, Chinese alpine rush, bamboo, jute hemp, kenaf, waste bags made from jute, hemp, fibres, cotton linters, cotton rags, etc.

These fibre raw materials are the material base for the pulp and paper industry. Their variety, quantity and quality not only relate to the grade, quality of the products produced and the developing speed of the industry, but also have a decisive influence on the size of the mills, the technology of the process, the treatment of pollution and the economic results of the mills concerned.

Because of the vast population, the scarcity of wood fibre, the availability of non-wood plant fibres and the low level of the national economy, China's paper industry had to build numerous small-scale paper mills using non-wood plant fibres for pulp and paper-making. Nowadays, China is the largest country using non-wood fibre raw materials for these industries. It can be seen from Table 2 that about half of the world total of non-wood fibre pulp was produced in China.

TABLE 2: Pulp Production in China and Estimated World Pulp Production 1986

*(1000 tonnes)*

| Grades | Estimated world total production | China's production | Estimated % of world total |
|---|---|---|---|
| Straw pulp | 5000 | 3761 | 75 |
| Reed pulp | 1400 | 704 | 56 |
| Bagasse pulp | 2000 | 257 | 13 |
| Bamboo pulp | 1300 | 114 | 9 |
| Rag, Jute pulp | 1300 | 147 | 11 |
| Total | 11000 | 5058 | 46 |

## 3. General Description of Small-Scale Paper Mills in China

In 1958 there was a mass movement in China to urge the government at all levels to make special efforts towards the establishment of small-scale paper mills with lower investment and shorter time schedules, in order to solve the problem of paper and board shortage. As a result, a number of small-scale paper mills were set up in a short time all over the country. There are more than two thousand countries in China and each built its small-scale mill so that the total number of these mills was more than two thousand at that time. The mills were simple in design and to be completed within one month. The capacity of such a mill was 2 to 5 t/day. Installed was a small rotary digester, a Hollander beater and a single cylinder vat, and a single dryer paper machine. Rice straw, wheat straw, reed and waste-paper were being used. The main products were wrapping paper, toilet paper, printing and writing paper. Under such conditions the quality of the product was not good, the technological level was low and the economic result poor. Since 1961 these mills have been overhauled and only five hundred further developed. Conditions improved as also did capacity and technological level. When in 1979 the policy of reform and opening up to the outside world was implemented, the authorities in the villages and townships were very interested in improving their economic situation so they chose the develop their paper industry as one of the industries which would help them improve their livelihood in a short period of time. Thus a number of small-scale paper mills with a daily capacity of 10 to 20 tonnes were again built. Two cylinder vats and two dryer paper machines replaced the previous ones. In some mills Foudrinier paper machines with a trim width of 1092 mm, 1760 mm and 2360 mm were installed. According to some incomplete statistics there are more than four thousand paper mills in China, of which most are small-scale mills with an annual capacity of less than 10,000 tonnes. There are 1600 paper mills under the supervision of the Light Industry Department. Of these 200 are large and medium paper mills with an annual capacity of more than 10,000 tonnes. The remainder are small mills with only 1 per cent of them using wood fibre as raw material. At the moment the total production of the small mills is about 60 per cent of the total production of the whole country. Thus small-scale paper mills currently play an important role in today's paper industry in China.

## 4. Characteristics of the Small-Scale Mills

Due to fibre raw materials being in ample supply locally, the price of raw materials and labour costs are cheap. The investment costs are limited and the process and technology simple, so that the construction of small mills has certain advantages; the mill can be completed in a short space of time, the investment problem easily solved by local government, technology and equipment are available, production costs are low and the products can be sold on local markets. Finally, such small mills can attain reasonable economic results and also solve the problem of the shortage of paper products in local areas. Even if small-scale paper mills have some disadvantages, such as the pollution problem, in certain areas the local governments would not close their small mills because they are the major force supporting the local economy. This is why so many small-scale paper mills are being preserved at the moment in China. Two examples demonstrate the importance of small paper mills in developing the paper industry. Shangdong and Henan are the provinces with the highest population in China. In 1952 the total output of paper and board in Shangdong province was very low, only 10,8 tonnes. After the small mills developed in 1987 the output had increased to 700,000 tonnes, that is 68 times more than in 1952. The situation in Henan province was similar. Before 1957 Henan was a blank spot on the paper industry map. The production of machine-made paper was zero. Then the small mills developed even more rapidly there than anywhere else. Some hundreds of mills were built and production has been increasing ever since. At present the output has increased to more than one million tonnes, which places the state at the top in the paper production ranks. These two examples demonstrate the power of the small-scale mills in the development of the paper industry in China.

## 5. Existing Problems and Measures to Improve Small-Scale Mills

The main problems existing in the small-scale mills are poor quality and only a few grades of product, heavy consumption of materials, backward technology and management, low production efficiency and high effluent pollution, which is a problem common to them all. The amount of effluent discharge of the paper industry is one tenth of the total amount of effluent discharge in the whole country. Most products from small-scale mills are low or medium grades such as writing and printing paper, wrapping paper, toilet paper, corrugated medium, straw board, container board etc. In general the quality of these products is not too good and materials and energy consumption are high compared with the same grades produced in large or medium sized mills. Productivity in the small mills is dramatically low. Pollution from these small mills is serious due to less chemical recovery and poor waste-water treatment. Most of the small mills have no chemical recovery facility and the disposal of black liquor from these mills presents a major problem. In fact, for economic and technical reasons it is difficult to operate chemical recovery systems in small-scale mills. Our efforts to alleviate the pollution problem of this industry are focused on the development of waste-water treatment and chemical recovery techniques for the black liquor from small mills. The major problems involved in the chemical recovery of non-wood plant fibre pulping are low washing and extraction efficiency, high silica content, high viscosity, low heating value of the black liquor and the limited size of the mills. A lot of research and development work has been carried out and some improvements have been implemented in this area. A horizontal belt vacuum washer for non-wood plant fibre brown stock washing has been developed and the extraction efficiency of black liquor can reach more than 95 per cent.

Research work has also been done on desilication, in which the flue gas from the boiler is used to precipitate the silica from black liquor at optimum pH of 10, 3 before evaporation. The precipitated sludge is then separated by a special centrifugal process.

A unique type of recovery furnace with a movable smelter has been developed to handle the high viscosity and low heating value of black liquor, using ammonium sulphite as cooking chemical, which is made by the waste flue gas from fertilizer or sulfuric acid factories. The waste liquor from pulping can be used as organic fertilizer to irrigate the fields and the results have been satisfying.

Other processes towards the abatement of pollution are still being researched and developed.

In order to further modernise our paper industry we have prepared an industry policy which aims at employing both wood and non-wood fibre raw materials, at gradually increasing the wood fibre proportion in the total, and enhancing the raw material basis for the paper industry. As for the size of mills, we will focus on large and medium sized mills, and reform and rebuild small mills as the conditions dictate. Some mills may be expanded and some may stop producing pulp and use market pulp. Some mills will be fitted with new technology to reduce effluent, and some will be discontinued if the effluent problem cannot be solved, in particular areas.

We would like to build large pulp mills producing market pulp supplying the integrated small mills. Thus the pulping process is these small mills can be discontinued and only paper produced. There is still much to be done regarding research and technology for small-scale mills and we hope to continue our work and achieve better results.

# *APPENDIX*

## LIST OF NAMES OF FIBROUS RAW MATERIALS USED IN CHINA'S PAPER INDUSTRY

| | |
|---|---|
| Spruce | Picea |
| Belsam | Abies fabri |
| Horse tail pine | Pinus massoniana |
| Larch | Larix dahurica turz |
| Pine | Pines koraiensis sieb |
| Poplar | Populas tremula, nigra<br>Populas cathayana |
| Birch | Betula plalyphylla |
| Eucalyptus | Saligna, Exserta, citriodora |
| Fir | Cuninghamia lanceolata |

# 13

OSCAR L. GARCIA HECTOR

# BAGASSE HIGH YIELD PULPING FOR SMALL-SCALE MILLS

## 1. Introduction

SINCE its inauguration in 1981, the Cuba-9 Pulp and Paper Research Center has been working on its originally conceived line of studying annual fibres for pulp and paper. Thus, the final markets are the developing countries, which is the area where most of the bagasse and other annual fibres are located.

In current times, where many financial schemes are being reappraised, the question of small mills is again being brought to focus.

High yield bagasse pulping is particularly well suited for small mills, solving many of the previous difficulties with conventional pulp technology.

The operational experience of the Cuba-9 demonstration plant, truly a small-scale mill with its capacity of 25 t/day, together with the possibilities of the technology, allow us to present another alternative in small-scale plants.

This document is intended to give an overall view of the process.

## 2. Background

During the work carried out in Cuba-9 on the development of a newsprint technology using bagasse as the main furnish, our philosophy was aimed at providing developing countries that import US $650 million of newsprint every year with a technology that would cut down imports in foreign currency and could be used by most of the countries, not only those, which by having government incentives and a vast population can benefit from the use of higher economies of scale. Instead of having a blend of pulps, which meant in practice several technological installations in one, Cuba-9 has been aiming at the use of chemi-mechanical high yield pulp from bagasse since way back in 1972. This means a simpler, less expensive investment. In December 1987 an international supervisory team on behalf of UNDP observed the production of newsprint made from 85 per cent bagasse high yield pulp, 8 per cent waste and only 7 per cent long-fibre, in the Cuba-9 experimental newsprint machine, which was later printed at 46,000 samples an hour without breaks or linting.

But even before these trials were scheduled, lab and pilot plant tests were taking place to produce printing papers using high yield pulp. At the end of the trials, 60 per cent high yield pulp paper for textbooks was made and the Education Ministry bought all the paper to make books for primary and technical schools.

Since Cuba-9 belongs to the Sugar Industry Ministry, and many of us have a sugar industry background, we realised that this technology, which used the smallest amount of bagasse per tonne of product, could be appealing for the sugarcane producers, now suffering a long-standing sugar price depression with a gloomy prospect for the future. Thus, the sugar industry, never very friendly with the pulp and paper neighbour who took away the bagasse fuel, now is looking around with an interest in "diversifying" the sugarcane industry.

Based on this, we came to the conclusion that the use of high yield pulp could have more potential applications and be of interest to more developing countries than newsprint. And all the research work to develop this pulp was already finished and the results at hand.

## 3. Printing Paper Situation in Cuba

Cuba has a population of ca. 10 million, and its paper per capita is around 23 kg. The main mills are, as of 1987:

| Mill | Paper grade | Tonnes per year |
|---|---|---|
| Tecnica Cubana | Writing and Printing (Bagasse) | 21 000 |
| Pulpa Cuba | Liner (Waste and kraft long-fibre) | 24 000 |
| Damuji | Corrugating Medium (Bagasse) | 18 000 |
| Uruguay | Writing and Printing (Bagasse) | 60 000 |

Pulpa Cuba produced bleached grades until 1986; it is unlikely it will produce them in the future.

Tecnica Cubana is providing most of the educational and cultural papers in Cuba. But it cannot increase capacity due to a shortage of bagasse in the area.

The mill at Uruguay sugar mill is the biggest and most modern, intended for export of both bleached pulp, in great demand, and writing and printing papers. In the first years of operation, the demanding quality standards of international paper trade allowed some paper to be sold locally, taking care of the deficit in the market. But as Uruguay mill is able to sell more paper abroad, some of this paper has to be diverted to the local economy in national currency, and with quality specifications way above the real requirements.

This situation in Cuba could also exist in many other developing countries.

That Cuba has a centrally planned economy is not a distinctive fact. Many developing countries also have it. The case could also be that there is no longer foreign currency available for importing paper to satisfy the demand, and no money to invest in new capacities.

It is typical situation that prompted us to study the feasibility of pulp and paper mills of small scale based on high yield bagasse pulp.

## 4. Process Description

Even though each technology may be modified according to the specific requirements of any investment, the development work carried out in the Cuba-9 research mill was focused from the very beginning on the goal of achieving a process, simple and economic enough, meeting adequate quality standards, so as to be attractive to the greatest possible number of countries.

Achievement of this result would, in our opinion, satisfy the goals and cope with the policy and purposes of UNDP and UNIDO, co-sponsors of the Project.

The technology of the Cuba-9 approach is based on the development of a high-yield chemi-mechanical pulp of sufficient strength so as to adequately run in the paper machine and pressroom, while at the same time meeting the requirements for printability, brightness and opacity.

Such a pulp, making up more than 80 per cent of the fibrous furnish, follows the concept shared at present by several firms of the so-called "Monopulp" from hardwood CTMP.

The advantages attributed to this process are in principle the same as those that have been claimed over the last 10 years by the Cuba-9 Project.

The starting point of the Cuba-9 Process is a bagasse with a high fibre content.

Fibre content of stored bagasse then reached values of 76-78 per cent, and 82-84 per cent after the second stage wet depithing, far beyond the fibre quality obtained by other processes. The bagasse is stored in a wet bulk form.

The problems arising from the liquid stream of suspended pith and fines were solved by installing a specially designed settler/clarifier that removes practically all the free suspended particles from the stream.

On the other hand, liquid effluents from the pulp mill have been used for irrigation of the surrounding cane fields for more than 3 years with good results. The only treatment is the above mentioned settler and a lagoon, giving a final effluent with 30 mg/L BOD and 25 mg/L suspended solids.

Wet depithed bagasse is pressed, 4-5 per cent NaOH being then added in the impregnation stage.

Refining is carried out in two stages at atmospheric pressure, which prevents harmful effects on brightness taking place at higher temperature.

Energy consumption in refining has been considerably lowered as a result of the fibre quality and due to improvements in the refiner feeding system, though still requiring additional small changes in order to satisfy the desired performance, as well as in the impregnation system.

After refining, the pulp undergoes latency removal in a chest, and is then screened and cleaned. Fibre rejects from the last stage screening are sent back to the feed of the second stage refiner because the small size of the mill does not justify a separate reject treatment refining system.

One of the most significant contributions of the Cuba-9 process has been the improvement of the peroxide brightening operation. Hypoclorite has also been used, depending on local prices. Twenty-five points increase in one stage have been obtained with peroxide. The pulp has brightness of 56-58 points. Table 1 shows pulp properties and Table 2 typical consumption data.

TABLE 1: Pulp Properties (Cuba-9 Process)

| Chemi-Mechanical | Bagasse |
|---|---|
| Freeness CSF | 125 |
| Basic Weight $g/m^2$ | 73 |
| Caliper, microns | 118 |
| Density, $g/cm^3$ | 505 |
| Tensile Index, Nm/g | 41,31 |
| Breaking length, m | 4215 |
| Brightness, Elrepho | 57 |
| Tear Index, $mN\ m^2/g$ | 3,89 |
| Opacity | 93,5 |
| Scattering Coefficient, $m^2/kg$ | 37,6 |
| Yellowness, % | 12,8 |

TABLE 2: Consumption Data for High Yield Bagasse Pulp

| | Tonnes/Tonne Pulp |
|---|---|
| Whole Bagasse, wet | 3,2 |
| Caustic Soda | 0,09 |
| Peroxide | 0,04 |
| Sulphur | 0,02 |
| Sodium Silicate | 0,04 |
| Steam | 4*<br>1,2** |
| Water | 100 $m^3$/Tonne |
| Electricity | 1,4 MwH/Tonne |

* Air Dry Pulp in Bales
** Wet Pulp in Bales

## 5. Process Economy for High Yield Pulp

Typical scale economy for an integrated pulp and paper mill using bagasse bleached chemical pulp, for the international market, is 200 tpd, costing more than 200 million USD. When scaled down to level it with the domestic cost market demand, chemical pulp still has a very high investment cost per tonne because of recovery boiler, effluent treatment (no longer overlooked, like in the past), steam plant and other ancilliaries.

A chemi-mechanical bagasse pulp mill is roughly half the investment cost of a chemical pulp mill.

Pollution is not a problem with high yield pulp. Cuba-9 takes water from wells which after a specially designed but simple mechanical treatment is sent for irrigation, maintaining a water balance in the area.

About 60 per cent of the pulp line equipment can be locally constructed.

A study was made of the minimum size mill using three different bagasse supply alternatives: 100 per cent substituted by oil, 70 per cent substituted and 100 per cent surplus bagasse. An Internal Rate of Return of 12 per cent was chosen, and the pulp price was obtained as a function of mill capacity.

The higher bagasse yield allows the use of more surplus bagasse, and as can be seen, for a selling price of $ 350/tonne, 20,000 tonnes is needed with substituted bagasse but only 12,000 tonnes with excess bagasse, even though it is not valued at zero price. In our case $ 8/tonne was taken. In actual operation bagasse yield per tonne of pulp was 3.26, based on wet bagasse. This included recycling back the pith to the whole bagasse conveyor coming out of the sugar mill. Since only 15-20 per cent excess bagasse is taken, only 6-8 per cent pith is added, which presents no difficulty to the boilers and saves bagasse. Pith is simply swapped for fibre.

## 6. Production Alternatives for Papers with High Yield Bagasse Pulp

Papers produced with this pulp fall into the category of uncoated groundwood papers.

We have several alternatives for producing newsprint and writing and printing papers:

*Case 1* Non-integrated mill, producing slush pulp for nearby paper mills, to substitute 40-60 per cent in the furnish.

*Case 2* Non-integrated mill, for wet bales processing.

*Case 3* Integrated mill, producing newsprint and uncoated writing and printing papers.

### *Case 1. Non-integrated Slush Pulp*

This case is very particular, as there should be an existing paper mill not far away from the bagasse supply, since pulp should be pumped. The use of surplus bagasse allows variable costs as low as $186/tonne, using $8/tonne for bagasse, $45/MwH for electricity, $356/tonne, caustic soda, $860 for peroxide and $110/tonne for fuel oil. Total price of the pulp is less than $250/tonne, lower than any other virgin pulp. These figures are given as indicative, since, as mentioned, this is a special case and will not be considered further.

*Case 2. Non-integrated Mill, Wet Bales*

This alternative supplies pulp at 50 per cent moisture for local consumption, at distances of up to 500 km.

It is not possible to export wet pulp due to rapid deterioration. Table 4 shows financial data on this investment. The price of the pulp was set at $325/tonne. ROI is 16.5 per cent and the Payback period 6 years. The investment cost uses second-hand wet lap machine, but the refiners and pulp equipment are new. Considerable savings could be obtained if rebuilt disc gravity refiners are purchased.

*Case 3. Integrated Pulp and Paper Mill*

Despite the benefits claimed for bagasse high yield pulp, we do not argue the fact that chemical pulp is more flexible. But in the field of newsprint and writing and printing papers, which covers a great share of the import demand in developing countries, the lower cost of papers based on bagasse high yield pulp makes it suitable if used properly. These paper grades need stiffness, dimensional stability, opacity, printability and brightness. As seen from Table 3, high yield bagasse papers have more than adequate strength, adequate opacity and lower brightness. A simple brightening scheme will not give more than 56-58 ISO in the pulp, but present if at 40-60 per cent in the furnish according to requirements can give a textbook paper which (according to the consumption pattern) can be satisfactory. The situation often seen in some countries in Latin America is to import bleached kraft pulp or high quality printing papers for school children, which of course is insufficient to cover the demand.

The paper can be used for offset printing. Table 4 again shows an investment, production and financial analysis of this alternative. In this case, second-hand machinery estimates were used for the paper machine, stock preparation and conversion facilities. The figures are more profitable than Alternative 2, but if the conditions are there to increase production in a mill with short imported pulp supply or substituting even partially a pulp worth $100-150 extra, then Alternative 2 cannot be disregarded.

TABLE 3: Paper Properties

(*60 gm Textbook*)

| | | |
|---|---|---|
| *Furnish*: | 70% Bagasse Chemi-mechanical<br>10% Bleached Kraft<br>20% De-inked Newsprint | |
| Basis Weight, $gm^2$ | | 60 ± 3 |
| Density, $kg/m^3$ | | 690 |
| Tensile Index, Nm/g | MD- | 39,2 |
| | CD- | 18,6 |
| Brightness, ISO | | 59 |
| Opacity, % | | 94 |
| Sizing, Cobb 60 | | 20/22,5 |
| Dennison Number | | 13-14 |

TABLE 4: Process Economy

| | Alternative 2 | Alternative 3 |
|---|---|---|
| Production | Wet baled pulp | 60 gm Textbook |
| Capacity, Tonnes/year | 20,000 | 20,000 |
| Investment Cost* | $11,000,000 | $14,400,00 |
| Capital Cost | $12,700,000 | $16,500,000 |
| Sales Price | $325 | $650 |
| Sales Income | $6,500,000 | $13,000,000 |
| Unit Cost | $220,12 | $408,44 |
| Annual Profit | $2,097,600 | $4,831,200 |
| IRR, % | 16,5 | 29 |
| Payback period, years | 6,0 | 3,4 |

* Without interest during construction.

## 7. Principles for the Success of Small Mills

Cuba-9 was conceived as an experimental mill but has its own production programme when not involved in research. But its daily capacity of 25 t/day puts it in the category of small mills. Therefore, the experience of operating the high yield pulp at this rate gave us some ideas on what should be done. Here are a few of those ideas:

- Small mills are very vulnerable to external inputs and often lack adequate warehouse space. Therefore, a technology with less materials required for operation – i.e., raw materials, spares, consumables – has a bigger possibility of uninterrupted production.
- The cost of recovery systems in chemical pulping is a necessary evil, with high investment cost and uncertain

performance.

- It is not a good idea to use multi-grade production with frequent changes. Particularly in areas where an established paper-making tradition does not exist, operators do not have time to acquire the necessary expertise, which is not given by theoretical training as in developed countries. Production is, therefore, less efficient.
- Contrary to popular opinion, we are in favour of using medium to high automation in the mill. Modern instrumentation is reliable, and all depends on the training and skill of a few maintenance people. In return, you get more quality control, less human error and more control of your inputs. The fact that instrumentation requirements of high yield pulping are simpler helps.
- The general engineering design of Cuba-9 mill could be used for up to 20,000 t/year, using readily available but not oversized equipment. This means the design is not a reduction in scale but a simplified, less expensive arrangement.
- A small-sized bagasse mill with the simpler technology of high yield pulping can benefit from the established services of the adjacent sugar mill. Even joint management is feasible, even though in this case somebody must arbitrate for bagasse quality standards, important in the process, and common use of utilities and services. The recent willing attitude of the sugar industry management makes this arrangements now feasible.

## 8. Conclusions

The high yield pulp developed in the Cuba-9 Research Center for bagasse adapts for some paper grades better than chemical pulps in small scale mills.

This technology allows greater use of surplus bagasse through higher yields, has almost no pollution, and lower investment costs. There is no need for recovery.

The use of second-hand machinery is encouraged and is more easily found than chemical pulp machinery for these sizes.

Even though the integrated mill for 60 g/m$^2$ textbook paper looks more attractive, in certain cases, a pulp mill can give great savings in foreign currency or increased production by substituting more expensive pulps. Newsprint could be within reach in small countries that cannot support a bigger plant. Cuba is starting feasibility studies for at least three plants with this approach.

Education is a right of mankind. And paper is the most widespread means of disseminating culture. This approach for small scale mills, the only hope for many countries, could be the answer to paper shortages. We are hoping to share our experiences.

## REFERENCES

Zegarra, Jose R. "Factibilidad de miniplantas productoras de Celulosa", *Boletin GEPLACEA*, Febrero 1988, Mexico.

Narby, M. "Monopulping, a new concept for developing countries". Seminar on comparative pulping processes, Alexandria, Egypt, 1986.

Kyrklund, B. "Printing and writing papers based on chemi-mechanical pulping — an economically viable proposition". Seminar on comparative pulping processes, Alexandria, Egypt, 1986.

Rao, P.J. Mahonar, "Establishment of minipaper plants based on surplus bagasse by the sugar factories". *XVI ISSCT Congress*, Sao Paulo, Brazil, 1977.

Hackl, Harry J. "Small pulp and paper mills in developing countries and their recovery system". *Pulpapel Conference*, Manila, November 1980.

# FOUR

# POLLUTION CONTROL AND PROCESS TECHNOLOGY

# 14

LOTHAR GÖTTSCHING

# POLLUTION CONTROL
## The West German Experience

### 1. Introduction

MOST of the activities of the societies of developing as well as of developed countries, contribute to pollution of water, soil and air. The specific pollutant load of the various types of pollution per capita, and/or per unit of area (e.g. per sq.km.), differs in average significantly between developing and developed countries due to the different extent of industrialisation, or due to the different level of living standards. Against this background, the developed countries are forced to fight overall more intensively against pollution in order to avoid severe damage to the natural resources (water, air, soil). This situation has also become serious in certain areas of developing countries, such as in rivers serving as drinking water source, where industry is densely concentrated and emits untreated or insufficiently treated effluent. However, the problems to be solved are more or less the same everywhere. Therefore, it is necessary to talk to each other, and to exchange expertise for the benefit of our countries and societies respectively.

### 2. Strategy of Environmental Protection

(a) The first step of successful environmental protection is the identification, monitoring and classification of the various sources of emissions in terms of effluent, flue gas and solid waste which are "produced" by -

- industries (including power plants)
- urban areas
- traffic.

Monitoring and classification is a prerequisite to identify the priorities of polluting sources according to their load and their damage potential. Keeping in mind that the financial means are always limited, governments (central and local), and private enterprises have to set priorities for the benefit of an effective environmental protection policy.

(b) The second step directed towards environmental protection should be realised by redevelopment of the polluting sources in such a way that emissions of effluent, flue gas and solid waste are reduced. The realisation of this approach requires modifications or even substitutions of applied technologies which, in the first instance, is often very costly, but which pays off in the long term because a reduction of energy and operation costs can be achieved.

(c) The third and last step (unfortunately this is often the only measure) is characterised by the treatment of effluent, flue gas and solid waste. Qualified technologies have been developed and are available, but they are rather expensive in most cases. Further optimization or innovative development of such technologies is needed to reduce operation costs, to improve efficiency and availability, and to minimize side-effects.

### 3. General Pollution Problems

Pollution is defined according to various parameters which are in most cases identical everywhere. On the other hand, the tolerated figures of such parameters differ from country to country of even within one country.

(a) Flue gas is mainly characterised by the parametres $SO_2$ and $NO_x$. Recently, another parameter has been under discussion, namely dioxine, the most dangerous toxic chlorinated compound which is created by combustion of waste.

(b) Waste-water which pollutes rivers and lakes partly utilised as drinking water sources, is characterised by the parameters of suspended solids, BOD and/or COD, heavy metals, temperature, pH and toxicity against first – to mention some of the best known parameters.

(c) Solid wastes originating from various sources – such as sludge of effluent treatment, ash from combustion plants or garbage from urban areas – are often characterised by the parameter heavy metals.

## 4. Pollution in West Germany

West Germany, with its population of 60 million inhabitants and with an area of 250,000 sq.km, is a densely populated country. The distance from the southern to the northern border is approx. 1,000 km. The most important rivers are the Danube (in the South), the Rhine passing through our capital Bonn (in the West), the Main passing through Frankfurt (central Germany), and the Weser and the Elbe (in the North). The water quality of our lakes and rivers is classified into four categories depending on the microbiological and fish population. The categories are also based on the oxygen content of the water. Category I is the best, not at all polluted and suitable for the most sensitive fish species like trout or even salmon. Water category I only exists in the very upper part of the river Rhine leaving lake Constance. Category IV is the worst being heavily polluted, almost devoid of oxygen and unpopulated by fish. This category can be in found in highly industrialised parts of the rivers Danube, Main and Rhine.

The national target in effluent treatment is directed towards the low polluted category II, characterised by a small content of organic and inorganic matter, not causing a significant oxygen demand.

The air pollution by the $SO_2$- and $NO_x$-content of flue gases (of power plants, private households, and traffic) is taken very seriously because the two pollutants are contributing to the damage of the forests by so-called acid rain. Damage to the forest was first noticed in 1975. In the following decade the situation became worse. In the Black Forest and in the forests of Bavaria more than 65 per cent of the trees are damaged. Such trees have lost a certain percentage of their needles and leaves, their annual growth is reduced to such an extent that it tends to be almost negligible.

As far as solid waste is concerned, each inhabitant of our country produces approx. 500 kg garbage per year, not including industrial solid waste. Industry has succeeded in incinerating a large amount of its waste in internal power plants. Nevertheless, a fraction of its waste has to be dumped in landfills. Increasing landfilling costs force industry to reduce its solid waste output by modifications of technology and by intensified incineration.

## 5. The West German Pulp and Paper Industry

Paper and board production amounts to 10 million tonnes (in 1987) which means that the paper industry of the Federal Republic of Germany (FRG) is the fifth largest in the world. The paper production is based on waste-paper (40%), chemical wood pulp (30%), mechanical wood pulp (15%), and fillers, pigments and additives (15%).

Paper and board are produced in about 180 mills. The average output of one paper mill amounts to approx. 50,000 tonnes. The largest mills produce almost 400,000 tonnes, the smallest ones only 20,000 t/year.

The chemical pulp industry with a production of 0.8 million tonnes is rather small, consequently 80 per cent of the pulp demand has to be imported. Chemical pulping is based exclusively on the acid sulphite process. Most of the pulp production is bleached either by conventional sequence (C-E-H-D) or by modified sequence (O- or P-E-H-D). The most serious environmental pollution problem are created by the conventional bleaching plant due to the highly chlorinated compound which are highly resistent to biodegradation.

## 6. Pollution Control of the Pulp and Paper Industry

By various governmental regulations, the pulp and paper industry amongst others is forced to treat its effluent and flue gas from internal power plant. Solid wastes have to be incinerated internally or disposal by landfilling.

### *6.1. Flue Gas*

The most important parameter for the control of flue gas from power plant is the $So_2$-concentration. The $So_2$-emission depends mainly on the sulphur content of the fuel and spent liquor. According to Fig. 14.1 the total energy demand on the West German pulp and paper industry amounted in 1980 to approx. 4 million tonnes calculated as hard coal units. Within the next five years, up to 1985, the fuel demand could be reduced by 8 per cent thanks to measures of energy saving, despite the fact that the pulp and paper production increased by 12 per cent in the same period of time. The total fuel demand is subdivided into hard coal, brown coal, fuel oil, natural gas and spent liquor. It can be stated that between 1980 and 1985 the amount of coal and fuel oil has been changed significantly by reducing the share of fuel oil and by increasing the share of hard coal.

Regarding the overall $SO_2$-emission, it is of interest to know the sulphur content of the various types of fuels:

- hard coal 1, 2 per cent S
- brown coal 0, 3 per cent S
- fuel oil 1, 6 per cent S
- gas 150 mg $S/m^3$
- spent liquor 3 - 4, 5 per cent S.

Thanks to energy saving and the reduction of the share of the fuel oil then total $SO_2$-emission of the pulp and paper industry had been reduced from 83,000 tonnes in 1980 to 67,000 tonnes 1985 (Fig. 14.2), which shows significant progress when taking the increased pulp and paper production into account. The overall $SO_2$-emission in our country amount to 3 million tonnes, of which industry contributes 25 per cent. Based on the national overall $SO_2$-emission the pulp and paper industry contributed only 2 per cent.

Nevertheless, a further reduction of the $SO_2$-emission has to be realised by the following measures:

- utilisation of fuel with less sulphur content (e.g. natural gas)
- partial desulphurisation of solid and liquid fuels
- desulphurisation of flue gas from all pulp mills.

### 6.2. *Solid Waste*

In the past solid waste such as bark, rejects, sludge and others, has been exclusively disposed of by landfilling. Shortage of landfill sites has forced industry to solve the disposal problem partially by combustion of suitable solids waste components in its power plants. This has the additional advantage of energy generation. Nowadays, both disposal procedures – the external as well as the internal ones – are applied but the tendency is directed towards an intensified internal disposal.

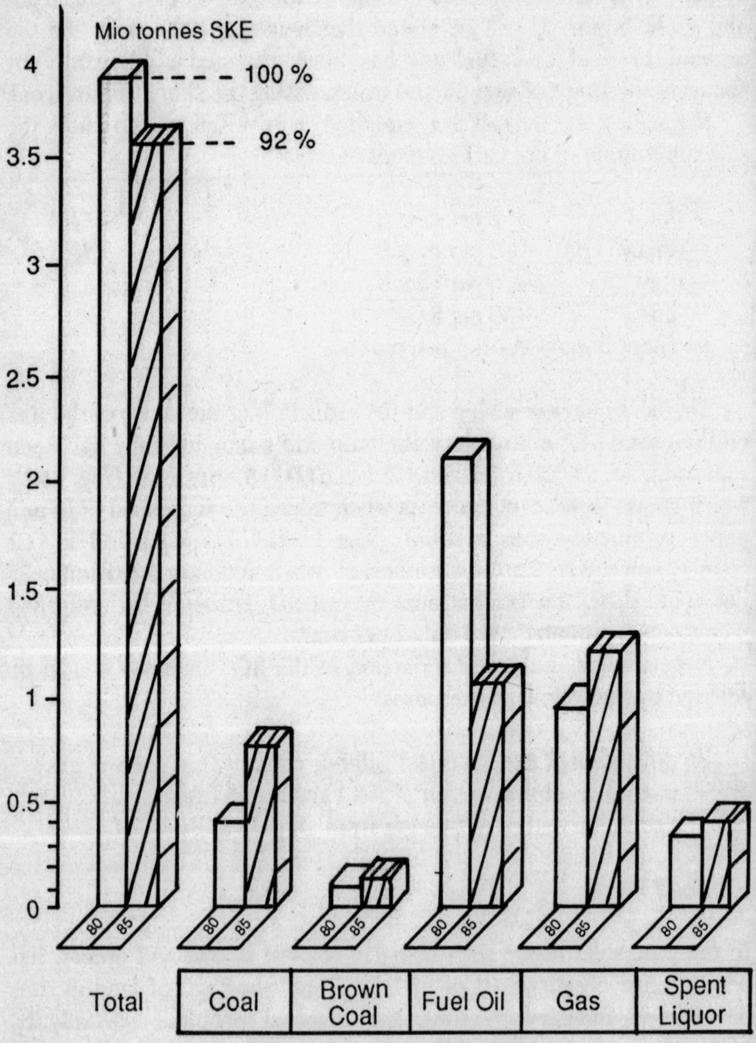


FIG. 14.1: Fuel Demand of the West German Pulp and Paper Industry

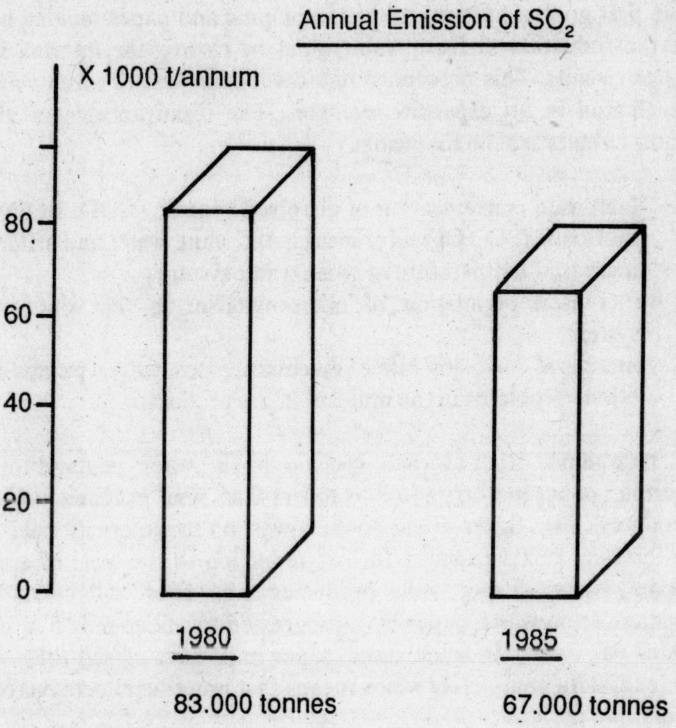


FIG. 14.2: $SO_2$-Emission of West German Pulp and Paper Industry

To avoid the creation of the most toxic chlorinated compound dioxine when combusting chlorinated solid waste, the combustion temperature has to be kept at least above 800°C. It is well known that dioxine has mutagenic and even carcinogenic effects.

In a few cases the sludge of effluent treatment plant is utilised as fertilizer on farmland or as additive in bricks to improve their porosity controls their thermal conductivity. To be used as fertilizer, certain requirements have to be fulfilled with respect to the concentration of heavy metals such as Cd, Cr, Cu, Hg, Ni, Pb, and Zn. Paper mill sludge contains less heavy metal contents then permitted, even in the case of sludge from deinking plant.

### 6.3. White Water System

The first goal of effluent control in pulping and paper-making has to be the reduction of fresh water input by closing the internal white water circuits. This procedure reduces the amount of waste-water to be treated in an expensive manner. The disadvantages of closed water circuits are the following:

- increased concentration of dissolved organic (COD, BOD) and inorganic ($SO_4$, C1) substances in the white water and effluent,
- increased temperature of white water system
- increased population of microorganism in the white water system.
- increased corrosion rate of machines, pipes, valves, pumps etc.
- odour problems in the mill and in the product.

Nowadays, the average specific fresh water demand of the German paper industry amounts to less than $30m^3$ per tonne of paper produced. This figure might be the lowest on the international scene. In the long run, I expect a further reduction to the level of approx. 20 $m^3$/tonne. Paper mills producing e.g. liner and corrugating medium from waste-paper have progressed to utilize only 5 $m^3$ fresh water per tonne. In some cases, paper mills have closed their white water system completely which means that no effluent gets out of the mill.

This ultimate steps means an optimisation in terms of effluent control because there is no need for any treatment plant. But one has to realise that all the disadvantages mentioned become evident. From my point of view, waste-paper based paper based paper mills run under optimal conditions with a specific fresh water intake of 5 to 10 $m^3$/tonne of paper produced.

The COD-load (calculated in kg $O_2$/tonne of paper) to be expected in the white water and in the effluent respectively can be evaluated under the following preconditions:

- the specific COD of solid fibre material based on wood, or of organic additives amounts to 1,300 kg $O_2$ per kg solid organic material
- one per cent of fibre material or additive input into a mill being dissolved in the stock preparation plant and getting into

the effluent via the white water system, leads to a COD-load of 13 kg $O_2$/tonne of paper produced.

Approx. 2 to 5 per cent of the fibre material entering the paper mill is dissolved in paper-making including mechanical pulping. The lower figure is for waste-paper utilisation, the higher figure represents TMP processing bleaching included. With the above mentioned figures and the figure of the specific fresh water intake, one can easily calculated the COD concentration (in mg/1) of white water and of effluent to be treated.

Progress has also been made in reducing the specific fresh water input in chemical pulp mills to a level of less than 150 $m^3$/tonne of fully bleached pulp. This figure seems to be still quite high compared with recently established sulphate pulp mills in Scandinavia and North America. But it has to be taken into account that our pulp mills are based on the sulphite process and were built thirty and more years ago. Nevertheless, our chemical pulp industry is internationally competitive, not as a supplier of market pulp, but as an integrated producer of wood free paper and soft tissue paper.

### *6.4. Effluent Treatment*

Now we will discuss how the German pulp and paper industry treats its effluents. Pressure to meet certain standards is imposed by two federal regulations. The comprehensive regulation – named Water Resources Policy Act – defines as a basic target that no effluent is permitted to be emitted without treatment.

In this context the recovery of Solids (fibres, fillers) in the effluent has been performed for many decades by sedimentation (most frequently used), filtration or flotation. Some of the paper mills re-use this so-called mechanical sludge in paper production (Fig. 14.3).

Since 1963, effluent treatment has taken place in a second stage by the activated sludge process. Nowadays, almost all paper mills are equipped with a two-stage mechanical-biological effluent treatment plant to fulfil the standard set by the authorities in terms of the parametres shown in Fig. 14.4. It is no problem to achieve lower figure than set for all parameters except COD. Heavy metals are not relevant for paper mill effluent because it is almost impossible to detect them even with very sensitive analyzers (like AAS).

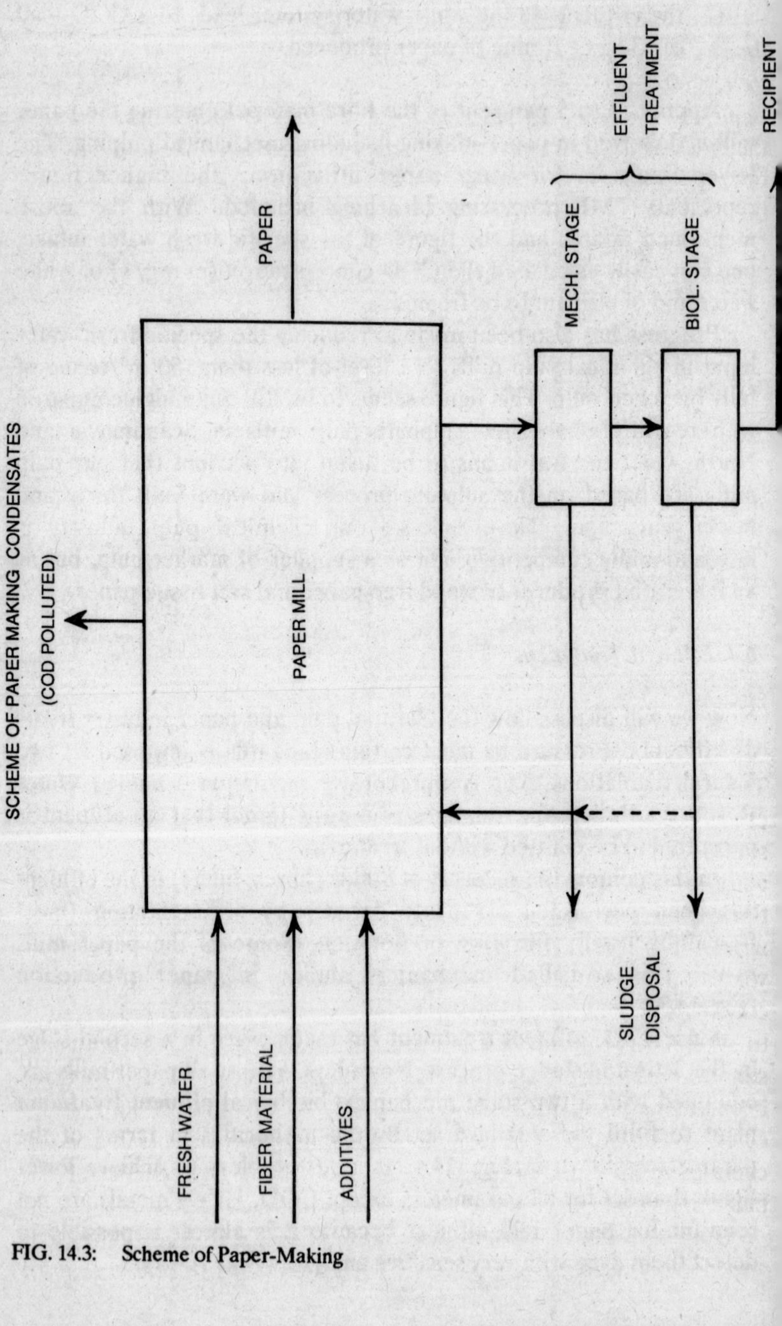


FIG. 14.3: Scheme of Paper-Making

As far as the pulp mills are concerned, the effluent treatment is limited to the mechanical stage, which means that no biological treatment is applied. But in the near future the situation will change thanks to the substitution of chlorine by oxygen and/or peroxide in the first bleaching stage. After having implemented these modifications the pulp mills invest in the second treatment stage to degrade the dissolved organic substance defined as COD and BOD.

| | |
|---|---|
| – SUSPENDED SOLIDS | (< 50 mg/1) |
| – CHEMICAL OXYGEN DEMAND | (< 200 mg/1) |
| – BIOCHEMICAL OXYGEN DEMAND | (< 50 mg/1) |
| – TOXICITY AGAINST FISH | |
| – HEAVY METALS (Cd, Cr, Cu, Hg, Ni, Pb) (not relevant for Pulp and Paper Industry) | |
| – ADSORBABLE ORGANIC CHLORINE COMPOUNDS | |
| – TEMPERATURE | (< 35°C) |
| – pH-VALUE | (6 - 8) |

FIG. 14.4: Effluent Characteristics (Treated by 2-Stage System)

All treated effluents of the industry have to be further improved. The so-called "Waste-Water Charge Act", established in 1980 as the other relevant effluent regulation in our country, sets more severe standards. According to his act, industry as well as the local authorities have to pay tax-like charges depending on the values of the parameters suspended solids, COD, heavy metals and toxicity against fish. Since this regulation has been in operation for eight years, the lakes and rivers of West Germany are in a much better condition than before; in general, transferred from water category III to water category II. To improve the water quality of the water sources receiving effluent, the Waste-Water Charge Act has recently been strengthened. The new parameter AOX (adsorbable organic chlorine compounds) is a significant challenge, particularly for the chemical pulp industry, to solve the problem of the effluent of the bleaching plants.

If a pulp mill does not treat its effluent with a high efficiency, the waste-water charge to be paid will overtake profits. In this case such a pulp mill has to be shut down, unless the effluent treatment is intensified or process modification are introduced.

In effluent treatment the alternative to be activated sludge process is the anaerobic process which is advantageous in respect of reduced sludge production, energy saving (no aeration required), and methane production (Fig. 14.5). A few paper and pulp mill in Western Europe have succeeded with this new technology. One of the most important prerequisites is a sufficiently high COD concentration of at least 1,500 mg/1 of the effluent to be treated. The most suitable effluent component of a pulp mill is represented by evaporator condensates, because the microorganisms are able to degrade acetic acid particularly well.

| AEROBIC | ANAEROBIC |
|---|---|
| AERATION REQUIRED | NO AERATION REQUIRED |
| ENERGY REQUIRED | ENERGY PRODUCED<br>(by methane formation) |
| SLUDGE GENERATION | LIMITED SLUDGE GENERATION |
| "ONE-STEP" DEGRADATION<br>(less sensitive bacteria) | MULTI-STEP DEGRADATION<br>(sensitive bacteria) |
| NOT DISTURBED BY<br>SUSPENDED SOLIDS | SENSITIVE SYSTEM<br>AGAINST S-COMPOUNDS<br>and $Ca\ SO_4/Ca\ CO_3$ |

FIG. 14.5: Comparison between Aerobic and Anaerobic Effluent Treatment

According to Fig. 14.6 the reactors for the anaerobic biodegradation differ in their design. The best known system are the UASB reactor and the Fixed Film reactor. The targets of the process are short retention time, high COD-load (in kg $O_2/m^3$ reactor volume and per day), high biogas production (methane and carbon dioxide), and effective COD-elimination of approx. 70 to 90 per cent, depending on the type of the substrate. The anaerobic process is sensitive against $SO_4$-concentration (less than 2,000 mg/1), Ca-concentration (because Ca contributes to $CaCO_3$ and $CaSO_4$ formation), and suspended solids (because they might plug the reactor in the long run). For a couple of years we have been involved in this technology. Three large reactors between 2 and 6 metres in

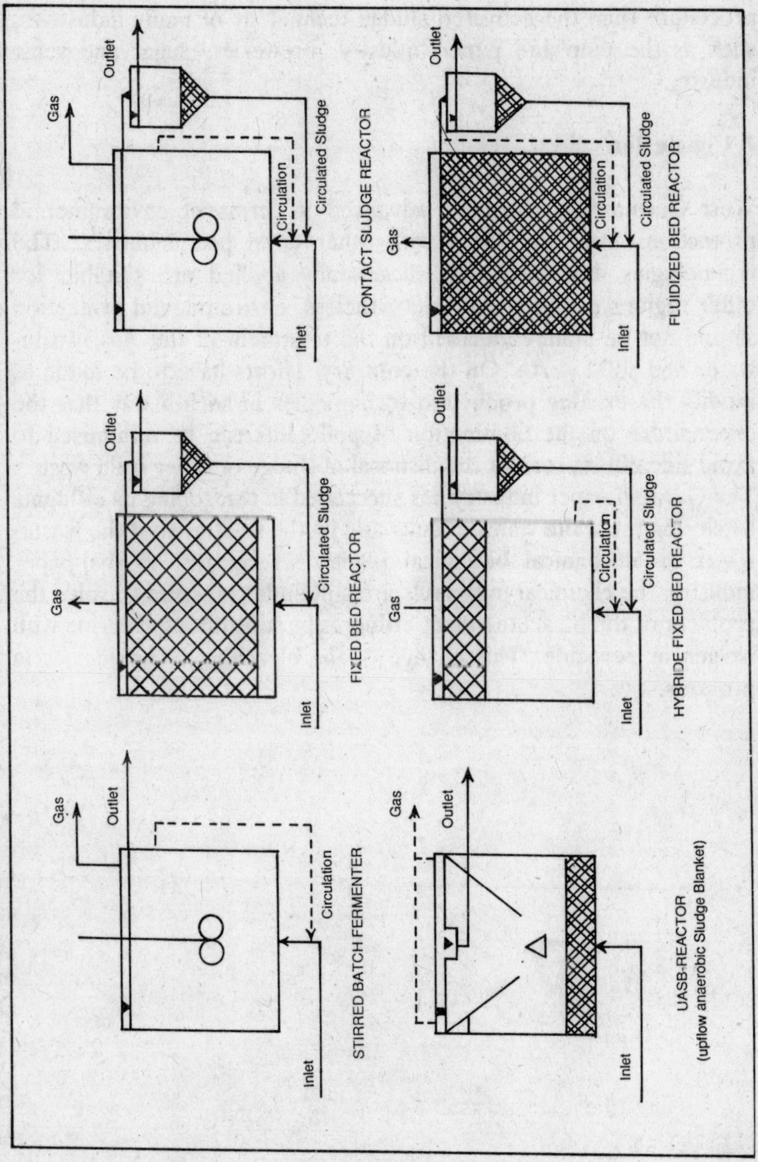


**FIG. 14.6: Anaerobic Reactors-Design and Process Variations**

height are now in use, along with five others having a volume of 10 litres. The anaerobic effluent treatment will be a more economic procedure than the activated sludge technology of many industries, such as the pulp and paper industry, breweries, sugar and yeast industry.

## 7. Conclusion

West Germany is relatively advanced in terms of environmental protection, even compared with other developed countries. The technologies developed and successfully applied are suitable for other regions of the world. Nevertheless, environmental protection should not be mainly focussed on the treatment of flue gas, waste-water and solid waste. On the contrary, efforts have to be made to modify the existing production technologies in such a way that the expenditure on the elimination of pollutants can be minimised to avoid side effects such as the disposal of sludge or other solid wastes. The German paper industry has succeeded in controlling its effluents by closing the white water circuits and by the treatment of the waste-water in mechanical biological plants. In contrast to the paper industry, the chemical pulp mills are still under pressure to solve the problem of the bleaching plant effluents by substituting chlorine with oxygen or peroxide. This change of the bleaching technology is in progress.

# 15

C.S. TRIPATHI & S.P. CHAKRABARTI

# PREVENTION AND CONTROL OF POLLUTION FROM SMALL PULP AND PAPER INDUSTRIES IN INDIA

## 1. Introduction

POLLUTION IS a backlash of unbridled industrialisation. Every industry directly or indirectly pollutes the environment. Small pulp and paper industries are not in exception. Pulp and paper is one of the largest groups of Industries in India. This is also one of the 20 highly polluting industries notified by the Government.

The quantum of paper consumption is increasing continuously throughout the world. In view of the steadfastly increasing demand for paper, it is unlikely that the production of paper natural wood/fibrous material, even if fully tapped, will be able to cope with the requirement of a growing number of mills. Moreover, constraints of large investment and the scarcity of bamboo are major causes for the mushroom growth small paper mills utilising non-wood fibres or agricultural residue in developing countries.

There are 271 Pulp and Paper Mills in India, out of which 38 are big with production capacity of more than 10,000 t/annum, most of which are provided with chemical recovery system, and 213 are small producing paper in the range of 1,000 to 10,000 t/annum, and the rest are very small. The 38 large units, although representing 15 per cent of the total number of units, produce 60 per cent of paper; but these mills contribute a lesser pollution load in comparison to small ones (Fig. 15.1).

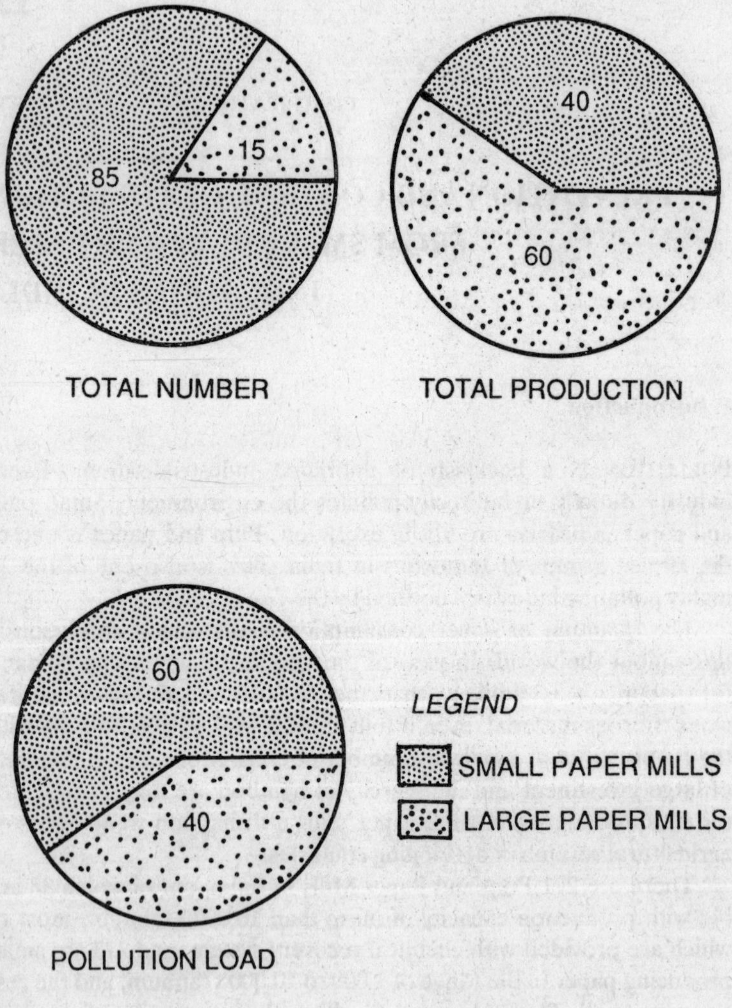


**FIG. 15.1:** Relative Number, Production and Pollution Load of Small and Large Pulp and Paper Mills on Percentage Basis

The small paper mills are highly water intensive. They consume 150-400 cubic metre water per tonnes of paper, and 100-350 cubic metre/tonne of paper is released as waste-water.

**2. Magnitude of Pollution Problems**

The small pulp and paper mills generate the maximum amount of pollution in the pulping, pulp washing and pulp bleaching stages. In sulphate and soda pulping, where chemicals are not recovered, black liquor in waste-water is the major contributing factor towards pollution because of high BOD, COD and very high colour/lignin content, which also imparts foaming potential that readily offers visual evidence of pollution. Waste-water from bleaching operations contains high BOD and dissolved organic and inorganic materials. Foaming is also a problem associated with the filtrate from the washing cycle in caustic extraction and hypochlorite bleaching stage.

The small pulp and paper mills, based on agricultural residue as raw materials and operating without chemical recovery units for economic reasons, generate obnoxious effluent which needs to be dealt with carefully. Pulp washing generates 20-25 per cent of the total waste-water and 70-80 per cent of pollution load. The effluent is discharged intermittently due to batch washing and hence alter the composition of combined waste-water.

Variations in flow, COD, BOD and lignin in the different of small paper mills based on agricultural residues are presented in Fig. 15.2.

The Central Pollution Control Board has published a comprehensive document for the small pulp and paper industry with the objective of formulating Minimal National Standards (MINAS) based on treatability of effluent and techno-economic feasibility of treatment system (Fig. 15.3). However, during implementation of the standards, two major problems are being experienced to be of concern, e.g. (i) removal of colour contributed chiefly by lignin in effluent, and (ii) recovery of chemicals from black liquor, which apparently has no appropriate cost-effective solution at the moment.

**3. Minimal National Standards (MINAS)**

The MINAS for small pulp and paper mill effluent have been evolved after looking into the characteristics of waste-water, treatability of various parametres, different treatments alternatives and their techno-economic feasibility, practical difficulties, impact on environment and economic impact on the industry.

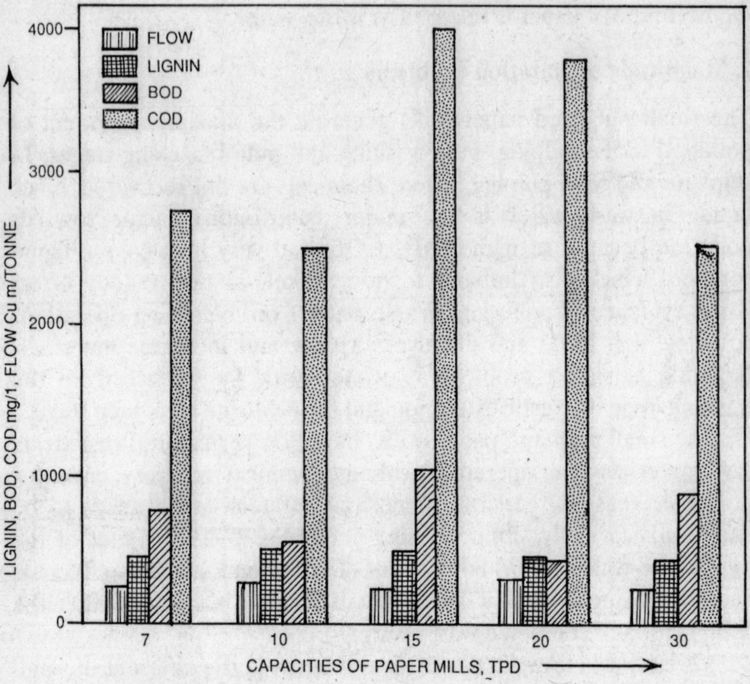


FIG. 15.2: Variation in Flow, Lignin, BOD and COD in Waste-Water from Small Paper Mills Based on Agricultural Residues

The tolerance limits for effluent, considering the above aspects, have been presented in Table 1. The permissible limits for COD and colour due to non-adoption of chemical recovery, for which no suitable economy technology is presently available, are not prescribed.

The prescribed limits will have to be achieved by all small pulp and paper mills in a phased manner.

TABLE 1: Minimal National Standards for Small Pulp and Paper Industry

| Parameter | Concentration |
|---|---|
| pH | 6.0 - 9.0 |
| Suspendid Solids | 100 mg/1 |
| Bio-chemical Oxygen Demand, 5 day 20°c | 50 mg/1 |

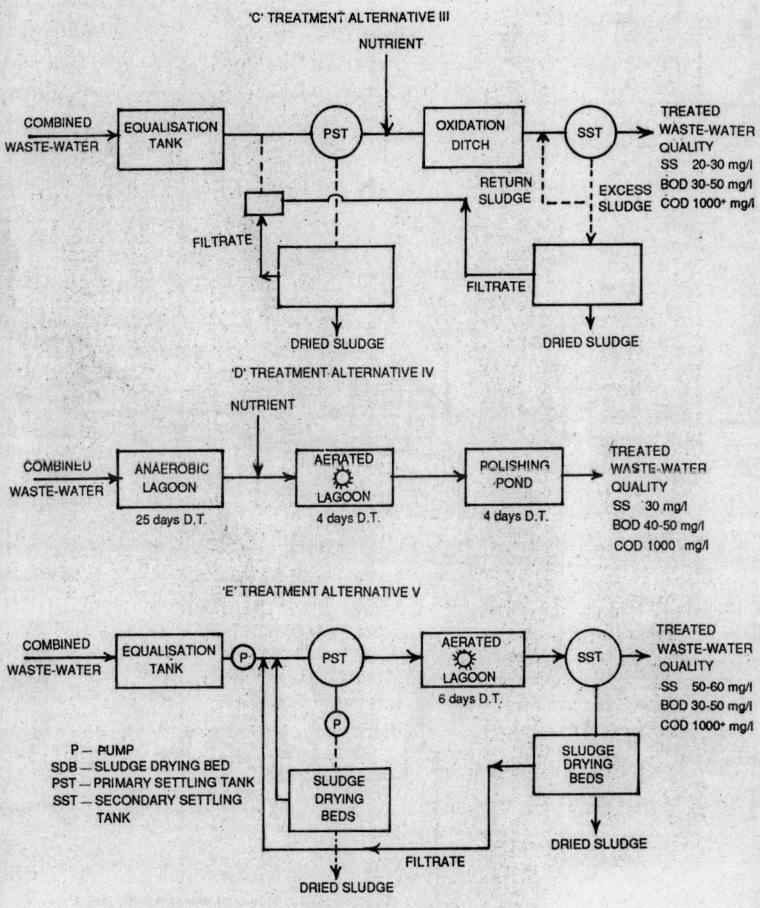


**FIG. 15.3: Waste-water Treatment Alternatives for Agricultural Residue Based-Paper Mills**

*Contd. on Next Page*

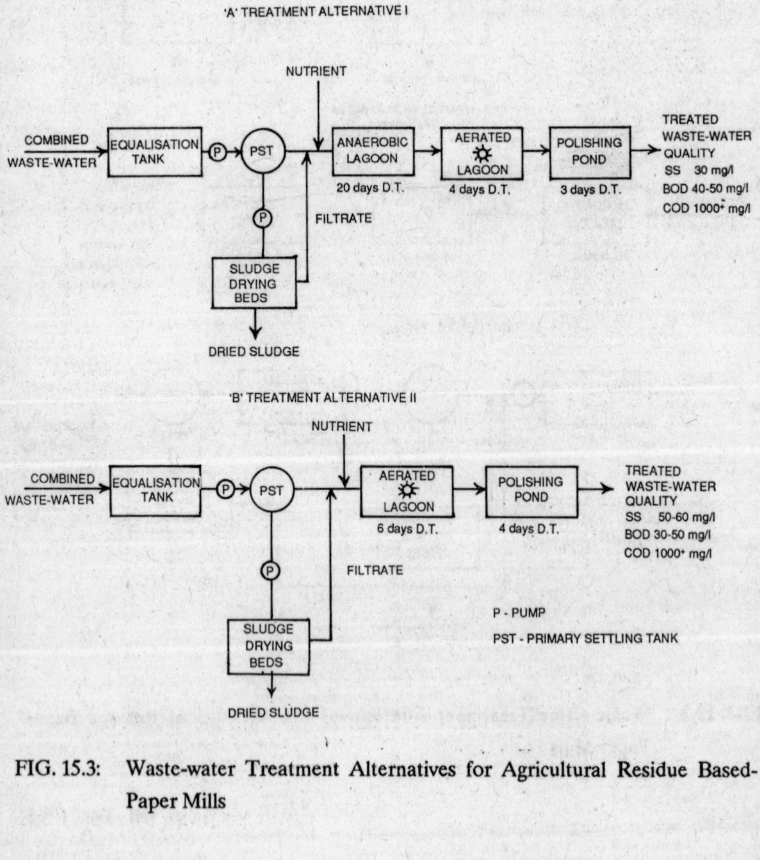


FIG. 15.3: Waste-water Treatment Alternatives for Agricultural Residue Based-Paper Mills

## 4. Pollution Control Status

The status of pollution control in small pulp and paper mills is not very satisfactory. Only 62 industries have a fully-fledged effluent treatment system and 79 industries have partial treatment. Latest status on pollution control through compliance with first and second phase of MINAS implementation is presented Table 2.

TABLE 2: Status for compliance with MINAS by Small Pulp and Paper Mills

| | |
|---|---|
| 1. Number of industries having complete effluent treatment plant (ETP) | 62 |
| 2. Number of industries having partial effluent treatment plant (ETP) | 79 |
| 3. Number of industries where ETP's are under construction | 25 |
| 4. Number of industries complying with MINAS | 25 |

## 5. Approaches of Pollution Control Authorities to Prevent and Control Pollution

*5.1.* The Central Board has constituted a national and four zonal task forces represented by members from State Pollution Control Boards, industry, and research institutions to provide thrust for the smooth and effective implementation of pollution control measures to meet the standards, also to look into various problems faced by the industries.

The Task Forces visited the various mills to assess and review the problems, and also examine the efficiency effluent treatment system for dissemination of information to other defaulting industries.

*5.2.* The Central Board, in association with the National Environmental Engineering Research Institute (NEERI) Nagpur, is working seriously for a solution to the colour problem from pulp and paper mill effluents. Under this project five (small and large) paper mills have been identified for the actual field-run on the coloured stream, on the basis of resulting obtained for removal of colour through different trivalent salts.

*5.3.* To reduce the pollution problem as well as to recover chemicals, applicability of chemical recovery process is being studied in association with the Central Pulp and Paper Research Institute, Dehradun, Parkhey Research Institute, Kopoli and

IIT, Bombay.

5.4. On the basis of experience acquired through performance studies on treatment plant and discussion on the aspects in Task Forces, inplant control measures are recommended to the industry to minimise pollution.

## 6. Inplant Control Measures

As prevention is always better than cure, the most techno-economic approach to reduce pollution is to minimise the quantity of water used by effective process control and inplant control measures which would result in a low waste-water volume for treatment. Some of the inplant control measures which may effectively prevent/reduce pollution, are as follows:

- Reduction of pollution at source and maximisation of reuse of water;
- Prevention of spillages, leakages and overflow of waste-water;
- Avoidance of overloading of machinery which may cause accidental spillages/leakages;
- Collection of all spillages, leakages, overflows etc. in a proper pit for recirculation or treatment;
- Adoption of good water management (sectionwise study of consumption and discharge) which would automatically result in good fibre and chemical management; and
- Use of efficient fibre recovery system for paper machine effluent and reuse of all water and fibre.

## 7. Concluding Remarks

Although expectations from the pollution control agencies are sky high, no pollution control programme can achieve success without the willing participation and cooperation of the industry which is causing pollution. Controlling pollution by recourse to legal prosecution in cases of industry's non-compliance with the provision for efficient effluent treatment facility is possibly the worst solution and is undesirable. While the pollution control agency should always be on the look out for innovative cost-effective and efficient technologies for dissemination of information to the industries, industries should also consider provision, operation and maintenance of the effluent treatment facilities as a social obligation which cannot be ignored. In the case of small pulp and paper industries this spirit is sorely missing. Paucity of funds to provide a moderate treatment plant to meet not-so-difficult-to-achieve effluents standards appears to be rather lame excuse. If there is a will there will certainly be a way out.

# 16

N.K. KUTTIAPPAN

# PROBLEMS OF BLACK LIQUOR TREATMENT IN INDIAN SMALL PAPER MILLS

## Possible Alternative Solutions

### 1. Introduction

IN ORDER to reduce the demand on the forest-based raw materials and at the same time meet the increasing demand for paper, the Government of India has initiated several steps to promote small scale pulp and paper mills based on non-wood agricultural residue raw materials.

Abundant availability of this renewable resource and the various incentives/subsidies offered by the Government have stimulated the installation of several small pulp and paper mills in the recent past. As of 1987, a total number of 260 such small mills, with a total installed capacity of 1.4 million tonnes/year (equivalent to more than 45 per cent of the total installed capacity of paper and paper board production in the country) are operating in India. The individual installed capacities of these mills vary from 2 to 30 t/day. Out of 260 units, 200 are based on waste-paper, 45 on cereal straws, jute, cotton rags and 15 based on bagasse and mixed raw materials. Waste-paper based mills do not discharge black liquor. It is in the straws, bagasse, jute, cotton rags, etc. based mills, that the problem of pollution load is severe due to black liquor. The Central Pollution Control Board has already prescribed "Minimum National Standards" exclusively for small pulp and paper mills. It stipulates that by June, 1988, all the units should comply with the following effluent disposal standards:

| | |
|---|---|
| pH | – 6.0 to 9.0 |
| Suspended Solids | – 100 mg/l |
| BOD | – 50 mg/l |

## 2. Manufacturing Process

Mills based on agricultural residues, jute, cotton rags, etc, follow chemical pulping using mostly sodium hydroxide. It's consumption varies with the type of raw materials, and normally 50-100 kg of NaOH is consumed per tonne of raw material (in the case of bagasse, it is about 120-140 kg/tonne). The digestion is carried out batchwise in a spherical/cylindrical digester at a material to liquor ratio of 1:2 to 1:4. Live steam is passed to the digester at an average consumption rate of 1.2 to 1.5 tonnes/tonne raw material, for cooking purpose. Mills using waste-paper adopt only hydropulping.

After cooking, the digested pulp, together with the spent liquor and condensed steam (black liquor), is either discharged into a blow pit having perforated bottom-floor or into a poucher. In the former case, the black liquor is drained and the pulp thereafter is manually loaded to the poucher/beater. The pulp received in poucher/beater is washed for 2 to 3 hrs by rotary vacuum drums. Since the drainability of spent liquor is very poor for agrobased cooked pulp, the black liquor is mostly washed off during pulp washing only. In mills with production capacity less than 25 TPD, only single stage washing is carried out. Thus the black liquor drained out is very dilute (< 1.5%) on account of higher water consumption.

The washed pulp is then passed through centricleaners, thickeners, refiners, etc. and bleached, in the case of writing and printing grade paper, using sodium/calcium hypo-chlorite solution. The bleached pulp is then conditioned by addition of alum, rosin, fillers, dyes, etc., and sent to paper machine. A generalised manufacturing process flow sheet adopted by Indian small paper mills is shown in Fig. 16.1.

Reported pulp yield for various raw material category is shown below:

| Raw Material | Yield (Avg.%) |
|---|---|
| Rice/Wheat straw, grass | 35-38 |
| Bagasse | 30-33 |
| Gunny or Jute | 60-70 |
| Cotton rags | 90-93 |
| Cotton linters | 85-90 |
| Waste-Paper | 70-80 |

## 3. Sources, Quantity of Waste-water and Pollution Load

The major sources of waste-water generation are shown in Fig. 16.1. In most of the mills, the effluents from the pulping section are segregated from that of paper plant within the factory. However, for final treatment and disposal, all the sources are mixed.

Depending on the extent of waste-water re-use, and the process followed, waste-water generation per tonne of paper produced varies from 225-300 $m^3$ for agricultural residue based mills and from 96-177 $m^3$ from waste-paper based mills.

The pollution loads from a waste-paper based mill compared to an agricultural residue based mill in terms of SS, COD, and BOD are found to be less by 18 per cent 80.4 per cent and 71 per cent, respectively. This is primarily due to the high organic pollution load from the chemical digestion/poucher wash in agricultural residue based mills. This can be seen from the following table, which gives typical characteristics of black liquor and combined waste-water from a straw mill, together with the characteristics for a waste-paper mill.

| Parameter | Black Liquor | Combined Agro Based Effluent | Combined Waste-Paper Effluent |
|---|---|---|---|
| pH | 10.0 | 8.5 | 7.5 |
| TSS, mg/l | 1100 | 758 | 618 |
| COD, mg/l | 74700 | 3442 | 674 |
| $BOD_5$, mg/l | 31000 | 644 | 187 |
| Flow, $m^3$/t | 5-8* | 285 | 116 |

* Computed figure based on material to liquor ratio and steam condensate.

The spent liquor from the digester and the poucher wash generally contribute only 25 to 30 per cent of the total waste-water flow, but account for more than 60 per cent of the total organic pollution load.

## 4. Problems of Black Liquor in Agro Residue, Jute, Cotton Rags Based Mills

Due to non-recovery of chemicals from black liquor, the small paper mills of this category caused severe water pollution problem. Although promising technologies are emerging, such as Direct Alkali Recovery System (DARS), Sulzer-Escher-Wyss, Copeland,

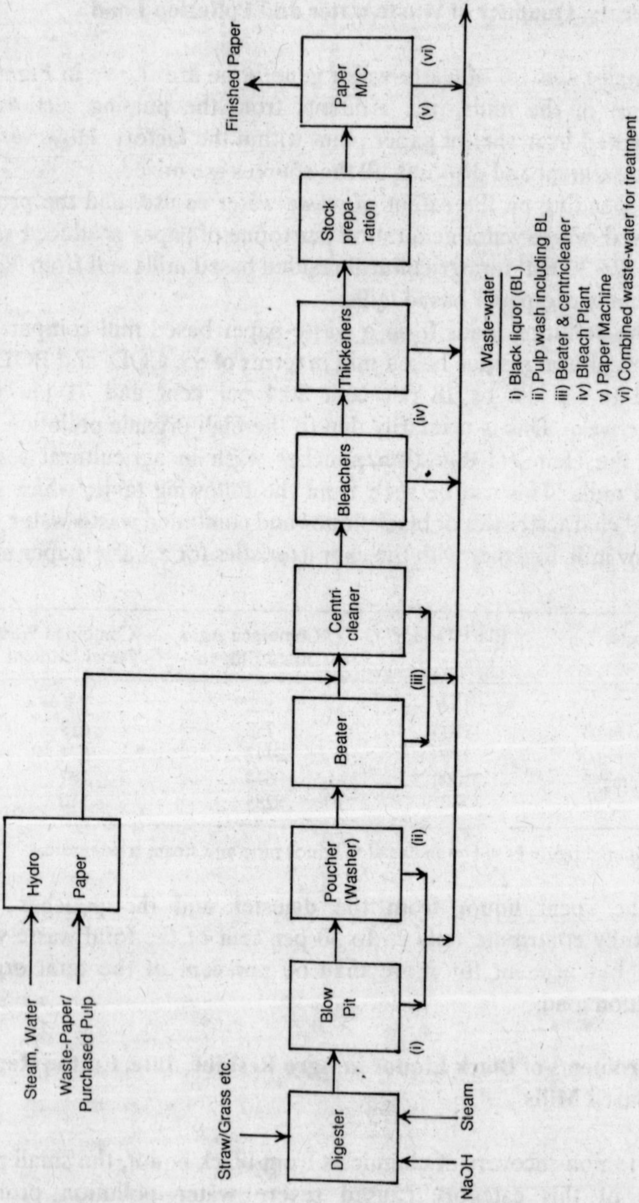


**FIG. 16.1: A General Manufacturing Process Flow Sheet Indicating Sources of Waste-waters**

Destromax, West Air Oxidation etc. for recovery of chemicals from black liquor of small mills, their commercial viabilities are yet to be proven, especially for mills with capacity < 25 TPD with the following general constraints:

- The production capacity of the mill should be more than 30 TPD on 100 per cent agrobased raw material. However, there are several mills having production capacity in the range 5 to 15 TPD only.
- Due to single stage pulp washing, the black liquor concentration is expected in the range 1 to 1.5 per cent, whereas the requirement is 10 per cent.
- The organic content of non-wood black liquor is about 30 per cent less than that of wood pulp, thereby the system requires auxillary fuel.
- High silica content in the non-wood black liquor (as high as 15-17 per cent $SiO_2$ in rice straw based). This will cause scaling in the evaporator.
- High viscosity of the black liquor at higher solids concentration. This limits the maximum attainable concentration in evaporators to 40 per cent solids.
- Requirements of high initial investment and skilled operation and maintenance attention.

On account of the above features, the application of chemical recovery system for low capacity mills appears to be non-viable. The presence of black liquor in the combined waste-water of such mills poses the following problems:

- Vast land area requirement for setting-up effluent treatment plant conforming to the MINAS. Many of the mills do not have adequate land area.
- Batch discharge of digester spillages (through blow pit) and poucher/beater wash cause severe foaming in aeration tank, thereby the biological treatment process is upset.
- Due to very high pollution load (3 to 4 times that of an integrated paper plant having recovery system), these small mills require high capital investments and have to meet operating expenditures.

*4.1. Status of Pollution Control*

The National Productivity Council conducted an on-the-spot study of 22 Small Paper Mills, which are located in Gujarat, Haryana, Uttar Pradesh and Himachal Pradesh regions, with a view to identifying areas for in-plant control measures and to assessing the present pollution control measures. Out of 22 Units, 7 are waste-paper based and the remaining are of the agro and mixed raw material category.

Excepting 3 units, the remaining (12 Nos) agro and mixed raw material based mills are with production capacity less than 15 TPD. Only 8 mills have partial waste-water treatment system, while the rest do not have any treatment. The units having treatment facility have the following problems:

- Foaming in aeration tank is severe, thereby the aerators are operated intermittently.
- The dissolved air flotation systems installed for fibre from paper plant effluent are not functioning properly due to frequent power failure, improper chemical dosing and poor operation and maintenance control.
- Return sludge recirculation is not practiced in most of the activated sludge process mode of treatment, due to poor process familiarity and absence of guidance from the system supplier.

## 5. Recommended Alternative Solutions

Considering the non-viability of chemical recovery systems for mills operating at lower capacity and the high investment required for exclusive pollution control measures, the following possible in-plant measure are recommended, which are yet to be fully exploited by Indian Small Paper Mills:

*5.1. Segregation of Digester Vents and Blow Pit Spillages*

Cooking of jute, cotton rags, etc. generate digester vents at the end of batch cooking. These vent gases normally carry spent cooking liquor (concentrated black liquor) in small quantity. After venting, pulp is spread on the floor for drainage of residual liquor.

Similarly, in the case of transfer of digested pulp into blow pit spent cooking liquor is generated. These sources of spills, overflows and washups together form a major source of pollution load. These should never be allowed to mix with the waste-water sources. It should be ensured that proper dykes, perforated floor-bottom and internal drainage system are constructed to contain the residual liquors and prevent the fibre loss.

### *5.2. Segregation of Black Liquor*

For pulps having good drainability, such as cotton linters, cotton rags, etc. maximum quantity of spent cooking liquor (black liquor) can be directly segregated from the digester. However, for this the digester should have built-in strainer for preventing fibre escape during discharge.

For pulps having poor drainability, such as agrobased pulps, it should be ensured to segregate maximum pollution load at minimum quantity of discharge during pulp washing in poucher/beater. For implementing this, the discharge pipe of poucher/beater should be installed with two outlets, one for concentrated wash water separation and the other for the normal discharge of wash water.

The above segregated black liquor and the digester vent and spillages should be collected together and evaporated in a solar evaporation pond. The residue thus obtained could be burnt along with the coal. In a tropical country such as India with very high solar incidence rate, the feasibility of separating the black liquor and increasing its solid content in a series of evaporation ponds for subsequent incineration of the solids in conventional equipment should be studied as an alternative.

### *5.3. Fibre Recovery*

The loss of fibres, both valuables and fines, is quite high in agro based mills. Systems like sedimentation savealls, floatation savealls are not only expensive but also require skilled operation and maintenance. Application of hydroscreen system will be a positive alternative, both for fibre recovery and for solid-liquid separation. In fact, the National Productivity Council has already recommended such a system for fibre recovery, which is in operational stage in one of the small paper mills. Removal of fibres will reduce the pollution load as well, thereby requiring less investment for exclusive pollution control.

### 5.4. Water Conservation

The water consumption in paper machine section is continuous and is always more than that of pulping section. Mostly recycled water is used for pulping process. Water conservation measures, therefore, should be stressed in paper machine section. It is feasible to reduce the water consumption by replacing the conventional perforated pipes by a nozzle spray system in the machine showers. Reduction in waste-water discharge will reduce the pump size and the area required for waste-water treatment.

## 6. Conclusions

Considering the small size of the paper mills and the low technical capabilities of the shop floor operators, it is not feasible to invest in an expensive complex waste-water treatment system, or to install and operate a conventional chemical recovery system. Therefore, the most attractive alternative is to implement in-plant pollution reduction measures discussed above.

Anticipated gains by implementation of the above few measures are highlighted in the following case study.

## CASE STUDY

The implications of meeting the Pollution Control Board's waste-water disposal standards, with or without implementation of in-plant control measures, in a 6 TPD unit, is discussed in this case study. The figures quoted in this case study are based on a project study conducted by the National Productivity Council.

## 7. Manufacturing Process

The unit produces 6 TPD of Cotton Linter Pulp Sheet (CLPS) per day using 100 per cent cotton linters as raw material. A schematic production process flow diagram indicating the major sources of waste-water generation, is shown in Fig. 16.2.

The following process discharges are occurring due to the production activity:

- Discharge of spent cooking liquor as black liquor directly from digester after cooking. The digester has build-in strainer (16

mm bore size).
- Washing of pulp within the digester for a period of 6-7 hrs/batch and discharged as "digester wash".
- Washing of pulp in poucher and discharged as "brown wash".
- Bleaching effluent consisting of hypo-chlorite wash and antichlor wash.
- Centricleaner rejects, vacuum pump seal water etc.

The entire waste-water flows by gravity into a common drain.

## 8. Waste-water Flow and Characteristics

The measured waste-water flow rate and the analytical results of process composite samples are given below:

TABLE 1: Waste-water flow and charateristics

| Source | Flow ($m^3$/day) | Parameters in mg/l, except pH | | | |
|---|---|---|---|---|---|
| | | pH | COD | BOD | TSS |
| Black liquor | 20 | 11.3 | 163304 | 35133 | – |
| Digester wash | 274 | 10.2 | 12500 | 3500 | 530 |
| Brown wash | 540 | 8.2 | 186 | 35 | 136 |
| Bleaching | 540 | 7.2 | 166 | 40 | 86.5 |
| Centricleaner | 137 | 7.5 | – | – | 150 |
| Combined effluent | 1511 | 9.5-10 | 4554 | 1127 | 189 |
| Combined effluent excluding black liquor | 1491 | 8.5-9 | 2425 | 670 | 192 |

In addition, measurement for active alkali content in the first 30 minutes of digester wash was conducted. It shows that the active alkali loss in the initial digester wash is 7.28 gm/l (as NaOH). Digester wash also contains recoverable fibre to the extent of 530 mg/l (refer the above Table 1).

The Table 1 shows that the black liquor alone contributes a flow of only 1.3 per cent of the total, but accounts for 41 per cent of the total BOD load. The BOD/COD ratio for black liquor is 0.2, indicating poor biodegradability. Since the black liquor contributes high pollution load and is poorly biodegradable, an evaporation test was carried out using a solar pan of size 0.5 m X 0.5m X 0.15m. Even

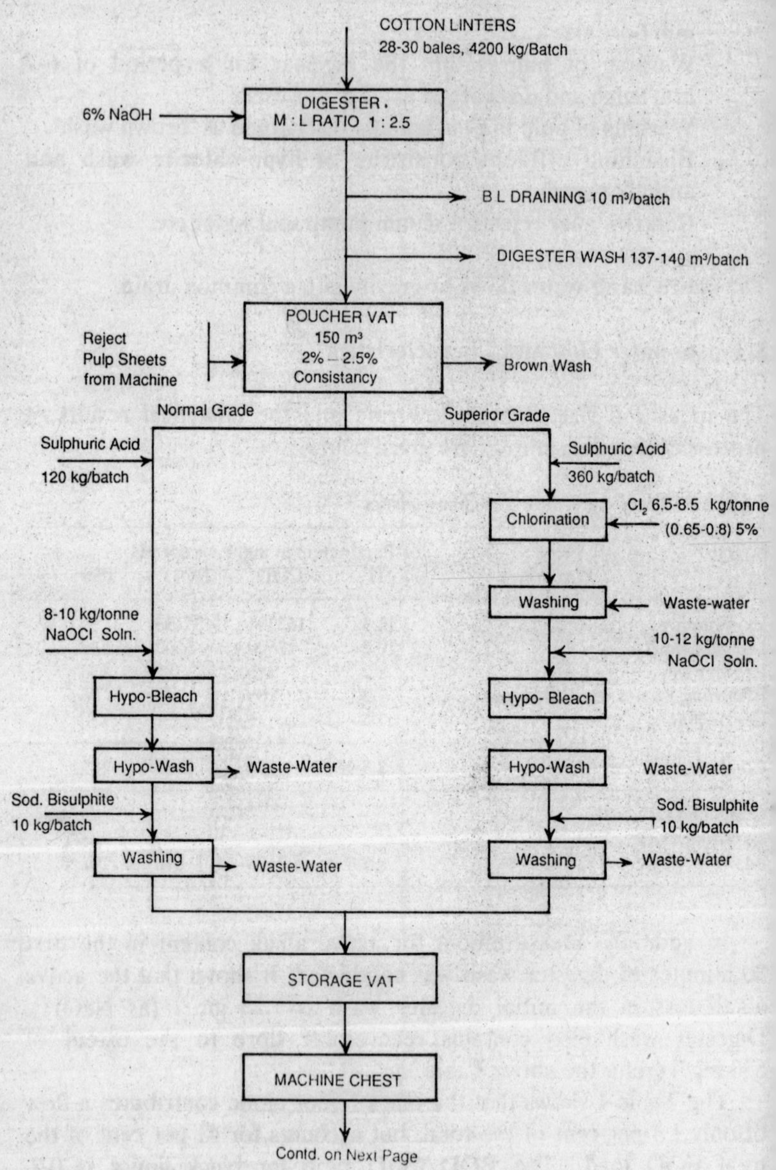


**FIG. 16.2: Production Sequence**

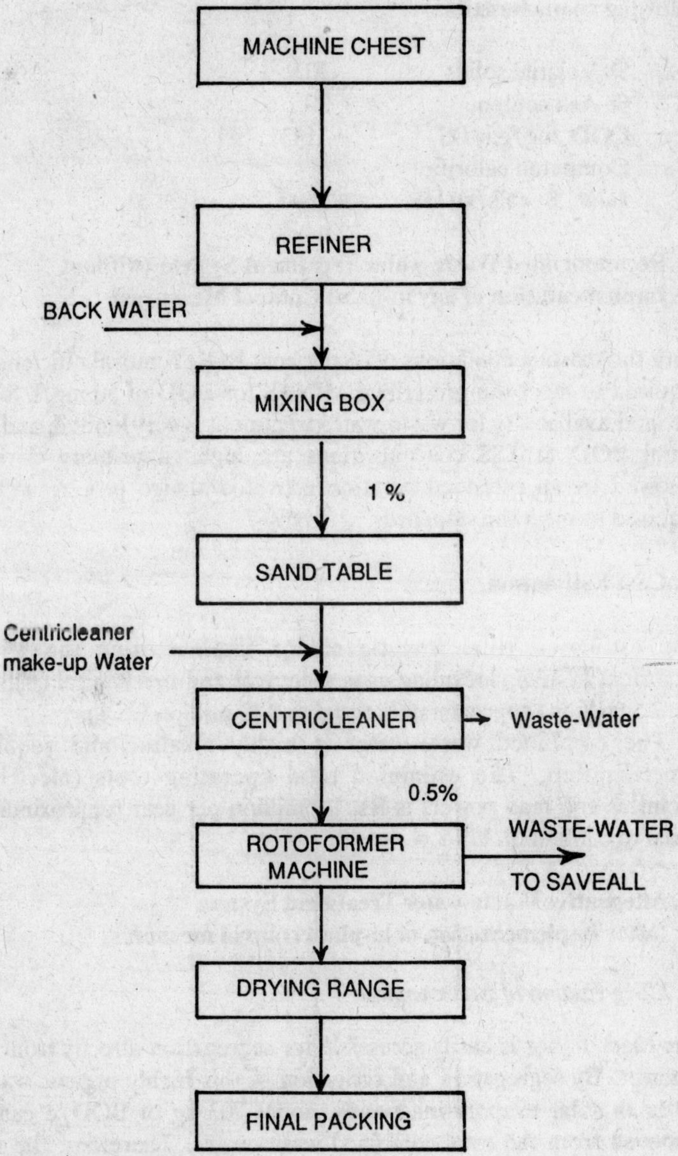


FIG. 16.2: Production Sequence

during winter period of Jan.-Feb. (Delhi), a net evaporation rate of 1.8 $m^3/m^2$. year was achieved for complete dryness with final solid concentration of 59 per cent +. The residue is analysed to contain the following characteristics:

| | |
|---|---|
| % Volatile solids | – 70.9 |
| % Ash content | – 29.1 |
| COD, mg/gm DS | – 1143 |
| Computed calorific value, K. cals/kg DS | – 3800 |

## 9. Recommended Waste-water Treatment System (without Implementation of any in-plant Control Measures)

With the existing conditions, 95.6 per cent BOD removal efficiency is required to meet the prescribed MINAS for BOD of 50 mg/l. Since the land availability for waste-water treatment is very limited, and the initial BOD & TSS concentrations are high, a primary clarifier followed by an extended aeration activated sludge process will be required to meet the standards.

## 10. Cost Estimation

The estimated total investment for implementing the above treatment system (including civil, electrical and mechanical costs) is Rs. 2.5 million (approximately equal to 0.19 million US $).

The combined waste-water is highly alkaline and requires neutralisation. The estimated total operating costs (electrical, chemical and man power) is Rs. 1.0 million per year (approximately equal to 0.1 million US $ per year).

## 11. Alternative Waste-water Treatment System (after implementation of in-plant control measures)

### *11.1. Segregation of Black Liquor*

The black liquor is easily accessible for segregation directly from the digester. By segregation and collection of this highly organic waste-water in solar evaporation ponds, about 703 kg of BOD/d can be removed from the total combined waste-water. Therefore, the unit will have to remove only 998 kg BOD/d, instead of 1703 kg BOD/d.

In addition, at an initial black liquor solids concentration of 121.8 gm/l and 70 to 75 per cent coal equivalent of the black liquor residue (after evaporation), it is possible to burn the solids in the existing boiler to save fuel cost, or it can be incinerated for recovery of chemicals. At a design evaporation rate of 1.8 $m^3/m^2$. year, the land requirement for solar evaporation is 3660 $m^2$. A pond of size 60m X 60m X 0.35m with 9 equal compartments has been recommended for evaporation. The compartments should be filled with 140 $m^3$ of black liquor (equivalent to 7 days of black liquor generation) and an evaporation and clearing time of 8 weeks will be allowed, which is adequate.

### *11.2. Recycling of Initial Digester Wash*

The digester wash during the initial 30 minutes of washing contain an active alkali content of 72.8 kg. Since currently fresh water is used for preparing the cooking liquor to achieve a material to liquor ratio of 1:2.5, it has been recommended to replace the same by recycling the above digester wash. This recycling will fetch a chemical saving cost of Rs. 0.2 million/year.

## 12. Recovery of Fibre from the Remaining Digester Wash

The composite digester wash sample contained a TSS content of 530 mg/l. Since the TSS are mainly fibres escaping through the strainer, a fibre recovery system was recommended. The total recoverable fibre content was computed based on the size requirement for recycling. According to this estimate, the unit will be in a position to recover about 100 kg of fibres per day, which is equivalent to a raw material saving of Rs. 0.132 million/year. This recovery scheme also reduced the TSS content in the composite effluent to 95 mg/l, from an initial content of 192 mg/l. Thus the waste-water treatment will not require primary sedimentation tank after the implementation of the in-plant control methods.

## 13. Treatment System

After implementation of the above measures, the unit is required to achieve a BOD treatment efficiency of 92.5 per cent only. Therefore, an extended aeration activated sludge process at a design F/M ratio of 0.15 $day^{-1}$ has been recommended.

### 14. Cost Estimation

The estimated total investment for implementation of both in-plant control measures and the waste-water treatment system (including civil, electrical and mechanical) will be Rs 1.6 million (approximately 0.12 million US $). The treatment system does not require neutralisation. Since the recycling of fibre and active alkali does fetch savings in material cost and the solar pond residue has fuel saving opportunity, the total operation and maintenance cost is offset by the savings. Therefore, implementation of the alternative treatment system suggested not only reduces the investment required for waste-water treatment by 36 per cent but also allows recovery of valuable materials and chemicals.

# 17

S.L. KESWANI

# INDIA'S EXPERIENCE IN BUILDING SMALL PAPER MILLS BASED ON RECONDITIONED PAPER MACHINERY

## 1. Need for Such a Concept

THE GAP between demand for and supply of paper has persisted for a long time in the Indian Paper Industry. Consumption of paper by an Indian is only 2 kg/annum compared to 252 kg. by an America. Total installed capacity for the production of paper and paper boards in India is of the order of 3.0 million tonnes while the licenced capacity exceeds 4.5 million tonnes.

There are certain inhibiting factors which have their origins in more investment from the private sector. They were basically in the form of heavy capital investments coupled with low return, long gestation period, inadequate availability of raw materials, and rising fuel costs.

The concept of setting up small paper-mills based on agricultural residues using reconditioned machinery, was to mitigate the severity of some of the above factors. How this concept overcomes the above mentioned inhibition is spelt out in the following paragraphs.

The capital investment for such mills was lower compared to large ones. Apart from the paper machinery, other pulping and utility equipment could be procured indigenously. Since these mills were using agricultural residues as raw materials, their processing involves equipment which is simpler in design, indigenously procurable and lower in cost.

Usage of agricultural residue is also a major factor in favour of setting up such mills. As these agricultural residues are difficult to be transported over long distances, localised use of it is best suited for small paper-mills.

Big mills requiring a huge quantity of such materials can not be conceived due to the same reason. Moreover, the conventional raw materials like bamboo and wood are so limited in supply that substantial usage of them in the near future appears doubtful and is becoming critical day by day.

The long gestation period of big mills is mainly due to the long delivery schedule of vital equipments like paper machines, finishing equipments and utilities like recovery and steam boilers etc. For small paper-mills the gestation period is considerably shortened due to quick availability of used paper machine from developed countries where they are lying idle due to economic reasons. The dismantling, shipping, renovations and re-erection takes about one-third of the total cost and delivery time of an equivalent new machine. The delivery period of other auxiliary items being of smaller capacity is also considerably less.

In this paper these points have been elaborated to highlight the need of small paper-mills which utilize readily available agricultural residues with reconditioned second hand machinery available at much lower cost.

## 2. Limitation of Forest Resources and Usage of Agricultural Residues

Since the beginning of paper-making in India, bamboo has been the basic source for fibrous raw materials. Hardwoods have also been used extensively mainly to provide the short fibred stock. The paper-making processes demand an adequate mixture of long fibred stock to impart necessary strength properties into paper, and short fibred stock to fill up the interstitial spaces between long fibres to impart uniformity. For too long a time this purpose has been met up by use of bamboo, hardwoods and sometimes by coniferous varieties from temperate regions.

The Paper Industry in India today faces a shortage of bamboo. Efforts have been made to augment the requirement by using more hardwoods. The optimum ratio of bamboo to hardwoods is taken as 2:1 keeping in view the quality considerations. However, some mills have achieved higher usage of Hardwoods by modernisation and rebuilding of their paper machines. On average about 2.7 tonnes of bamboo and hardwoods with 10 per cent moisture content is required to produce one tonne of paper.

There are 297 Pulp and Paper Mills in India out of which 53 account for almost half of the total production. Over and above this, the newsprint mill at Nepanagar, Mysore and Kerala and Rayon Grade pulp mills are also using bamboo. The existing installed capacity is 2.9 million tonnes/annum and the actual production was about 1.7 million tonnes in 1988. Based on the above figure, estimated consumption of bamboo and hardwoods comes to 3.0 million tonnes and 1.5 million tonnes respectively.

Systematic data regarding availability of bamboo and hardwoods are not available. An estimated figure puts it as 5000 million cubic metres. There is no correct estimated of total area of growth for bamboo but as a responsible estimate it is believed to be more than 10 million hectare. Based on this figure annual potential availability may be reckoned at about 5 million tonnes. This figure however, is quite misleading if actual availability is to be gauged for fulfilling future demand. This is due to the fact that bamboo plantation is concentrated mainly in Orissa, Madhya Pradesh, Andhra Pradesh, Karnataka and the north eastern states like Assam, Arunachal Pradesh, Tripura, Mizoram etc. Whereas some infrastructure is available in States like Orissa, M.P, A.P. and Karnataka, there is hardly any in the north eastern states where the major concentration of bamboo plantation lies.

Projecting the demand of paper in A.D. 2000 with per capita consumption of 3.0 kg and a total population of about 1000 million, we arrive at a figure of about 3.0 million tonnes of paper per annum.

If this augmentation in production is to be met by conventional raw materials alone the requirements of bamboo and hardwoods will rise to the tune of 7.0 million tonnes after allowing for reasonable circulation of such paper.

On the basis of a reasonable level of capacity utilisation the present demand of hardwoods is about 2.0 million tonnes/annum. This demand is estimated to rise to 2.6 – 2.8 million tonnes by A.D.

2000. In the context of this alone, the shortage of bamboo is inevitable.

The solution to this problem therefore lies essentially in the utilisation of non-conventional raw materials like wheat and rice straw, bagasse, waste-paper, rags, etc. Cereal straws are abundantly available in this country with vast amounts of agricultural land available. The present availability of wheat and rice straws comes to 86 million tonnes. Other cereal straws may be placed roughly at 24 million tonnes. Allowing for 10 to 15 per cent of the total available straws being consumed as cattle feeder and 10 to 15 per cent as fuel, still an enormous amount to the tune of 60.0 million tonnes is available for paper-making. Taking 30 per cent yield over the raw material for paper-making, the total potential of paper-making from such cereal straws works out at 18.0 million tonnes.

There are certain inherent problem too, in, utilisation of the cereal straws for paper-making. They are broadly classified as follows:

(a) Cereal straws cannot be transported over long distances due to their bulk and heavy constraints on the transportation system of this country. Long distance transportation, therefore, becomes quite uneconomical.
(b) Cereal straws being seasonal materials, a large amount of storage at the mill also has its own problems. Due to its high bulk storage area required per tonnes of cereal straw is much higher when compared to that of bamboo or timber. It has also been experienced that a larger spacing between stacks is required in the case of cereal straw, due to fire hazards especially during summer.

Considering the above factors we come to the logical conclusion that paper-mills based on non-conventional raw material cereal straws have to be limited to a capacity of 30-50 TPD, expandable to 75 to 100 tonnes, keeping in view the benefits of economic of scale to maintain increasing share of market and cost competitiveness. This means that small paper-mills up to a capacity of 50-100 TPD should be made to utilise the agricultural residue as basic fibrous raw materials for paper-making.

Small paper-mills are further justified due to their low capital investment, apart from being potential utilisers of agricultural residues which otherwise cannot be utilised in a large sized paper-mill.

It may however be pointed out that small paper-mills cannot be solely based on agricultural residue as fibrous raw materials due to the fact that length of fibre obtained from these sources much smaller compared to that of wood-stock or bamboo, and thus they do not withstand sufficient beating or refining before paper-making. These raw materials are, therefore, normally supplemented with long fibred stock from rags or purchased pulp to make a reasonably good paper stock. However, in practice, it has been found possible to use agricultural residue to form 80-85 per cent of the total pulp stock for paper-making.

**3. Low Capital Investment**

The capital investment required for a small paper-mill is of vital importance for its economic viability. Utilisation of agricultural residue coupled with use of reconditioned second hand machinery have contributed to lower capital investment in the following manner:

(1) The use of agricultural residues calls for simpler equipments like straw or grass cutter, duster, batch digesters, etc. These items are much cheaper and indigenously available on a short delivery schedule compared to those of chippers blowers, centrifugal screens (for wood based mills) which are much costlier. Chippers etc. are still imported with a long delivery schedule and have a high price tag.

(2) Power consumption for refining agricultural residues is quite low compared to that of wood or bamboo pulp. This means less refining equipment too.

(3) The use of imported reconditioned machinery considerably reduce the project cost. A typical 30 to 50 TPD writing and printing machine imported for reconditioning costs about Rs. 10.0 million, whereas the same machine procured new from indigenous sources with some imported items like suction couch, may cost about Rs. 30 to 40 million. The fact

that a reconditioned paper machine has a substantial effect on the total project cost is beyond controversy.

(4) The lower gestation period for such mills (this is elaborated further in the next section) also reduces the project cost considerably. The pre-operative expenses like establishment cost and interest paid during construction are considerably reduced.

It has, therefore, been established that both aspects, viz, utilisation of agricultural residues and use of imported reconditioned machinery, are complementary to each other for reducing the investment for mills of capacity ranging from 20 to 50 TDP.

This becomes clear from the case studies which follow:

*Case-I* includes minimum of reconditioned machinery i.e. only paper machine and finishing equipment. This results in the highest capital investment per annual tonne of installed capacity.

*Case-II* has larger share of imported reconditioned machinery i.e. stock preparation equipment in addition to paper machine and finishing equipments. Although cost figures in this case data back to 1974, the apparent effect of this case can be seen in capital investment per annual tonne of installed capacity.

*Case-III* refers to a mill with more than 80 per cent equipment which has been imported and reconditioned. The cost figures are based on a mill commissioned in October 1980, and showing a substantially low investment figure per annual tonne of installed capacity. The cost figure in 1988-89 is likely to be around Rs. 150 million.

*Case-IV* refers to a 30 t/day saleable writing and printing paper mill. This was commissioned in January 1981. The mill has a Fourdrinier paper machine having a size press. The other imported reconditioned equipment are stock preparation units. It has about 30 per cent imported equipment while raw material preparation, pulp mill equipment and utilities are of Indian origin and new. Current cost of such investment would be to the order of Rs. 100 million.

These case studies also prove beyond doubt that a larger share of reconditioned machinery considerably reduces the capital investment.

**4. Short Gestation Period**

One of the most important aspects of a paper-mill using second-hand imported, reconditioned machinery is its short gestation period. From our experience of setting up such units, it was established that an imported paper machine takes about 12 to 15 months for dismantling, shipping, reconditioning and re-erection. For a new paper machine of similar capacity total time taken between placement of order and commissioning may be as long as 24 to 30 months.

Total project implementation schedule of a 20 to 30 TPD paper mill using imported reconditioned machinery has been found to be about 20 to 24 months. For a similar mill using new machinery it may be anywhere between 36 to 40 months.

A short gestation period considerably reduce the preoperative expenses incurred in the form of establishment costs and interests payment. This further contributes to a lowering of projects cost, apart from the fact that reconditioned machinery, re-erected, costs about one third of its new indigenous counterpart.

**5. Case Studies**

We have taken up four cases of small paper-mills to study different aspects in particular project cost, extent of utilisation of agricultural residue, gestation period, etc.

*Case-I* refers to a mill of 20 TPD capacity producing M.F. kraft and writing/printing on a second-hand reconditioned machine utilising straw and hessian as primary raw materials. Total project cost was reported to be Rs. 35.5 million. (Projection No. 6).

The profitability statement in Case-I shows negative cash accrual. However, if cash accrual from depreciation is also taken into consideration, the net cash accrual shows a healthy return. It may be noted that the mill was paying the interest on debt which was dissipated gradually with repayments. This meant better cash accrual in the following years.

*Case-II* refers to a mill of 30 TPD capacity producing posters, kraft and writing/printing varieties on a combined machine. All stock preparation equipments, paper machine, finishing equipments and boiler were imported and reconditioned. The total project cost was reported to be Rs. 20 million. The estimation of profitability shows a healthy return of 48.3 per cent on investment. This was due to the fact that capital investment was quite low and short term loans had been repaid.

*Case-III* refers to a mill of 50 TPD capacity commissioned at the end of October 1980. The mill produces kraft and writing/printing grades on a Fourdrinier combined machine. Complete pulp mill with separate streets for straw and wood handling, stock preparation, paper machine, finishing equipments etc. were imported and reconditioned. The total project cost was Rs. 50 million.

*Case-IV* refers to a mill of 30 TPD capacity commissioned in March 1981. The mill produces writing and printing grades on a Fourdrinier multicylinder machine. The paper machine is imported and reconditioned. The total project cost works out at about Rs. 70 million (Projection No. 7).

Most of the above mills have since expanded to higher levels and their performance has been satisfactory despite recessionary trends in the paper industry over the past 3-4 years. The scenario is however, fast changing in view of the spurt in demand and improved profitability. The capacities therefore, are being further expanded to keep pace with market demand and to take advantage of emerging healthy scenario.

## 6. Problems and Prospects

### *6.1. Prospects*

In the foregoing sections we have tried to emphasise the main problems and advantages of setting up small paper-mills in India based on reconditioned machinery. The main advantages like low capital investments and short gestation period are incentives in themselves for small entrepreneurs to invest in the paper industry.

Another important fact is that these small mills are potential consumers of agricultural residues abundantly available in India. As we have pointed earlier, due to transportation and storage problems, agricultural residues cannot be economically utilised on a large scale by big paper-mills. Small paper-mills up to the capacity of 50 to 100 TPD, are the only ones which can utilize these cheap and abundant resources. This, therefore, can be considered to be one of the immediate benefits of this concept. India being one of those countries where the supply of paper has always been lagging behind the demand, it becomes all the more necessary to explore all the available sources of raw materials. Conventional raw materials like bamboo and wood available in India can not be immediately utilised for paper-making due to many constraints like higher economy of scale, poor transportational infrastructure in remote areas where such raw materials are available etc.

The gap between demand and supply is already quite apparent where some immediate short-term solution is urgently required. The concept of small mills of the nature described above is probably the only viable solution.

It is also noteworthy that India's immediate need lies in the writing/printing and packaging varieties of paper. These small mills using short fibred raw materials like agricultural residues are more suitable for such varieties for mass consumption.

Immediate benefits of this concept can therefore be listed below:

(a) Scope of utilisation of agricultural residues which otherwise is not possible on a large scale,
(b) Lower capital investment to attract private sector to invest in the paper industry,
(c) Short gestation period which means quicker realisation of objective to meet the market demand,
(d) More employment opportunities in the form of direct and indirect employment.

### *6.2. Constraints*

So far we have discussed the benefits of the concept of small paper-mills based on reconditioned machinery. However, there are quite a few problems which have been nagging the entrepreneurs in this field. We take them up for discussion in the order of priority.

The second-hand machines in the capacity range of 15 TPD to 50 TPD or even 100 TPD for writing/printing or packaging varieties are available with difficulty, thus increase in the scale of operation may have to be considered by adopting continuous pulping etc. as described in Case-III.

The small paper-mills do not incorporate chemical recovery systems for economic reasons. This results in much higher chemical input, like caustic soda, per tonne of paper compared to that of a big mill. This substantially increases the production cost in comparison to big mills with chemical recovery.

Non-recovery of chemicals results in a higher load of pollutants in effluent and thereby increases the cost of treatments. In the course of time, discharge of effluents from mills without chemical recovery can be a major source of pollution. It is, therefore, necessary to plan for effective recovery systems for small paper-mills and ensure that the small paper-mills install such recovery system to prevent wastage of chemicals and pollution. This scene is changing fast and serious attempts are being made with necessary R & D effort to incorporate a recovery system at least at the level of 50 TPD or above which may become mandatory in the near future.

The third problem lies in the area of quality. Given the fact of small scale production and the inherent nature of the agricultural residues as poor in quality compared to bamboo or wood as raw materials, there is a risk of small paper-mills not being competitive with the existing or new paper-mills based on forest raw materials. This lacuna can however be overcome to some extent if these small mills are prepared to take up the manufacture of speciality and superior varieties of papers. However, in view of shortages of normal grades of writing or printing papers which can be satisfactorily made from these raw materials, this problem may not be of prime importance. In case suitable technology is made available, superior quality of writing and printing varieties can also be manufactured by these mills.

## 7. Status of the Industry

Table 1 gives the distribution by percentage contribution of production in various sizes of plant capacities. It shows that above 40 per cent of the output was contributed by smaller paper-mills in 1986.

Table 2 shows the growth of paper-making capacity, by size of paper mills, for the years 1982 to 1987. There were 141 small paper-mills in 1982 (annual capacity up to 10,000 tonnes) which contributed 586,000 tonnes of capacity.

In 1987, the number of such mills has risen to 241 with a total production capacity of over 1.12 million tonnes. Aggregate output from these units now matches the total production from the larger units. This is a major achievement of the last one decade, giving substantial relief to meet paper shortages in the country.

The demand of paper and paper boards in India (at a modest growth rate of 5 per cent per annum) is likely to increase annually by 80,000 tonnes to 100,000 tonnes, during the next 6-7 years. If the small paper-mills maintain their present share in domestic production of paper, their contribution of 40,000 – 50,000 t/annum would require the setting up of at least 4-5 small units (average capacity 10,000 tonnes) every year. It can, therefore, be confidently predicated that higher percentage share of such mills in gross national production of paper will play a crucial role in the years to come.

Table 3 shows the changes in pattern of production of paper in India from 1970 to 1987.

TABLE 1: Production of Paper and Paper Boards in 1986 by Category of Mills
*(Projection No. 1)*

*(in tonnes)*

| Mills (tonnes per annum) | No. of Mills | Production | Percentage Share |
|---|---|---|---|
| 1000 to 2000 tonnes | 56 | 90,960 | (5.8) |
| 2000 to 5000 tonnes | 93 | 185,080 | (11.8) |
| 5000 to 10000 tonnes | 75 | 338,780 | (21.6) |
| 10000 to 20000 tonnes | 18 | 133,310 | (8.5) |
| 20000 to above | 29 | 820,270 | (52.3) |
| Total | 271 | 1,568,400 | (100) |

*Source*: Directorate General of Technical Development, New Delhi India.

TABLE 2: Growth of Paper Capacity By Size of Mills

*(000's tonnes)*

| Mill Category (tonnes per annum) | 1982 | | 1983 | | 1984 | |
|---|---|---|---|---|---|---|
| | No. of units | Capa-city | No. of units | Capa-city | No. of units | Capa-city |
| Above 20,000 | 22 | 1127.0 | 23 | 1160.8 | 23 | 1139.0 |
| 10,000-20,000 | 10 | 148.8 | 11 | 160.3 | 14 | 153.0 |
| 5,000-10,000 | 40 | 326.2 | 41 | 336.2 | 54 | 398.0 |
| 1,000-5,000 | 85 | 249.8 | 100 | 324.9 | 130 | 270.0 |
| Grand Total | 157 | 1853.8 | 175 | 1982.2 | 221 | 1960.0 |

*Contd.*

| Mill Category (tonnes per annum) | 1985 | | 1986 | | 1987 | |
|---|---|---|---|---|---|---|
| | No. of units | Capa-city | No. of units | Capa-city | No. of units | Capa-city |
| Above 20,000 | 23 | 1172.3 | 29 | 1357.3 | 29 | 1357.3 |
| 10,000-20,000 | 15 | 235.8 | 18 | 278.6 | 18 | 278.6 |
| 5,000-10,000 | 68 | 565.2 | 75 | 622.2 | 84 | 702.0 |
| 1,000-5,000 | 143 | 376.6 | 149 | 396.5 | 157 | 420.6 |
| Grand Total | 249 | 2349.9 | 271 | 2654.6 | 288 | 2758.5 |

TABLE 3: Variety-Wise Production of Paper
*(Projection No. 3)*

*('000 tonnes)*

| Year | Printing & Writing Papers | Industrial and Other Papers | Total |
|---|---|---|---|
| 1970 | 444.7 | 313.6 | 758.3 |
| 1975 | 503.8 | 325.2 | 829.1 |
| 1980 | 627.6 | 430.8 | 1058.4 |
| 1981 | 714.0 | 490.8 | 1204.8 |
| 1982 | 741.6 | 501.6 | 1243.2 |
| 1983 | 674.4 | 463.2 | 1137.6 |
| 1984 | 805.2 | 553.2 | 1358.4 |
| 1985 | 866.4 | 596.4 | 1462.8 |
| 1986 | 942.0 | 628.0 | 1570.0 |
| 1987 | 990.0 (E) | 660.0 (E) | 1650.0 (E) |

E = Estimated.

*Note*: Variety-wise production of paper slightly differs from mill-wise production of paper.

*Source*: Central Statistical Organisation, Govt. of India.

TABLE 4: Summary of Installed Capacity of Paper and Paper Board Industry Category-wise as on 1.1.1988

*(Projection No. 4)*

| S.No. | Category | No. of Units | Annual Installed Capacity (tonnes) |
|---|---|---|---|
| 1. | Above 20,000 tonnes | 29 | 13,57,300 |
| 2. | 10,000 to 20,000 tonnes | 24 | 3,79,100 |
| 3. | 5,000 to 10,000 tonnes | 83 | 6,93,690 |
| 4. | 2,000 to 5,000 tonnes | 103 | 3,49,020 |
| 5. | Less than 2,000 tonnes | 58 | 88,619 |
| | Total | 297 | 28,67,294 |

*Source*: Directorate General Technical Development, India, New Delhi.

TABLE 5: (Projection No. 5)

| Unit Size (tonnes per day) | Total Investments (Rs. in million) | Investments per Annual tonne (Rs.) |
|---|---|---|
| 30 | 150 | 15,000 |
| 100 | 800 | 24,200 |
| 200 | 1500 | 22,700 |

*Note*: Rs. 100 equivalent to U.S. $ 6.6.

# *ANNEXURE-I*

## Case Studies of Four Small Paper Mills

| Sl. No. | Particulars | Case-I | Case-II |
|---|---|---|---|
| 1. | Production Commenced | 1978 | 1974 |
| 2. | Capacity Installed (TPY) | 6600 | 10000 |
| 3. | Production Range | M.F. Kraft or writing/ printing of 50-100 GSM. | Creamwave, posters, of 32-400 GSM |
| 4. | Details of Reconditioned Machinery (Imported) | (a) Paper Machine<br>(b) Slitter rewinder & sheet cutter.<br>(c) Finishing equipments<br>(d) Boiler. | (a) Stock Preparation equipments<br>(b) Paper machine |
| 5. | Cost of Project (Rs. in million) | | |
| | 5.1 Land & Site Development | 0.46 | 0.70 |
| | 5.2 Buildings | 4.32 | 6.20 |
| | 5.3 Plant & Machinery: (including foundation, erection) | 14.59 | 7.80 |
| | 5.4 Miscellaneous fixed assets (utilities, office equipments, vehicles etc.) | 8.30 | 2.00 |
| | 5.5 Pre-operative expenses | 6.07 | 2.30 |
| | 5.6 Contingencies | — | — |
| | 5.7 Margin money for working capital. | 1.70 | — |
| | Total Project | 35.44 | 19.00 |
| 6. | Investment/Annual tonne (Rs./tonne) | 5370 | 1900 |
| 7. | Remarks | Investment per tonne of annual production is high as the extent of imported reconditioned machinery is limited to paper machine and finishing equipments. | The cost figures are pertaining to 1974. Due to higher proportion of re-conditioned machine the investment per annual tonne is low. |
| | Courtesy | Nath Pulp & Paper | Laxmi Board and Paper Mills. |

| Sl. No. | Particulars | Case-III | Case-IV |
|---|---|---|---|
| 1. | Production Commenced | 1980 | 1980 |
| 2. | Capacity Installed (TPY) | 16500 | 10000 |
| 3. | Production Range | kraft & writing/printing | Writing/Printing (50-250 GSM) |
| 4. | Details of Reconditioned Machinery (Imported) | (a) Complete pulp mill with continuous digesters, washing & bleaching equipments.<br>(b) Stock preparation equipments.<br>(c) Paper Machine & finishing equipments.<br>(d) Boiler & Turbo-generators. | |
| 5. | Cost of Project (Rs. in million) | | |
| | 5.1 Land & Site Development | 0.70 | 1.50 |
| | 5.2 Buildings | 6.50 | 9.50 |
| | 5.3 Plant & Machinery: (including foundation, erection) | 15.00 | 22.86 |
| | 5.4 Miscellaneous fixed assets (utilities, office equipments, vehicles etc.) | 7.00 | 10.88 |
| | 5.5 Pre-operative expenses | 13.30 | 8.24 |
| | 5.6 Contingencies | — | 2.80 |
| | 5.7 Margin money for working capital. | Included in pre-operative expenses | 3.30 |
| | Total Project | 42.50 | 59.08 |
| 6. | Investment/Annual tonne (Rs./tonne) | 2575 | 5900 |
| 7. | Remarks | Considering the fact that figures relate to 1979-80 prices, investment per annual tonne is quite low as proportion of reconditioned machinery is very high. | Investment per annual tonne is the highest as the extent of reconditioned machinery used is only the paper machine. |
| | Courtesy | United Pulp & Paper | Shiva Paper Mills. |

# 18

MANUEL DELGADO & ENRIQUE ESCUDERO

# THE "SAICA" PROCESS
## Semi-Chemical Pulp from Straw

### 1. Introduction

STRAW, AS fibrous raw material for paper and board making, has been used for many years, even long before wood. Later, despite the fast and spectacular growth in wood utilisation, the use of straw went on, particularly in countries with scarcity in wood resources, because straw was cheap and plentiful.

At the beginning of the 40s, there were many small mills throughout Europe producing different grades of paper with variable amounts of straw in the furnish. As the years went by, many of those mills were forced to close down for a variety of reasons; either because they could not compete with wood, because they could not comply with the ever increasing strict environmental regulation and, most important, because they became technologically obsolete when virtually all research and development efforts carried out by industrialised nations were entirely devoted to the wood-based pulp and paper industry. Today, when it is internationally recognised that wood is no longer cheap and plentiful, an ever increasing interest in the utilisation of non-wood fibres is shown by the international pulp and paper industry, and a promising future is ahead of the few straw mills that managed to survive despite all adversities.

One of these small mills, SAICA, located in Zaragoza (Spain), strongly believed in the future of straw and, driven by a remarkable enthusiasm, has dedicated a continuous effort to the development and improvement of their own technology, with their own resources, not only in the processing of straw itself, but also in all associated aspects such as paper-making, energy conservation, environmental protection, etc. The results are there; from a small mill of less than 1,000 t/year of straw based paper, SAICA has become, in less than 30 years the world's largest producer of straw based paper with a production of over 1,000 t/day of fluting, including nearly 400 t/day of straw based semi-chemical pulp. In addition, SAICA has been the first mill of its kind in the world to adopt the anaerobic treatment of its effluents, producing biogas equivalent to over 7,200 t/year of fuel oil. Last but not least, the new co-generation plant recently started has provided SAICA with a generating capacity of approx. 50 MW of electric power, of which close to 70 per cent is sold to the public grid.

The fact that such a modern, high-capacity mill by any standard, has been able to achieve these levels of quality and economic performance is striking evidence that straw does not need to be restrictive to production in terms of scale or efficiency. With a total labour force of 250, including 25 university graduate, SAICA has one of the highest productivity rates in the world, 1,400 t/man-year.

## 2. The "SAICA" Straw Pulping Process

### *2.1. General*

Of all aspects of SAICA, the most exclusive one, and the main reason for this presentation, is the Straw Pulp Mill. The basic plant was designed by SAICA and since the first 40 t/day SAICA continuous digester was installed in 1958, it has evolved through progressive improvements to economic and qualitative standards which are considered to be unequalled for the grades of paper involved. Today, four pulping lines of 80 t/day of nominal capacity are in operation with an effective production of near 400 t/day of high yield semi-chemical pulp.

Loyal to its innovative principles, SAICA maintain through a pilot plant located at the mill, a regular research programme, testing a variety of raw materials, cooking chemicals and operating procedures in order to determine the optimum treatment for any given conditions.

### *2.2. Process Description*

The basic process is described below and illustrated in Block diagram N-1.

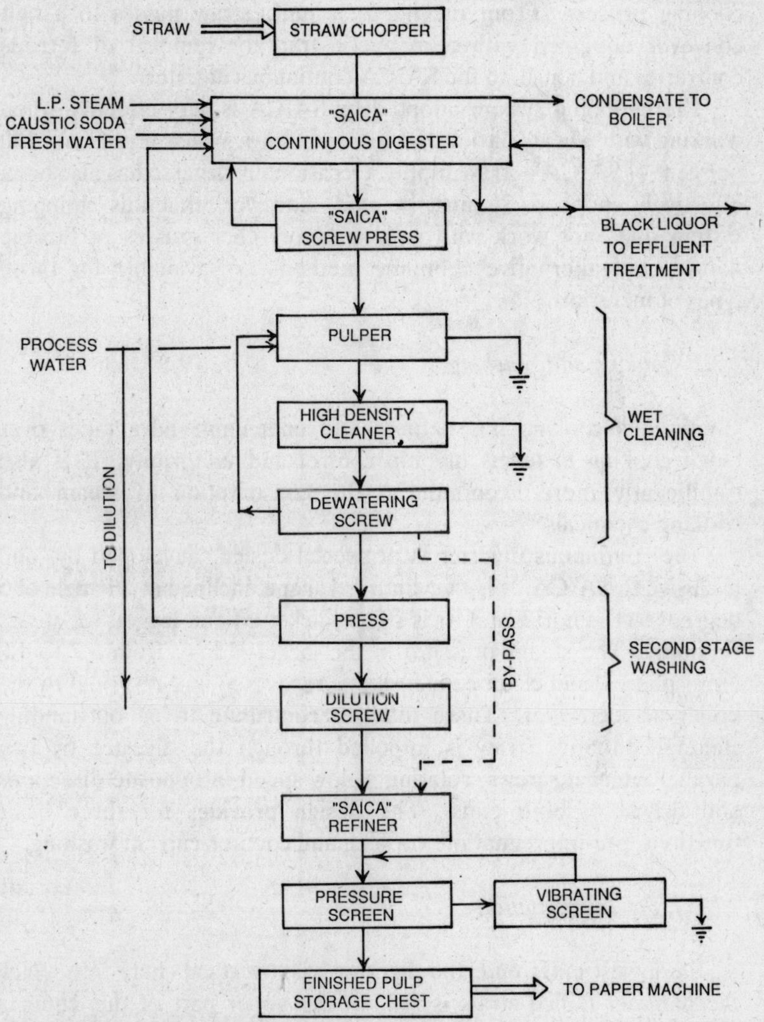


**DIAGRAM N-1: The "SAICA" Straw Pulping Process**

### *2.2.1. Straw Feeding*

One man, operating a front-end loader supplies all four pulping lines pushing the straw into the below-ground hopper of a rotary hammer mill, simple but remarkably effective and of very little maintenance. In this hammer mill, straw is cut in smaller pieces and also bruised so that a better chemical impregnation is obtained, thus improving the cooking process. From the hammer mill, straw passes to a belt conveyor equipped with a magnetic trap for removal of ferrous contraries and hence, to the SAICA continuous digester.

The chopping system adopted by SAICA is very effective when working with wheat, barley, oat and rye straw, which represents 100 per cent of SAICA's straw supply. Occasionally bagasse has also been effectively chopped. It must be said, however, that this chopping system does not work with rice straw or other grasses of flexible nature, but alternative chopping methods are available for those types of materials.

### *2.2.2. Cooking and Washing*

Continuous cooking has definite and undeniable advantages over batch cooking in terms of pulp control and uniformity. It is also significantly more economic in the consumption of steam and cooking chemicals.

The continuous digester is of special design, developed by, and exclusive to SAICA. It is of cylindrical shape, inclined at an angle of 5 degrees to the horizontal. It is steam-jacketted and lagged for steam economy. The steam pressure in the jacket is low, from 1.2 to 1.8 atmospheres, and clean condensate is recovered and returned to the boiler as feedwater. These features contribute to an outstanding steam economy. Straw is impelled through the digester by two parallel internal screws, rotating at low speed in opposite directions and driven at both ends. The design provides for three basic functions, pre-impregnation, cooking and counter-current washing.

#### *2.2.2.1. Pre-Impregnation*

At the lowest entry end, the digester has a vertical chute into which the hammer-milled straw is fed. In the upper part of this chute a regulated quantity of spent cooking liquor is injected to provide pre-impregnation which is an aid to absorption of the fresh cooking liquor when it is applied. It also increases the specific weight of the straw which improves feeding conditions and utilises any active chemical residual in the spent liquor, thus reducing chemical consumption.

### *2.2.2.2. Cooking*

Cooking is carried out at low-temperature and atmospheric pressure conditions. Live steam does not come into contact with the fibre but it is fed only to the jacket and condensate is returned to the boiler giving feedwater and energy economy. It has been established that the low-temperature, pressureless and slow cook is ideal for straw pulp, retaining to the maximum extent the most desireable fibre characteristics. The process is also simple and safe. The digester is built for outdoor operation, reducing the costs of buildings.

Cooking chemical, normally caustic soda at 50 per cent concentration, is introduced at mid-point of the digester together with a controlled quantity of "brown" liquor obtained from the washed pulp after pressing at the discharge end of the digester. This feature, with pre-impregnation, substantially reduces chemical consumption by maximum utilisation of active residual chemical.

### *2.2.2.3. Counter-Current Washing*

Although it is recognised that pulp washing is desirable for semi-chemical wood pulp, the equivalent of the straw pulp used by SAICA, it is not a universal feature of production because of the capital and operating expense which the low margins for corrugating medium can find difficult to afford. It is an inherent feature of the SAICA digester and it imparts two valuable characteristics. Clean pulp, with minimum corrosive effect on plant is one; the other is that the pulp leaving the digester does so free of pressure. No blow tank to release pressure is required and the pulp is stronger because the explosive nature of sudden pressure release is avoided.

Pulp washing is carried out in a counterflow manner by adding washwater at the discharge end. Washwater requirements are around 4.5 cubic metres/tonne of pulp produced. It is not essential to use freshwater; paper machine backwater can be used with economies in fibre and water. Spent liquor is continuously extracted from the digester at the lowest, feed entry end, and is collected in a small tank from which a regulated quantity is pumped to the feed chute for pre-impregnation; the remainder is pumped away for treatment and disposal.

Washed pulp discharges from the digester into a screw conveyor with two or more outlets according to capacity. Each outlet is connected to a screw-press of SAICA design. The pulp is pressed to a consistency of approximately 25 per cent and extracted liquor is returned to the digester.

*2.2.3. Wet Cleaning*

The SAICA digester can process straw without previous cleaning, however, as straw gets dirtier for various reasons, it becomes necessary to remove heavy contaminants such as stones, sand, etc., in order to protect downstream equipment. The most common practice is to do dry cleaning before cooking but the excessive maintenance and power cost of the standard method available represents an economic burden difficult to afford for corrugating medium. After a careful evaluation, SAICA decided to adopt a "wet cleaning" system after cooking and pressing.

Pressed pulp is sent to a pulper where it is diluted down to 3.2 per cent consistency. At the junk box, most of the large heavy contaminants are removed. From the pulper, pulp is then pumped through a high density cleaner where residual small size contaminants are further removed. Depending upon the characteristics and precedence of the straw, for a daily production of 100 tonnes of pulp, the amount of heavy contaminants can vary from 150 kg up to 2000 kg. The removal of these contraries improve the quality of the pulp, lengthen the life of refiner segments and reduces wear in other areas of the mill.

*2.2.4. Second Washing Stage*

For the corrugating medium normally produced at SAICA, the counter-current washing done at the digester is considered sufficient. However, for specific applications of the corrugating medium, additional washing is required. A simple method adopted by SAICA consists of passing the pulp, after the wet cleaning stage, through a single press where consistency is raised up to 25 per cent and liquor extracted is sent to the digester. From the press, pulp passes through a screw conveyor where it is diluted and homogenised before being fed to the refiners. With the washing done at the digester, the efficiency in the removal of total suspended solids is approximately 67 per cent; after the second stage, the efficiency is increased up to 88 per cent. Provision is made to by-pass the second washing stage when manufacturing corrugating medium of less strict applications.

### *2.2.5. Refining and Cleaning*

From the screw conveyor, pulp is discharged into disc refiners designed by SAICA to operate at 8 to 10 per cent consistency for optimum pulp characteristics. Refined pulp is collected into a chest where it is diluted to about 4 per cent consistency before it is pumped through a pressure screen where shieves, uncooked matter, etc. are removed. Pressure screen rejects discharges into a vibrating screen. Accepts from the pressure screen are collected in a storage chest from where they are finally pumped at controlled consistency directly to the paper machine.

### *2.3. Operating Conditions*

For a typical 80 t/day straw based semi-chemical pulping line as described above, the operating conditions, consumptions and yields are set out below:

| | |
|---|---|
| Straw consumption; | 1.62 tonnes of straw as received (14% moisture) per BDMT of pulp produced |
| Yield: | 71.7 per cent |
| Chemical consumption (Caustic soda as NaOH) | 6.0 per cent on BD straw input. |
| Steam consumption: | 0.65 t/BDMT of pulp |
| Steam pressure: | 1.2-1.8 atm. |
| Cooking pressure: | Atmospheric |
| Cooking temperature: | 98°C |
| Power consumption: | 220 kWh/BDMT of pulp. |
| Washwater consumption (process water) | 4.8 $m^3$/BDMT of pulp. |
| Fresh water consumption | 1.5 $m^3$/BDMT of pulp. |
| Water Retention Value | 2.8 |
| CMT index of pulp | 2.12 N.$m^2$/gr. |

### *2.4. Advantages of the SAICA Process*

By comparison with batch or non-continuous processes, continuous pulping for straw or similar grasses offers the following advantages:

- Better quality control
- Lower chemical consumption
- Lower steam consumption
- Lower power requirement
- Lower manpower requirement
- Higher efficiency
- Lower investment cost in equipment and buildings.

By comparison with other continuous processes available for straw or similar materials, SAICA offers a number of outstanding advantages which make the SAICA pulping process unique. The most significant advantages are set out below:

*2.4.1. Steam and Feedwater Economy*

The avoidance of direct steam cooking by the use of a steam jacket provides these benefits. 1.5 to 2 tonnes of steam per tonne of pulp common to most existing processes, represents more than double the SAICA consumption of 0.65 t/tonne of pulp. For a pulping line of 80 t/day, such a difference represents a yearly saving of nearly 1.500 tonnes of fuel. In addition, clean condensate with its inherent heat is returned to the boiler feedwater system with the subsequent saving.

*2.4.2. Lower Steam Pressure*

The SAICA process uses steam at 1.2 to 1.8 atmospheres which should be compared with steam pressures 5 to 12 atmospheres, deemed necessary for high temperature, fast cook typical for other continuous processes. This factor represents lower capital cost for boiler plant, greater power generation (if this a feature), a single process steam pressure system for pulp mill and paper mill, or a combination of all these benefits, representing economy in cost and simplicity in operation.

*2.4.3. Quality Control and Uniformity*

The higher liquor ratio employed and the longer retention time (2 hrs. as against 15 to 20 minutes) minimize the effects of variation in straw quality, promoting closer uniformity. The low temperature cooking cycle and the incorporated pulp washing, eliminate the adverse effect of sudden pressure release on the fibre. Pulp freeness and strength are enhanced.

### *2.4.4. Incorporated Washing*

The fact that washing is done at the SAICA digester represents considerable economy in capital and operating cost. Due to the relatively slow drainage rate of straw pulp, conventional washers with vacuum filters are larger and expensive in capital cost and building requirements. On this account, some corrugating medium pulp mills do not incorporate washing, but then chemical consumption and plan maintenance suffer.

### *2.4.5. Covered Space Requirement*

It is normal for continuous straw cooking and washing plant to be installed in a covered building. The SAICA equivalent is designed for outdoor, uncovered operation, to the maximum extent.

### *2.4.6. Simplicity of Operation*

Operating at low temperature and atmospheric pressure contributes to simplicity and safety in working conditions. These factors, plus the longer retention period, minimize training requirements so that operators with no previous experience can very quickly assimilate the process and produce good quality pulp.

## 3. Summary

The SAICA Mill has been producing corrugating medium based on straw pulp for nearly 30 years. Following a strict policy of research and development, they succeeded in developing a straw pulping process with supporting equipment, very competitive, in terms of product quality and viability, with any other process available.

Recently, the SAICA Process was made available to potential users around the world and the first SAICA semi-chemical pulp mill outside Spain was installed at MODERN KARTON SANAYI fluting mill in Corlu, Turkey. After one year of successful operation, a 50 per cent expansion is under consideration. Soon, more SAICA straw pulp mill will be erected in several parts of the world.

Inquiries can be addressed to:

Enrique Escudero
SAICA.
San Juan de la Peña 140. Zaragoza. Spain
Phone: 51-43-33
Telex: 58127 Saica-E
Fax: 51-54-65

Manuel Delgado
Infanta Mercedes 92-304.
28020 Madrid. Spain
Phone: 571-20-52
Telex: 47589 Elsit-E
Fax: 571-22-17

GÜNTHER SCHILDHAUER

# DESILICATION OF ALKALINE BLACK LIQUORS–DIGESTION OF RICE STRAW

## A Brief Test Report on a Pilot Plant Project at the Rakta Pulp & Paper Mill in Alexandria, Egypt

### 1. Test Objectives

IN INDUSTRIAL pulp production from wood, it has been general practice for many years to recover the cooking chemicals, as well as energy, from the spent liquor, thus contributing towards a cleaner environment.*

At this chemical recovery process has been successfully employed in wood pulping, its use suggests itself also for pulp production from annual plants. Compared with wood, these annual plants feature, however, a considerably higher silicic acid content ($SiO_2$). This is exemplified by the following table:

TABLE 1: Silicic Acid Content of Various Raw Materials

| Raw material | $SiO_2$ in % related to DS content |
|---|---|
| Coniferous wood | 0.002 – 0.007 |
| Rye straw | 0.5 – 1.5 |
| Bagasse | 1 – 2 |
| Bamboo | 1 – 3.5 |
| Wheat straw | 2 – 4 |
| Reed | 2 – 4 |
| Rice straw | 8 – 14 |

* This paper represents the personal view of the author and not necessarily the view of LURGI AG.

In the sulfate process, which takes a predominant position in the pulping of annual plants, the major part of the silicic acid is obtained in the black liquor thus causing considerable problems in the chemical recovery system.

1. In the evaporation unit, the $SiO_2$ forms a scale which is extremely difficult to remove. This scale impairs heat transfer and reduces the capacity of the evaporation unit, eventually resulting in frequent downtimes of the unit for scale removal.
2. In the liquor incinerator, $SiO_2$ increases the melting temperature of the ash and favours the formation of accretions.
3. In the causticizing unit, $SiO_2$ interferes with the process by forming calcium silicates and thus increasing the lime consumption.
4. In the lime kiln $SO_2$ causes the formation of glassy deposits reducing the conversion efficiency and bringing kiln operation to a standstill due to the build-up of accretions.

In some bagasse or reed-based pulp mills, these difficulties are encountered every day. Moreover, in such mills, the silicate-laden lime sludge obtained in the causticizing unit has to be dumped, since reburning is not feasible.

In the pulping of rice straw, economic operation of a chemical recovery unit has so far not been possible. This means that in several thousand pulp mills worldwide, the cooking chemicals are still wasted resulting in heavy pollutant loads on the surface waters.

## 2. Purpose of this Pilot Plant Project

This deplorable situation, both from economic and ecological aspects, will continue to persist until commercial-scale separation of the troublesome silicic acid has become possible.

## 3. Test Prerequisites

A special feature common to all black liquors is that their characteristics will change as a function of time, transport and storage thus being crucial factors. For this reason, tests with black liquor should always be conducted at their point of origin, i.e. a pulp

$$\epsilon_M = \frac{s_1 - s_2}{s_1 - s_E} = 1 - \frac{s_2 - s_E}{s_1 - s_E}$$

This means that the separation efficiency of the laboratory centrifuge has to be taken as a basis and assumed to be complete. Consequently, the desilication efficiency $\epsilon_{lab}$ downstream of the laboratory centrifuge directly indicates the degree of completeness (related to total $SiO_2$) of the precipitation reaction (precipitation efficiency).

Thus, the total desilication efficiency is obtained by the interaction of the precipitation efficiency $\epsilon_{lab}$, the decanter efficiency $\epsilon_{dec}$ and the separator efficiency $\epsilon_{sep}$ in accordance with the following algebraic interrelationship:

$$\epsilon = \epsilon_{lab} \times [1 - (1 - \epsilon_{dec}) \times (1 - \epsilon_{sep})]$$

The expression in brackets corresponds to the total separation efficiency of the two centrifugal separators connected in series. With such a combination multiplication of the individual pass percentages will give the total pass percentage which is subtracted from the value to determine the total separation efficiency. Multiplication of the latter by the precipitation efficiency yields the total desilication efficiency, this relationship directly reflecting the basic prerequisite for $SiO_2$ removal, i.e. that only such material can be removed that has been both precipitated and separated.

Additional examinations carried out within the scope of the subsequent evaluation of the test results in Frankfurt comprised the determining of the measuring error for the pilot tests, the ascertaining of the correlation between the black liquor properties determined, the setting up of mass balances and computation of the alkali losses of the process, the examining of the characteristics of the precipitation reaction, as well as the drawing of conclusions as to how the observations made will have to be considered in the design of an industrial-scale plant.

## 7. Test Results

### *7.1. Desilication Reaction*

It can be assumed that the silicic acid is present in the black liquor in the form of sodium silicate.

On mixing with flue gas, the carbon dioxide reacts with the silicate forming a $SiO_2$ precipitate and soda.

To obtain information on the velocity of the above reactions, a special test was conducted. For this purpose, the charged reactor was operated without black liquor throughput.

While 93 per cent of the initially available total $SiO_2$ are precipitated after a reaction time of only 20 minutes, the further increase of the separation efficiency to 97.5 per cent takes about 3 times as long.

In practice, this means that reactors of considerable size will be required if desilication efficiencies of this order of magnitude are to be attained.

In contrast with this non-steady state test, all other tests were conducted with continuous liquor flow under steady-state conditions, since this corresponds to the actual operating conditions of a continuous process.

By means of the liquor feed rate, mean black liquor retention times in the reactor between 50 and 100 minutes were adjusted. Shorter retention times which would have required a correspondingly higher flue gas rate were not practical due to the limited delivery rate of the Roots fan available.

The temperatures of 40 to 80°C in the reactor were manually adjusted via the vapour pressure in the steam beating jacket. Evaporation was controlled in such a way as to supply the reactor with different black liquor concentrations varying between 5 and 15 per cent DS. The pH was controlled by manual adjustment of the bypass valve on the flue gas fan. pH measurement was conducted at operating temperature, temperature compensation in the pH metre being set to 50°C at all times.

The samples taken from the reactor were separated in the laboratory centrifuge at 4000 rpm for a period of 20 minutes followed by the examination of the precipitate and the clear liquor.

Based on the $SiO_2$ content $s_E$ of this clear liquor and that of the reactor feed liquor $s_D$, the so-called laboratory desilication efficiency was determined according to the formula

$$e_{lab} = 1 - \frac{s_E}{s_D}$$

The measured values $\epsilon_{lab}$ along with the experience gained from the field experiments enable the following qualitative statements:

1. Temperatures above 65°C result in considerably higher residual silicic acid concentration than measured with temperatures around 50°C.
2. The best desilication efficiencies are attained within a pH range between 9 and 9.5.
3. Retention times of the black liquor in the reactor beyond 75 minutes only bring about minor improvements in the desilication efficiency.
4. An influence of the dry substance content of the feed liquor on the residual silicic acid concentration is not recognizable for the range 6 to 15 per cent.
5. An influence of the silicic acid concentration of the fed liquor on the residual silicic acid concentration is not recognizable in the silicic acid concentration range 0.35 to 1.65 per cent.
6. A correlation between the residual silicic acid concentration and the silicic acid to dry solids ratio in the feed liquor is not recognizable in the range 4 to 15 per cent.
7. In the range of optimum pH values, a correlation of the residual silicic acid concentration and the specific carbon dioxide supply kg $CO_2$/kg $SiO_2$ or the content of free NaOH is not recognizable.
8. The mean value of the residual silicic acid concentration downstream of the laboratory centrifuge determined as 50°C and optimum pH adjustment is 0.035 per cent related to the liquor. The maximum deviation was +0.023 per cent, –0.02 per cent, 90 per cent of all measured values were below 0.05 per cent. Included in these measured values are also the values determined during a 3-day continuous operation. Their mean value 0.033 per cent hardly differs from the mean value computed for the remaining tests.

Thus, information on the residual silicic acid concentrations obtainable in the reactor under the given test conditions is now available. The question as to what extent these values can be realised in a commercial-scale desilication plant will depend on the performance of the centrifuges.

*7.2. Losses*

In judging the efficiency of a desilication process, the volumes of alkalis and organic matter discharged with the $SiO_2$ sludge will also play an important role.

The data obtained in the present tests enable a quantitative assessment of this point. One prerequisite in this connection is that the very fluid separator sludge which has a $SiO_2$ content of only 1 per cent and, in fact, greatly resembles the black liquor, is admixed to the preconcentrated black liquor upstream of the precipitation reactor. On the one hand, this measure prevents excessive loads of diluted alkali and organic matter in the sludge treatment process, and on the other, it can be assumed that the precipitate present in the sludge will act as a nuclei former and thus favour the $SiO_2$ precipitation reaction.

If the sludge were dumped untreated, this would imply alkali losses of the order of 5 to 6 per cent and losses in organic matter of 3 to 4 per cent.

However, according to the findings 94.6 per cent of the alkali and 65.5 per cent of the organic matter can be recovered from the sludge. Thus the actual alkali losses are reduced to below 0.5 per cent and the losses in organic matter to about 1 per cent.

Accordingly, an indispensable prerequisite for a desilication process which is to be both economical and environmentally beneficial can be met.

**8. Economic Use of the Findings**

The economic attractiveness of chemical recovery is demonstrated by the mere fact that, in wood-based pulp mills, this process has been widely applied throughout the world for a long time, even when pollution control was not of itself a reason for investment.

Further evidence for the benefits of the chemical recovery process is provided by the fact that it is also employed for liquors from annual plants with moderate silicic acid contents, despite the problems it poses in this type of application. In the case of rice straw liquors, these problems become so substantial that there chemical recovery from the cooking liquor has so far not been possible at a dependable yield.

The findings made in the course of the pilot plant project have demonstrated the feasibility of building and operating a plant for black liquor desilication and thus for the recovery of chemicals from the cooking liquor of annual plants. This means that the chemical recovery process so successfully employed in wood pulping is to be also used for processing of liquors from high-$SiO_2$ annual plants.

In the following, some figures will be given to provide an idea of the monetary value of the recovery chemicals: A large scale rice straw-based pulp mill requires 87 tpd sodium hydroxide (NaOH) for the production of 200 tonnes pulp per day.

According to "Chemical Marketing Reporter, New York", of March 1986, the price for 50 per cent caustic soda solution ranges between US$ 350 and 390 per tonne anhydrous NaOH.

Unless chemical recovery is applied, the pulp mill will have to buy 26,000 tonnes NaOH/year. At an average price of $ 370 per tonnes, this runs to $ 9.62 million/year which, after all, accounts for 36.7 per cent of the world market price per tonne of produced pulp.

Rough cost estimates for a chemical recovery plant made so far suggested that the savings in chemicals of $ 9.62 million/year will be more than sufficient to cover the capital and operating costs of a chemical recovery plant.

Even if the more exact cost estimates still to be made should result in less favourable prospects, if can at least be expected that the savings in chemicals will balance out the capital and operating costs quite apart from the beneficial effect on the environment.

Finally, brief mention should be made of a third cost saving factor which is brought to bear in the chemical recovery process: the power and steam generated by the incineration of the concentrated liquor. The amount of steam produced is sufficient to evaporated the black liquor to the concentration required for incineration. Electric power is produced in quantities sufficient to meet the total demand of the chemical recovery plants.

## 9. Conclusion

Based on the orientative findings obtained from preceding development projects, it was possible in the present empirical tests to determine the most suitable method of silicic acid removal from black liquor and to demonstrate the feasibility of the corresponding process in a pilot plant.

The process does not require any additional chemicals, desilicates the black liquor under favourable conditions up to about 97 per cent, and can be realised with practice-proven equipment.

Thus, the way has been paved for the well-proven chemical recovery process to be also applied in the pulping of annual plants.

# 20

HANS RAHM

# ENERGY USE AND CONSERVATION IN PULP MILLS

## 1. Introduction–Major Terms and Definitions

TALKING ABOUT energy use and saving potentials in pulp for this audience certainly means "carrying water to the well", as the subject is not new, and engineers and economists in India and all over the world have already given tremendous thought to the subject particularly during the last decade.*

I therefore wish to be understood as

(a) summing up the developments and achievements up to now, and
(b) spotlighting potential for further progress in the years ahead of us, and correlating this with the situation of the Indian pulp industry.

As for the latter, the relation to Indian conditions, this is not an easy task for me, as my knowledge on mills in India is based on information received indirectly, i.e. from reading and from talking to people. I do, however, have profound experience in Middle East countries, and in neighbouring regions, such as Bangladesh and Sri Lanka, as well as South East Asia, the Philippines and Malaysia, and of course, Europe and North America.

---

* Paper given at the UNIDO Technical Workshop on Energy Conservation in the Indian Pulp and Paper Industry at the Annual Convention of IPPTA in New Delhi, 19-21 March, 1985. We would like to thank the author for permission to print his article in this reader.

Talking about pulp mills means, in the first instance, chemical pulp mills, and here again, predominantly Kraft-or Sulfate–and Soda pulp mills, as they prevail in India.

I will, however, also specifically refer to the potential of the newly developed, and still developing, chemi-thermo-mechanical pulping processes, as they clearly indicate enormous potential for larger and larger percentages of pulp produced in the future.

For the purpose of clarity and to avoid over diversification, the convential mechanical pulping (i.e. grinding) process has been excluded from this paper.

In my following presentation I have attempted to follow generally the split between

- electrical energy use and conservation, and
- heat consumption and savings potential, followed by a number of recent energy conserving sub-processes.

It is, however, not always possible to maintain this split as interrelations exist in many process sections.

So, I may ask you not to become impatient at hearing things you have heard before. They are presented in an attempt to show the whole width of the spectrum of using energy more carefully in the future.

## 2. Indian Situation as Identified in the Sectoral Report, Energy Audit Studies, Prepared by the National Productivity Council for the Inter-Ministerial Working Group, and Corresponding Savings and Conservation Potential

To use my time rationally I shall concentrate on major items which are very pronounced, and where appropriate, corrective measures would immediately show impressive saving effects.

### *2.1. Electrical Energy Use and Savings Potential, General for all Pulp Mill Departments*

A major, obvious potential lies in the use of electrical power for pumping water, white water and stock within the pulp mill.

Three consecutive steps are to be envisaged here:

(a) Reducing the flows by an internal closing of water recirculation and, consequently, reducing the use of fresh water. This includes:

- checking circuits for unnecessary recirculation and corresponding reduction of pump capacities,
- avoiding unnecessary losses of static and dynamic energy in the fluid pumped, and
- checking that the working point in the Q-H diagram of pumps is not too far from a reasonable efficiency and change pump size or impeller diameter accordingly.

(b) Checking actual power consumptions of pumps versus the motor size, and recalculate pumps. The motors are often heavily oversized, and simple interchange of motors and corrections of pump impeller sizes are required, and

(c) Replace a control valve at the pump discharge, particularly at large pumps, by a frequency control of the AC-drive motor. This way the motor takes only the amount of power corresponding to the actual flow and pumping head conditions, and energy losses due to the throttling effect of the control valve are avoided.

The overall power saving effect for pumping alone can easily reach 50 per cent of that of the present mill.

Furthermore, actually all electrical drives in the mill, i.e. also those used for conveyors, blowers, screens, etc., should be investigated with the goal of determining the proper motor size to avoid losses of electrical power.

### 2.2. *Stem Use and Saving Potential, General for all Pulp Mill Departments*

The very obvious improvements possible in steam generation and the combination of stem and electrical energy generation are not dealt with here but are presented independently and will, to an extent, be spotlighted later on in my paper in other connections.

As far as steam consumption goes, the highest potential for saving is identified in the areas of heat recovery systems, condensate recovery, control of steam flow and insufficient insulation of equipment.

The means to remedy the situation are again obvious: Identify quantitatively, the sources of losses, adapt available designs for the recovery or heat saving systems, install the equipment and control the operation with proper modern instrumentation.

The heat input into the typical Indian digester house is approx. 5.700 M J/t pulp, while a good average pulp mill, i.e. not an optimised one to newest technology, needs 3.500 M J/t of pulp only.

The saving potential is obvious.

Here again, the identification and remedy principles as outlined above are to be applied to all mill departments, whereby, through heat recovery and recirculation systems, as much as possible secondary heat is to be used to reduce primary heat inputs. The saving potential is estimated to be 30 to 50 per cent magnitude, when comparing the heat consumption figures as shown in the "Sectoral Report" to actual operation figures in Europe.

More specific new sub-processes are outlined further down.

### *2.3. Capacity Utilisation*

The sectoral report indicates, for 1979, an overall capacity utilisation of the Indian pulp and paper industry of 67 per cent only, with the tendency to further decline due to raw material shortages.

This low utilisation is one of the very important and most obvious reason for high energy consumptions. Most of the drives, the water quantities pumped to the mill, and all secondary and auxiliary equipment continues to run at full speed and load, but has to be correlated with a reduced product output. This certainly boosts the specific consumption figures for steam and power.

To remedy this situation at least partly, and as far as energy consumption is concerned, it is better to shut down the mill completely during raw material shortage periods, and collect sufficient quantities to run the mill at full production rates during certain periods only.

## 3. Modern Energy Conservation Tends in European and American Mills

### *3.1. Potential for Mill wide Application*

#### *3.1.1. Improved Automatic Control*

During the past decade, a fundamental change in instrumentation and control techniques has taken place, and is still developing rapidly:

- The replacement of the basically pneumatic transmission of control signals by electronics,
- the improved reliability of transmitters for standard values such as level, temperature, pressure, and the rapid improvement of the reliability of sensitive, analytical transmitters, such as for pH, redox, brightness, conductivity etc.,
- the availability of all-electronic solid state control elements and fast introduction of new and simplified computer techniques, and the availability of relatively low cost hardware, and ready-to-adopt (with minimum knowledge of programming) software, permitting practically unlimited possibilities of adopting digital control systems for almost all applications in a pulp mill, including sophisticated multiple loop interlocking and sequencing.

Such systems are, in fact, ideally suited to control–

- steam and condensate systems in the digester house and evaporators,
- steam and warm water use in brown stock washing,
- steam and warm water use in bleaching,
- collecting, storing and diverting secondary heat containing back waters for reuse, and
- the distribution and recovery of heat for dewatering and drying (steam, warmwater, condensate, air flows) (I do not elaborate on the latter for reasons of similarity to the situation at paper machines, which are dealt with by others).

*3.1.2. Optimising Electric Drives and Drive Controls*

This subject has already been touched on and is, therefore, not repeated here. But again, the availability of newly developed, reliable features like solid state frequency converters (fc), working practically without power losses, open up new application areas.

For example, a number of recently installed new paper machines use fc-AC motors as fan pump drive, but even smaller pumps in control circuits use this new technique. For instance, we have designed, approx. 2 years ago, a linters pulp mill of 25 t/day, in which all controls of stock, white water, water and liquor flows are by fc-AC motors driving the centrifugal pumps. The investment, of course, requires verification by R.O.I. calculations individually for each case, and we have found wide variations here: from 1/2 year to 4 years, mostly depending on energy cost at the specific mill, and the size of the drive.

#### *3.1.3. Steam Savings*

The task is to reduce the primary heat input to the pulp mill system, i.e. to save steam produced from oil, coal, or other fuels.

The principles to be applied are:

- Increase the recuperation and use of secondary heat as contained in condensates, filtrates, cooling waters, fumes and warm exhaust air, and
- keep the temperatures in the individual process steps as equal, and as high as possible.

Useful, effective means of doing this are:

- Indirect heating wherever possible, and collection/return of condensates at the highest possible temperature level while trying to avoid flashing to atmosphere (insulation!),
- counter-current flow of wash waters through bleach plant and brown stock washers as far as process conditions allow,
- recuperation of heat in filtrates, before discharge, by using heat exchangers with fresh or recycles wash water (The latter has recently been done with the E-stage filtrate of a bleach plant in Germany),
- cold blow and displacement heating in batch digesters (details follow further down),
- utilise heat contained in exhaust air by means of heat exchangers with water or cold air. The economics of such systems have to be studied in detail, as many cases–such as bleach plant exhausts-require expensive heat exchanger materials and may thus not (yet) be viable,
- the counter-current use of evaporation vapours is well

established, the increase of the number of evaporator stages (in many cases up to 6) and the integration of the concentrator stage into the vapour heating sequence are means of optimising the live stem consumption.

### *3.1.4. Water Consumption*

The often repeated advice – reduction of fresh water consumption – has basically a threefold effect, two of which ar directly energy conserving:

*Firstly*: The electric energy consumption is reduced due to the smaller quantities pumped. The saving potential is considerable: the "Sectoral Report" states water consumptions of 250-450 $m^3$/tonnes of paper for integrated mills, and from examples in neighbouring countries we know that the consumption of a bleached pulp mill may reach approx. 2/3 of this quantity, i.e. 150-300 $m^3$/tonnes of pulp. Modern pulp mills actually do not need more than a tenth of such quantities, and often less. Certainly, the electric power consumption for pumping does not drop in the same ratio: Recirculation of filtrates and back waters also requires pumping. However, the expected gain may average in the range of approx. 50 per cent, and as pumping consumes roughly about 50 per cent of the mill's total power an all-over 25 per cent reduction is realistic.

*Secondly*: The heat lost with the enormous quantities of effluent is reduced. Again, the heat losses cannot be brought down to 1/10 of the present, as the temperature of the effluent goes up with progressive closing of mill water circuits.

How far this can go is demonstrated in a very advanced German market pulp mill, which has now reached such a reduction of water consumption and effluent flow that discharging unavoidable excess process heat becomes a problem: The mill effluent becomes too hot. The use of cooling water from a nearby small river is not permitted. The discharge of excess heat into the air by means of a cooling tower has also been objected to by the local environmental protection authorities.

*Thirdly*: The loss of fibres, fines, additives and chemicals, drops substantially. This has no direct influence on the mill's energy balance, but after all, the production of fibres and chemicals consumers power as well, so consequently the economic use of those items conserves energy.

Another effect is the reduced effluent volume, i.e., less mass has to be conditioned, mechanically treated, aerated etc., in the effluent plant.

### *3.1.5. Materials Handling*

I only briefly touch on this subject, as its energy conserving elements are by no means new:

In principle, pneumatic conveying systems (for chips, bark, fluff pulp, coal, etc.) consume approx. 10 times more electrical energy than mechanical conveyor systems.

The latter ones are, however, in many cases less flexible and more expensive to install and to maintain, but the power cost savings usually do more than compensate for this (Secondary benefits are less noise, less dust and sometimes less degradation of the material.)

### *3.1.6. Exhaust and Flue Gas Scrubbers and Absorbers*

The subject is also touched upon only briefly. The major feature is the elimination of venturi scrubbers with high electric energy consumption, by modern low energy-high efficiency equipment, namely:

(a) electrostatic precipitators for particulate matter, mainly for recovery boiler and lime kiln flue gases. The power demand of an electrostatic precipitator is negligible as compared to a venturi scrubber, its efficiency is as high as to reach 30–40 mg of particulate matter per $Nm^3$, over a much wider range of flue gas flow fluctuations than possible with a venturi,

(b) direct contact, spray-type or packed tower absorbers, where gaseous matters are to be washed out of a gas stream, such as for acid preparation systems in sulfite mills and for flue gas desulfurisation. The power consumed this way is approx. 1/4 for the packed tower system, to 1/2 for the spray absorbers, as compared to the venturi.

### *3.2. Specific Pulping Sub-process Alteration Potentials*

I am now coming to a few of the more recent and important process developments in chemical pulping, particularly in the kraft mill, which have effects on the mill energy consumption pattern:

### *3.2.1. Woodhandling and Chipping*

As mentioned before, one of the major items is avoiding pneumatic conveyer systems and the use of mechanical conveyers instead. Also, chippers undergo changes in detail design: Knife angles, cutting speeds etc. are carefully studied and selected for the specific cases, to avoid unnecessary power input.

More important, power-consumption wise, however, are operational matters, such as–

- the proper knife setting and grinding intervals, and
- the provision of equal feed of logs or poles to the chipper, to avoid extreme chipper operation fluctuations. Chipper motors belong to the biggest single drive units in a pulp mill and load fluctuations consequently have a negative effect on the mill's overall power balance.

The application of dry debarking and the use of heavy duty bark and other wood debris presses for wet rejects, in order to obtain fuel, is well known. The special new furnaces developed for hog fuel are not dealt with in further detail here.

### *3.2.2. Digester House*

Two new developments for the batch kraft digester operation have been introduced recently and result in substantial energy savings:

(a) The "cold blow" system, and
(b) the "displacement heating".

They may be briefly explained as follows:

(a) *The new cold-blow cooking* technique is closely similar to the conventional method. The primary differences are the introduction of cooking liquor drainage and cold blowing.

Chip filling and steaming is performed in the conventional manner.

This is followed by the liquor charging stage. The white liquor is preheated in a heat exchanger before being pumped to an accumulator. The black liquor is charged from the accumulator to the digester. The black liquor charge from the accumulator has a temperature slightly below the cooking temperature used in the process.

When the liquor charge is completed, the temperature blend is 135 to 140°C, as opposed to 90°C in conventional batch cooking. The increased starting temperature in the digester plays a crucial role in reducing steam consumption and cooking time.

When the cooking temperature is reached the digester is kept at a constant pressure and temperature up to a targeted kappa number.

At the end of the cook, cooled, first washer filtrate is pumped into the bottom of the digester, while the hot cooking liquor is simultaneously drawn off from the top of the digester and conveyed to the strong liquor accumulator. This stage is halted when a pre-set liquor volume is drawn off. Full cooking temperature and pressure are maintained in the digester top during the entire cooling stage.

Cold blowing then takes place. A steam cushion is maintained in the digester top by means of liquor vapour from the strong liquor accumulator connected to the digester top.

Cold blowing takes place at 80 to 100°C during the main discharge stage. This provides a major environmental benefit, since most of the odorous pollutants normally released during conventional blowing remain in the liquor to the evaporator.

The principle of the low-energy, cold-blow process is to utilise the heat in the final cooking stage to preheat the fresh liquor charge. The higher starting temperature shortens a normal cooking cycle by approx. 30 minutes.

Compared with conventional batch cooking, the steam consumption is reduced by 40 to 50 per cent, making the new process a highly attractive alternative to the continuous process for a new or for the rebuild of an existing batch digester system.

(b) The displacement heating is a refinement of the Cold blow system and works as follows (Fig. 20.1):

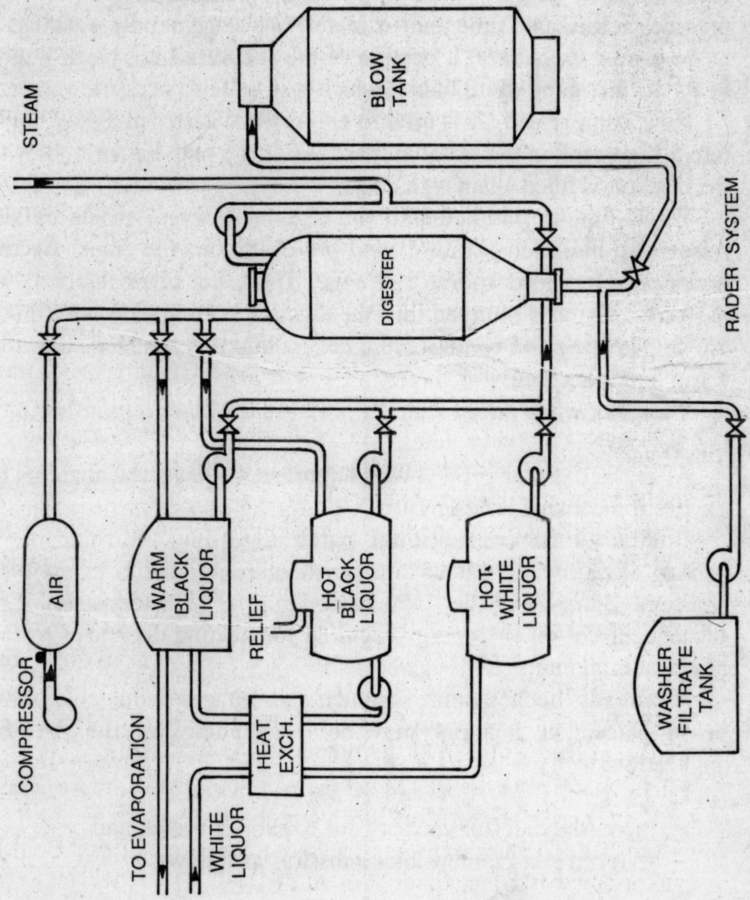


FIG. 20.1: Displacement Heating Diagram

At the end of the cook, first washer filtrate pumped into the digester bottom cone pushes the hot spent liquor up through the chip column. The hot liquor discharges into a hot pressurised accumulator, as described before for the cold blow system. When the temperature of the discharged liquor drops to a pre-set level, the discharge flow switches to a warm black liquor accumulator. This transfers more heat from the chip mass to the displacing liquor and provides at the same time approximately one stage of pulp washing.

In a heat exchanger, a portion of the recovered hot black liquor heats the incoming white liquor, which is stored in a pressure vessel.

Now, compressed air is used to empty the digester in a cold blow, into a blow tank in the usual manner. After the pulp has been blown, the digester is filled again with chips.

Warm liquor, pumped into the digester bottom, displaces air, raises chip mass temperature, and pre-conditions the chips. Excess liquor transfers to evaporator storage. Then, hot black liquor from the accumulator is pumped into the digester bottom. This continues the chip heating and conditioning. Excess liquor is transferred to the warm liquor accumulator.

Then, hot white liquor is mixed with the hot black liquor flow into the digester.

After the digester is filled with liquor, steam heats the contents to the desired cooking temperature.

Compared to conventional batch digesting, "displacement heating" is claimed to reduce digester steam requirements by up to 75 per cent. By re-using the spent black liquor at high temperature in subsequent cooks, the energy required for heating decreases to the practical minimum.

As already touched upon, secondary advantages of the "cold blow" or "displacement heating" may be, depending on the specific application:

- increased digester capacity due to shorter cycles, and
- reduced non-condensibles emission, as follows:

| Cook | $H_2S$ | MM | DMS | DMDS | Total |
|---|---|---|---|---|---|
| Conventional | 0.04 | 0.90 | 0.11 | 0.03 | 1.08 |
| "RHD" | 0.00 | 0.00 | 0.01 | 0.01 | 0.02 |

This results in a simplification of the odour abatement system, and the deletion of the blow heat recovery system.

### *3.2.3. Brown Stock Washing*

Here, the introduction of multistage belt washers has been observed recently. They use a Fourdrinier type wire, or in some instances, perforated steel belts, and gravity, suction boxes, vacuum and press rolls for drainage, according to individual designs (Fig. 20.2).

Besides the process advantages over the conventional drum washers, such as

- better washing (up to 7 stages have been realised on one belt)
- low dilution factor (1.0 $m^3$ wash water per tonnes pulp against the conventional 2.5 $m^3$) and thus higher liquor concentrations and less evaporator steam requirements,
- no fumes emission due to closed, and partly pressurised hoods,

The electrical power consumption is considerably reduced: One system claims to consume 14 kWh/tonnes only, as compared to approx. 50 kWh/tonnes pulp for a conventional drum washing plant of similar capacity. The main reason for the electric power reduction is the elimination of the inter-stage dilution and the much lower pumping energy for the reduced filtrate quantities.

### *3.2.4. Bleaching*

The continuous displacement bleaching system is well enough introduced, and sufficiently known and not further detailed here. Basically, the same features as for brown stock belt washing, i.e. displacement washing without interstage dilution and reduced dilution factors, result in savings in electric (pumping) power and reduced effluent volumes. Particularly in peroxide bleaching (which is important in CMP/CTMP pulping processes and which will be dealt with later on), very high consistencies (20 to 25 per cent and more, depending on the type of stock), can be obtained, and are process-wise desirable, by applying wash presses of various designs (twin wire, drum etc.). The result is reduced steam requirements: By raising the consistency in the bleach tower from 10 to 20 per cent, the volume of stock and water is reduced to half, and so is the heat requirement for the bleaching stage.

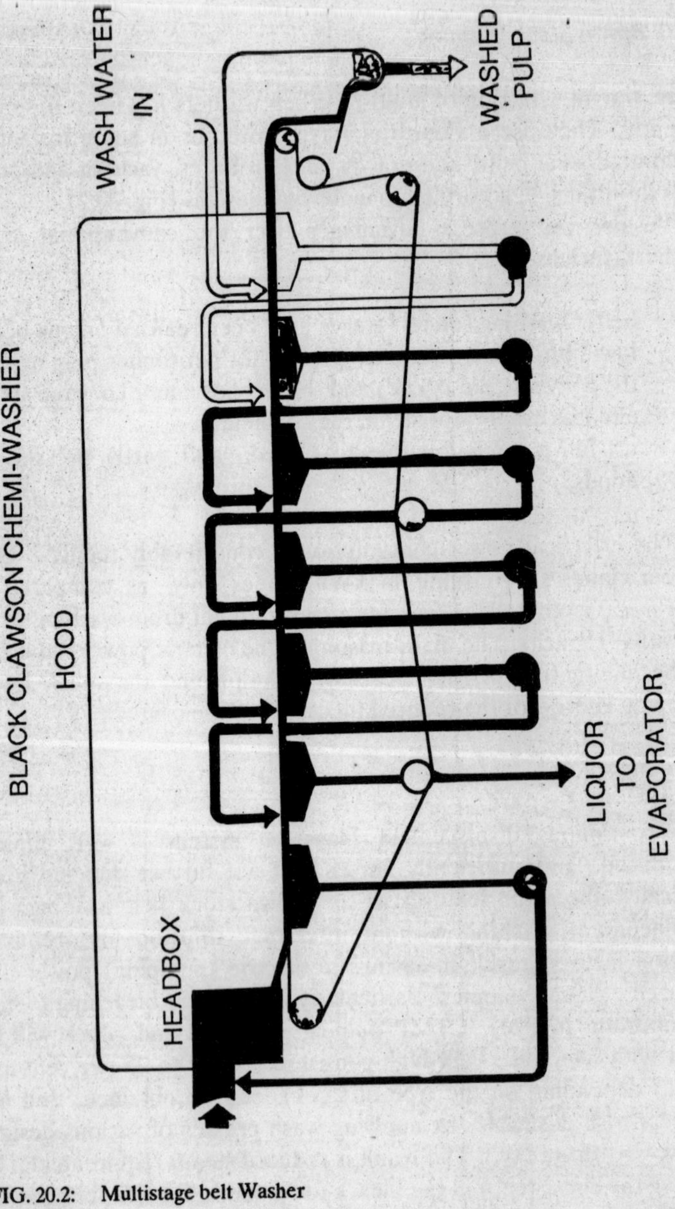


FIG. 20.2: **Multistage belt Washer**

In Europe in particular, the paper consumers realise more and more that super-high brightnesses of ordinary writing and printing paper are not really necessary, and the increasing environmental protection consciousness triggers acceptance of less bright papers for daily use. Besides the reduced electrical energy (about 20 to 40 per cent electrical power is required to prepare a bright grey waste-paper pulp as compared to virgin fibre pulp), the bleaching to only 86 or 88°C ISO brightness instead of 90-91°C would save a 500 t/day American mill close to 500,000.–$/year out of which approx. 1/3 is energy costs.

In general in bleach plants it is attempted to run with temperatures as equal as possible in the various stages, thus allowing extensive use of secondary heat contained in the filtrates, either directly or via heat exchangers. Nowadays, generally over 80 per cent of the total heat input in a modern European bleach plant is covered by secondary heat.

### *3.2.5. Dewatering and Drying*

As mentioned earlier, the energy saving potential is not discussed here, for reasons of similarity with the paper mill potentials.

### *3.2.6. Chemical Recovery Systems*

Looking briefly at the standard Kraft of Soda recovery block, the main energy saving measures are optimisations such as

- increased number of evaporator stages and modifications in the sequence, including integration of the concentrators. Just to repeat known facts: The water evaporated per tonne of live steam of 3.5 barg in a sextuple effect evaporator is approx. 40 per cent higher than in a quadruple effect.
- the revival of thermo-compression in evaporation, particularly in sulfite mills,
- the lowering of flue gas temperatures of the recovery boiler with the aim of higher steam output, and the increasing of steam pressures for higher electric power generation per tonne of steam.

These subjects are not further dealt with now, as they rather belong to the power generation theme.

### 3.2.7. Anaerobic Effluent Treatment

Unlike aerobic systems, which require large amounts of energy and produce substantial quantities of biological sludge, anaerobic systems do not need an external energy source. On the contrary, they convert the soluble organic material in the waste-water to methane gas, which is a high grade fuel. Since so much of the organic materials is converted to methane gas, very little residual sludge is discharged from the process. To sum up, the advantages of anaerobic treatment systems are:

- Minimal space requirements
- Low sludge yield
- Minimal power requirements
- Low nutrient requirements
- Production of methane gas as a by-product
- Effluent easily treated in conventional secondary systems with limited power consumption.

The only power requirements are for pumping the waste-water into the anaerobic reactor and for sludge pumping. All of the aeration power of approx. 1 kW of aerator capacity required for 20–25 kg BOD removal is saved. Over and above, methane gas is produced which may be burnt in the mills power boilers.

Because of the extremely low sludge yield, the need for supplemental nutrient addition to stimulate biological growth is far lower than that of aerobic systems. Effluents from anaerobic pre-treatment systems are easily treatable in conventional, secondary aerobic treatment plants. This can be a major advantage when a municipal treatment facility is available for secondary treatment.

A number of different anaerobic processes already exist for other industries (breweries, sugar mills, slaughter houses etc.) and will be available, with proper adaptations, for our industry as well.

The capital and operating costs of each of these processes should be carefully evaluated, with consideration given to the particular characteristics of the effluent and the recipient, before a process is finally selected.

In a North-American project study, an anaerobic treatment, which would be designed for evaporator condensate, treats 23,000 kg COD/day, removes 83 per cent of the same by producing an 80 per cent methane containing biogas of 600 $m^3$/min. It would cost an investment of US $ 3.5 million. The projected pretax capital payback would be 3 years.

The principal components of an anaerobic digestion system are shown schematically in Fig. 20.3.

The effluent waste-water (1) either flows by gravity of is pumped into a mixing tank (3) which, if necessary, could also serve as an equalisation or a pre-acidification vessel, depending upon the particular characteristics of the waste-water. pH-adjustment and, if necessary, supplemental nutrient addition (2) takes place in the mixing tank. From the mixing tank, the waste-water is pumped into the reactor vessel (4) through a series of inlet manifolds. If any temperature adjustment is required, it is usually carried out in this loop. The treated effluent from the reactor can be recirculated (9) to the mixing tank for purposes of reducing the incoming COD concentration and/or retaining some alkalinity within the system to save pH-adjustment chemicals. The remainder of the treated effluent (6) is discharged.

A surplus sludge vessel (8) can be provided for the storage of the biological sludge mass on site, in the event that replacement of some of the sludge in the reactor is desirable. The vessel serves to decant the sludge that is discharged (5) from the reactor. The sludge bed within the reactor is typically compacted to a concentration of about 10 per cent, and the sludge in the surplus sludge vessel should decant to at least that density. The supernatant overflow (10) from the surplus sludge vessel is of the same quality as the reactor effluent and can be discharged along with it.

Routine disposal of sludge is normally drawn from the surplus sludge vessel, not from the reactor.

The gas generated (7) from the process is piped from the reactor through an entrainment separator and defoamer and via a pressure regulator to a discharge point from which it can either be flared or piped to the mill as fuel for the boilers.

There are types and design of anaerobic systems in use, such as the BVF (bulk volume fermenter), with relatively low investment cost, where the reactor is a flat basin, constructed from earthwalls, covered with simple plastic sheeting.

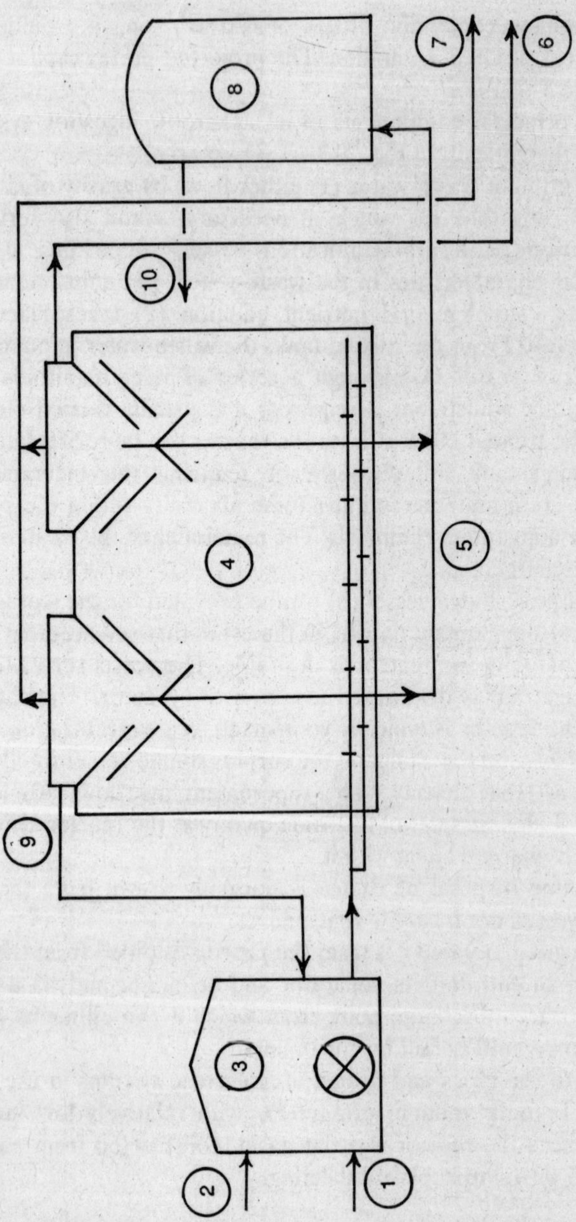

FIG. 20.3: Anaerobic Effluent Treatment Diagram

Pulp mill effluent streams suitable for anaerobic treatment are–

– evaporator condensates (these contain approx. 80 per cent of the soluble BOD load from an unbleached sulfite mill), while for bleach plant effluents investigations are in an advanced stage.

Further research work is being carried out on–

– NSSC spent liquor and white water
– clarified groundwood mill effluent and others
– Soda pulp mill spent liquor
– E-stage filtrates from bleach plants.

## 4. Outlook: Changes in Pulping Technology and their Impact on the Energy Situation

Up to now I have purposely restricted myself to well established pulping processes.

Before finishing my presentation, I would like to mention the new developments of CMP (chemi-mechanical) and CTMP (chemi-thermo-mechanical) pulping.

Starting from RMP (refiner mechanical-) pulping many years ago, the processes have developed via TMP (thermo-mechanical-) pulping to CTMP and CMP, which may be characterised by approx. the following values for yield, power requirements and chemical charges (Fig. 20.4).

| Abbreviation | Type | Yield % on wood | Power requirements (kWh/t pulp) | Chemical charges (kg/t wood) |
|---|---|---|---|---|
| GW | mechanical pulp (groundwood, made on stones | ↑ 99-100 | ↑ 1600-2000 | ↑ nil |
| TMP | thermo mech.pulp | 97/98 | 1800-2400 | nil |
| CTMP | chemi-thermo mech.pulp | 91-97 | | 30-50 |
| CMP | chemi-mechanical pulp | 82-96 | min. 930 | |
| SCP | semi-chemical pulp | 62-82 | | 70-110 |
| CP | chemical pulp | 40-60 | 800-900 | 160-200 |

FIG. 20.4: Yields, Power Requirements and Chemicals Used, for Different Grades of Pulp Increasing Increasing Decreasing

This new development features some outstanding results which, in their tendency, appear to be revolutionary:

- The yields are over 85 per cent, mostly 90 per cent, thus eliminating the costly conventional recovery processes. Effluent treatment only is required,
- The effluents appear to be suitable for the energy-generating anaerobic treatment (investigations are underway),
- The chemical charges are as little as 1-6 per cent on wood, – mostly $Na_2SO_3$ and NaOH,
- The electrical power required can be recovered, to a substantial degree, in the form of steam, which is applicable for paper machine heating,
- Bleaching can be done without chlorine – by peroxide and hydrosulfite use, to approx. 75 to 80 per cent ISO, thus avoiding the generation of toxic chlorinated organic compounds in the effluent.
- The minimum size of a pulping line can be rather small (approx. 50-60 t/day), to be economically viable, and thus suit the conditions of the Indian pulp and paper mills much better than many of the newer developments in chemical pulping aiming at very large units.

The CMP/CTMP processes are still in full development, also with regards to further reduction of energy consumption.

A very advanced example in this respect is in operation in a Swiss mill:

At approx. 40-45 t/day capacity it produces an unbleached pulp from a mixture of spruce and beech chips at 90 per cent yield, which fully substitutes the unbleached sulfite pulp in a newsprint furnish. Chemical consumption is 6 per cent sodium sulfite ($Na_2SO_3$) charge on b.d. wood, and the power consumption is altogether 930 kWh/t of pulp! This is only slightly more (approx. 5%) than required for conventional chemical pulp mills with around 50 per cent yield!

These processes can in principle be adopted for raw materials available in this country. In fact, and to my knowledge, refiner TMP is already being produced for quite some time at the Kerala mill. In my estimation the CMP/CTMP/TCMP technology will, in the coming years, take over a considerable share of pulp produced for wide variety of writing and printing papers boards, tissue and fluff

# FIVE

# OUTLOOK

# 21

MICHAEL LAVIN

## RESULTS AND RECOMMENDATIONS OF THE NEW DELHI WORKSHOP

IN ORDER to adequately understand and analyse the problems involved in paper production in developing countries, it is necessary to develop a concept embracing a whole network of systems. According to the perspective with which one approaches the problems involved in paper production, one can arrive at different results. For example, if the perspective is that of raw material then the tendency is to develop and further programmes for the industrial development of agriculture in regions where there are raw materials suitable for paper production. If, however, the perspective is that of paper products then one tends to support the importation of paper from the industrialised countries because the quality of the paper produced there is usually much better than that achieved in the developing countries. If, however, to mention just one last example, the perspective is that of ecology then the tendency is to encourage large paper mills as the problems of environmental pollution associated with small mills have in no way been properly solved.

The workshop in New Delhi did not achieve a consistent overall perspective, and up till now it has not been possible to develop a type of overall matrix of the interrelated problems of paper production, be it from the point of view of the practicians, the engineers or the theoreticians. To say nothing of the difficulty of providing directives for action, on the basis of any such matrix, which would clearly outline the financial, social, cultural and ecological advantages and disadvantages of any one field of the matrix.

For these reasons controversies arose throughout the course of the discussions and will be presented here without any attempt to conceal them.

## 1. Results

### *1.1. Economy*

It became clear that the various economic problems of the paper production industry in the developing countries differ greatly due to the fact that the macro-economic perspective of economic rationalism and world market conditions is in no way compatible with the operational point of view of an individual mill. Even though an economic analysis can argue convincingly that a government subsidised small-scale pulp and paper mill means a large foreign currency saving for a country, and furthermore, provides many thousands of related jobs, an operations manager with his management-criteria can at the same time clearly show that the operation of such a small mill can be very questionable. This contradiction between macro- and micro-economics permeated the whole discussion on economic aspects of paper production. The following problems were dealt with in detail:

- On the world market some paper producers from the industrialised countries work with dumping prices and thus make realistic estimations of the market very difficult,
- Local paper mills certainly contribute to savings in foreign currency and to the creation of local jobs. The question is whether this effect should not be aimed at more appropriately in other branches rather than paper production. Furthermore one must ask whether the saving of foreign currency and the creation of jobs might not be achieved by other means than the establishment of government subsidised paper mills,
- In almost all developing countries there is no harmonisation between foreign trade policy on paper and pulp imports on the one hand, and the establishment of local paper production on the other,
- In most developing countries there are not sufficient economic reserves to profitably use local raw materials,
- The economic and technological span between paper production capacities in the industrialised countries and those in the developing countries seems to be widening continually. Many developing countries fear their increasing dependency on foreign monopolies,

(Interestingly enough the former Prime Minister Rajiv Gandhi announced shortly after his assumption of office that in India wood fibre was no longer to be used for paper production),

- Kenaf is basically viable, if the problems of related land use and reliability of supply can be solved. Special problems related to Kenaf are: drying takes 50 per cent more time than other materials; its bulk requires large-scale storage place; as a cash crop it must be treated as a commodity, meaning that it must be bought under market conditions so that this strategy can in turn be undermined by international market conditions,
- The pros and contras of plantation economy, of the cultivation of large eucalyptus forests, need to be examined much more closely,
- Also the question of the conditions under which waste-paper can be used as raw material needs further consideration.

*1.5. Pollution*

The pollution problems in India and West Germany were discussed on the basis of comparative studies in these countries. Special points of discussion were the problems of fibre and chemical recovery, and water and energy recovery. The emission standards for both countries are almost identical, but in India they have been only partially implemented. The pollution problem is particularly acute in small-scale pulp and paper mills, and demands urgent solutions. For example, in the People's Republic of China 10 per cent of the industrial waste accumulating there comes from the paper industry (which consists mainly of small mills). The following points were discussed in detail:

- There is less internal mill pollution control than external control, although internal control would contribute to the economic efficiency of the small mills,
- Pollution costs must be carried jointly be governments and producers. Clear conditions for definitely outlined periods must be set for producers,
- The multiplicity of responsible authorities for pollution matters hinders effective regulation of the problem,

- The Indian Central Pollution Control Board has set June 1988 as the deadline for the introduction of minimum control measures, but progress in this regard has been unsatisfactory. There are difficulties in enforcing minimum national standards, and particularly in relation to taking court actions,
- Priority must be given to recovery of fibres, chemicals, water and energy, in the paper production process (recovery is the best form of pollution control),
- Separation of the black liquor is of great importance.
- Use of waste-paper is to be increased where possible, to avoid the pulp process.
- The bleaching process should be modified as far as possible; $O_2$, $H_2O_2$ etc. should be used instead of $Cl_2$,
- Small units have more difficulty in implementing pollution control measures than larger units. About 10 per cent of the total investment must go into pollution control,
- The re-utilisation of by-products and their conversion into other products should be a subject for future research and development work,
- Appropriate treatment technologies must be implemented more systematically, such as anaerobic treatment systems with energy recovery (methane gas). Alternative solutions for smaller units, such as solar evaporation ponds etc. should be tested for suitability.

### *1.6. Chemical Recovery*

This was a central theme, due to the fact that on the one hand the known technical installations are not realised in existing small mills, and on the other hand advanced processes for complete chemical recovery are still not available, due to the problem of silicic acid from one-year plants.

All participants were in agreement that solutions to this problem are conceivable and will more than likely be realised. However, unfortunately the research capacities of developing countries are much too limited for such development work, while the dominant mill-designers and developers in the industrialised countries have little interest in this specific problem, which is of such importance to developing countries.

The workshop participants agreed that chemical recovery should be given preference over pollution control as it alleviates the financial and raw material problems.

### *1.7. Research and Training*

The great interest in this workshop, especially on the part of India, demonstrated clearly the need for increased research work as well as the exchange of ideas, training and advanced training. Emphasis was placed on the following points:

- There is a need for intensified dialogue at a south-south level, but also at the level of the various institutions within any one Third World country,
- What is missing is a continuous and practically relevant dialogue between research and industry,
- Due to the existence of different aid-doners, differing standards of testing have emerged. This lack of uniform testing standards has led to confusion. Harmonisation in this field is very necessary.

## 2. Recommendations

Throughout the discussions a series of recommendations emerged; they have already been referred to in the re-capping in the course of the various discussions, and will not be repeated in detail here. On the last day of the workshop another series of general recommendations was worked out. There was no formal vote on these recommendations. They were more the expression of a wide concensus:

- For a limited period of time the government should promote and protect the establishment of a national paper production industry,
- Process technology should be developed for the efficient saving of raw materials, for social and environmental compatibility, for saving energy, water and chemicals, that is to say recovery process technology, plus installations which are easy to use and maintain,
- Economic efficiency could be improved by (a) increased horizontal and vertical integration of this production sector

into the economy of the country in question, and (b) by improved management methods,

- A training concept should be developed for all areas concerned in this industry to ensure both formal and internal training and continuation training. This should be a joint effort by government and producers,
- Manpower training strategies should have priority over exclusively technical training strategies,
- Within the production sector emphasis should be placed on self-motivation of the workers instead of on bureaucratisation and hierarchical structures,
- Support is needed by the R&D institutes in developing countries in the field of pulp and paper, towards achieving uniform test standards, improvement in communications between different research institutes, improvement in cooperation between research and industry and the promotion of joint research programmes.

22

JÖRG BECKER

# A FAREWELL TO ARTHUR W. WESTERN (1913-1988)

ON APRIL 8, 1988, just a few days before the New Delhi workshop began, my friend and colleague Arthur W. Western died at his home in England. I met Arthur in 1982 when he was a consultant with Intermediate Technology Consultants Ltd., London. Without him, his specialised knowledge, his professional experience and his untiring dedication to the cause of small-scale paper mills, I would not have been able to carry out my paper technology projects for the German Agency for Technical Cooperation (GTZ).

Arthur was born on 7.12.1913. His professional career was dedicated entirely to paper. In 1937, at 24 years of age, Arthur entered the St. Annes Board Mill in Bristol, where he was involved in the design and construction of the 5th and 6th machines. After the second World War, during which he spent some time in India, Arthur worked in different paper mills in England, until he became Chief Engineer, later Deputy Chief Engineer, with Reed International. From 1957–1960 he was Chief Engineer and Production Manager with the Tasman Pulp and Paper Mill in New Zealand. After that, he returned to Reed International, where he was active until he retired in 1978, his last positions being Managing Director, Chairman, and Chief Executive with Reed Engineering and Development Services. During this time he was responsible for mills in Norway, Italy, Canada, France and South Africa. For Reed International Arthur built, commissioned and managed three bagasses-based mills in Iran, totalling 100,000 t/annum of writing and printing paper, a similar mill in South Africa, with coating included, two tissue mills in Iran and South Africa, and modifications to mills in Canada and the US. He was also involved in major projects in Indonesia, Egypt and Syria.

After his retirement in 1978, he worked as a consultant, in particular for Intermediate Technology Consultants Ltd, London, which was founded by the economist Ernst Schumacher (*Small is beautiful*, 1973). In this context he was involved in feasibility studies for pulp and paper projects in Chile, Colombia and Nigeria.

Cooperation between myself and Arthur was probably so intensive and successful because of the fact that we were, by nature, almost total opposites. When we first met Arthur was 69 years old and I was 36; whereas I was more theoretically and analytically orientated, Arthur was above all a man of practice; I was a social scientist, Arthur an engineer; while Arthur was proud to say he was politically conservative, my position is on the other side of the political spectrum. A small anecdote may serve to illustrate the difference between us: When Arthur presented his manuscript for our first book to me I was quite shocked to find that although it was 100 pages long, it did not contain a single footnote. When I spoke to him on the phone about this and asked him to provide some, it was he who was then shocked: "I can't give you any footnotes. Everything I wrote is in my head. It is the sum total of my professional experience. You can't read it anywhere!" However, this is not quite true. The following three publications by Arthur W. Western are still worth reading:

- *Small-Scale Paper-making*, London: Intermediate Technology Development Ltd, 1979.
- "Paper, Paper Products and Pulp Mills", in : *Appropriate Industrial Technology for Paperproducts and Small Pulp Mills*, ed. by the United Nations Industrial Development Organisation, New York 1979, pp. 108-122.
- "Fabricas de pasta y papel de pequency capacidad para paises en vias de desarrollo", in: *Il Congreso Latinoamericano de Celulosa y Papel "Nuevas Materias, Procesos y Productos Derivados"*. Seccion Tecnica No. 2, Torremolinos, Spain, 22.-26. June 1981, pp. 185-199.

The reasons for Arthur's commitment to the cause of small-scale paper mills were very different from mine. He often commented: "In the last decades our paper machines have become bigger and bigger. We must have gone totally wrong somewhere. Our whole philosophy seems to have been committed to the ideal of the gigantic. In Third

World countries such huge machines simply cannot work, as I know from my own painful experience." Self-critically, Arthur admitted that he had spent his whole professional life developing such large machines. Thus, after his retirement, he wanted to work on concepts which would be more adapted to the needs of the Third World, without his being bound to the interests of any group or firm. His motivation was based on personal experience. I myself had come to similar conclusions as he had, but as a result of theoretical study of the problem of under-development.

In September 1985, Arthur and I stayed at the guesthouse of Shree Warana SSK Ltd., Paper Division, where we were made very welcome by the Managing Director, Mr. N.K. Naik and his colleagues. Every evening the two of us discussed the third, the eight and tenth stage of our project at great length. Our wish and aim was to help in setting up the "ideal" paper mill somewhere, sometime. Whereas I often could not go on talking due to tiredness, Arthur, although in his seventies, became more and more lively and involved in our discussions as time went on. Unfortunately, after that sojourn in India I had to stay in bed for a whole year with hepatitis, while Arthur enjoyed the best of health. His recipe for his good form throughout that stay in India was to eat only omlettes, where possible, and to drink 2 or 3 scotches each evening.

I cannot and shall not forget our research sojourn in India that autumn. In Arthur I have lost a very important, close friend and colleague.

[illegible] ... [illegible] with his wife ... [illegible]

[illegible] ... [illegible]

[illegible] ... [illegible]

[illegible] ... [illegible] and ... [illegible] of

[illegible] ... [illegible]

[illegible] ... [illegible] third ... [illegible]

[illegible] ... [illegible]

[illegible]

## LIST OF CONFERENCE PARTICIPANTS AND AUTHORS

**Ahuja Vinod K.**, Indian Institute of Management, Ahmedabad, India

**Amarasinghe Y. Ranjith**, Institute for International Studies, Peradeniya, Sri Lanka

**Auansakul Aroon**, Ministry of Agriculture, Bangkok, Thailand

**Becker Jörg**, Technical University of Darmstadt, Darmstadt, and KomTech GmbH, Frankfurt and Solingen, FRG

**Burman A.K.**, National Productivity Council, New Delhi, India

**Chakrabathi S.P.**, Central Pollution Control Board, New Delhi, India

**Delgado Manuel**, Consultant, Madrid, Spain

**Escudero Enrique**, SAICA, Zaragoza, Spain

**Garcia Hector Oscar Luis**, Cuba 9 Pulp and Paper Research Institute, Havana, Cuba.

**Göttsching Lothar**, Technical University of Darmstadt, Darmstadt, FRG

**Grant Roger L.**, Consultant, Cranbrook, Kent, United Kingdom

**Gupta Tirath (†)**, Indian Institute of Management, Ahmedabad, India

**Ivanov Georg**, GTZ and National Productivity Council, New Delhi, India

**Jahn Walter**, GTZ and GATE, Eschborn, FRG

**Jain Parmod**, Agro-Based Indian Pulp & Paper Mills Association, New Delhi, India

**Judt Manfred**, UNIDO, Vienna, Austria

**Kauppi P.K.**, FLEDIC Engineering Ltd., Vancouver, Canada

**Keswani S.L.**, Chemprojects Design & Engineering Ltd., New Delhi, India

**Krist Helmut**, GTZ and Central Pollution Control Board, New Delhi, India

**Kuttiappan N.K.**, National Productivity Council, New Delhi, India

**Kyrklund Borje**, FAO, Rome, Italy
**Lavin Michael**, KomTech GmbH, Frankfurt, FRG
**Meyhöfer Bernhard**, GTZ and National Productivity Council, New Delhi, India
**Mukundan P.G.**, Indian Agro Paper Mills Association, New Delhi, India
**Nyati K.P.**, National Productivity Council, New Delhi, India
**Pant Rajesh**, Central Pulp & Paper Research Institute, Dehra Dun, India
**Pitroda Sam**, Centre for the Development of Telematics, New Delhi, India
**Rahm Hans**, Hans Rahm Ingenieurplanung, Männedorf/Zürich, Switzerland
**Rao N.J.**, Institute of Paper Technology, Saharanpur, India
**Schildhauer Günter**, LURGI AG, Frankfurt, FRG
**Shouzu Hu**, Ministry of Light Industry, Beijing, People's Republic of China
**Soe U Myint**, Printing and Publishing Corporation, Rangoon, Burma
**Srinivasan S.**, Technological Information Pilot System (TIPS), New Delhi, India
**Tiwana N.S.**, State of Punjab Pollution Control Board, Patiala, India
**Tripathi C.S.**, Central Pollution Control Board, New Delhi, India
**Tyagi P.C.**, Central Pollution Control Board, New Delhi, India
**Vallamattam John**, Indian Catholic Press Association, Muvattupuzha, India
**Western Arthur W.** (†), Consultant, Maidstone, Kent, United Kingdom